ALLAN J. LICHTMAN is a Distinguished Professor of History at American University in Washington, DC, and is the author of many prize-winning books including *The Keys to the White House* and *Predicting the Next President*.

thecaseforimpeachment.com

THE
CASE FOR
IMPEACHMENT

Allan J. Lichtman

WILLIAM
COLLINS

William Collins
An imprint of HarperCollins*Publishers*
1 London Bridge Street
London SE1 9GF

www.WilliamCollinsBooks.com

First published in Great Britain by William Collins in 2017
First published in the United States by Dey Street Books in 2017

1

A catalogue record for this book is
available from the British Library

ISBN 978-0-00-825740-8

Printed and bound in Great Britain by
Clays Ltd, St Ives plc

MIX
Paper from
responsible sources
FSC® C007454

FSC™ is a non-profit international organisation established to promote
the responsible management of the world's forests. Products carrying the
FSC label are independently certified to assure consumers that they come
from forests that are managed to meet the social, economic and
ecological needs of present and future generations,
and other controlled sources.

Find out more about HarperCollins and the environment at
www.harpercollins.co.uk/green

Contents

Acknowledgments

Above all I would like to thank the light of my life, my wife, Karyn Strickler, for her patience and invaluable help. I would also thank those who contributed significantly to this book: Amanda Brower, Jake Assail, Rebecca Brenner, Scott Vehstedt, Dan Ballentyne, John Schmitz, and Sam Lichtman. Special thanks go to my outstanding agent, Bridget Matzie, my superb editor, Julia Cheiffetz, and the incredible team at HarperCollins that made this book possible.

Author's Note

———

Impeachment will "proceed from the misconduct of public men, or, in other words, from the abuse or violation of some public trust," and "they relate chiefly to injuries done immediately to the society itself."
—*Alexander Hamilton,* The Federalist, *1788*

I began thinking about impeachment before the November 2016 election. For weeks, my students had been asking who I thought would be our next president, Hillary Clinton or Donald Trump. Finally, on a late evening in mid-September 2016, I leaned back in my chair and peered out into the hall at the mostly darkened offices of American University in Washington, D.C. I had just finished my analysis: Donald Trump would win the presidency. My forecast ignored polls, debates, advertising, tweets, news coverage, and campaign strategies—the usual grist for the punditry mills—that count for little or nothing on Election Day. I had

———

used the same proven method that had led me to forecast accurately the outcomes of eight previous elections, and I'd kept my eye on the big picture—the strength and performance of the party holding the White House currently. After thirty-two years of correctly forecasting election results, even I was surprised by the outcome.

Among those who noticed my prediction was Donald J. Trump himself. Taking time out of preparing to become the world's most powerful leader, he wrote me a personal note, saying, "Professor—Congrats—good call." What Trump overlooked, however, was my "next big prediction": that, after winning the presidency, he would be impeached.

Here I did not rely on my usual model, rather I used a deep analysis of Trump's past and proven behavior, as well as the history of politics and impeachment in our country. In the short span of time between Trump's election and this book's publication in April 2017, his words and deeds have strengthened the case considerably. History is not geometry and historical parallels are never exact, yet a president who seems to have learned nothing from history is abusing and violating the public trust and setting the stage for a myriad of impeachable offenses that could get him removed from office.

America's founders, who had so recently cast off the yoke of King George's tyranny, granted their president awesome powers as the nation's chief executive and commander in chief of its armed forces. Yet they understood the dangers of a runaway presidency. As James Madison warned during the Constitutional Convention, the president "might pervert his administration into a scheme of peculation or oppression" and "betray his trust to foreign powers," with an outcome "fatal to the Republic." To keep a rogue president in check, delegates separated constitutional powers into three independent branches of government. But knowing that a determined president could crash through these barriers, they also put in place impeachment as the rear guard of American democracy.[1]

After exhaustive debate, the framers agreed on broad standards for impeachment and assigned this absolute power not to the judiciary, but to elected members of the U.S. House and Senate. By doing so they ensured that the fate of presidents would depend not on standards of law alone, but on the intertwined political, practical, moral, and legal judgment of elected officials. Hamilton explained that impeachments broadly cover "the abuse or violation of some public trust" and are properly "denominated POLITICAL."[2]

This book will escort you through the process and history of impeachment; as your warning about the dangers of Trump's rogue presidency; and as your guide to the myriad transgressions that I predict will lead to his impeachment. I invite you to follow each chapter and decide for yourself when Trump has reached the critical mass of violations that triggers the implosion of his presidency.

In *The Case for Impeachment,* I'll look beyond the daily news cycle of events which will have continued to evolve to focus on the big picture of the impeachment process and the Trump presidency. I'll take you through constitutional debates and the gritty politics of past impeachments. I'll explain how Trump threatens the institutions and traditions that have made American safe and free for 230 years, and I'll make clear why a Republican Congress might impeach a president of its own party. I also include a personal memo to President Trump on how he might dispel the clouds of controversy overhanging his presidency and avoid impeachment. I am not calling here for a witch hunt against an unconventional presidency or for snaring Trump on some minor or technical violation. The point is to assess at what point impeachment becomes necessary to protect America's constitutional liberties and the vital interests of the nation. An impeachment of a president need not imperil the institution of the presidency. "The genius of impeachment," said historian Arthur Schlesinger Jr. is "that it could punish the man without punishing the office."[3]

The impeachment of an American president is rare, but not exceptional. The U.S. House of Representatives has impeached two presidents, Andrew Johnson in 1868 and Bill Clinton in 1998; another, Richard Nixon, only averted impeachment with a timely resignation. Counting Nixon, one out of every fourteen U.S. presidents have faced impeachment. Gamblers have become rich betting on longer odds than that.[4]

But forget historical odds. Trump has broken all the usual rules of politics and governing. Early in his term, he has stretched presidential authority nearly to the breaking point, appointed cabinet officials dedicated to destroying the institutions they are assigned to run, and pushed America toward legal and constitutional crises.

No previous president has entered the Oval Office without a shred of public service or with as egregious a record of enriching himself at the expense of others. Trump's penchant for lying, disregard for the law, and conflicts of interests are lifelong habits that will permeate his entire presidency. He has a history of mistreating women and covering up his misdeeds. He could commit his crime against humanity, not directly through war, but indirectly by reversing the battle against catastrophic climate change, upon which humanity's well-being will likely depend. His dubious connections to Russia could open him to a charge of treason. His disdain for constitutional restraints could lead to abuses of power that forfeit the trust of even a Republican Congress.

What are the ranges and limitations of presidential authority in a system of separated power? What are the standards of truthfulness that a president must uphold? Where should the line be drawn between public service and private gain? Can a free press continue to function in the United States? How can America guard against foreign manipulation of its politics? What responsibility does the president have to protect the earth and its people from catastrophic climate change? When should impeachment be invoked or restrained? These are timeless issues that will decide the future of American democracy. The case for impeaching Donald Trump must be situated in the history of past impeachments—but if you're really anxious, you can jump ahead to chapter 3 and start right in on Donald Trump.

In his inaugural address, Trump slammed his favorite target, Washington politicians. "For too long," he said, "a small group in our nation's capital has reaped the rewards of government while the people have borne the costs." Yet this small group holds in their hands the power to impeach and remove the forty-fifth president.

It is our responsibility to arm ourselves with the knowledge needed to protect our great nation and keep alive its most precious traditions. Already millions of Americans and many more people worldwide have risen in protest against the dangerous presidency of Donald Trump. His impeachment will be decided not just in the halls of Congress but in the streets of America.

———

CHAPTER 1

High Crimes and Misdemeanors

The President, Vice President and all civil Officers of the United States, shall be removed from Office on Impeachment for, and Conviction of, Treason, Bribery, or other high Crimes and Misdemeanors.

—*Article II, Section 4,*
Constitution of the United States of America

IMPEACHMENT 101

The first thing you need to know is how impeachment works: The impeachment and removal of a president begins under the Constitution in the United States House of Representatives. An impeachment typically begins with an investigation by the Judiciary Committee. If the committee decides to investigate, it may then by majority vote recommend articles of impeachment to the full House. Members then vote up or down on each article. The House may also proceed with impeachment regardless of the Committee's recommendations. If a majority of the House ratifies one or more articles of impeachment, the case against the president proceeds to a trial by the Senate, presided over by the chief justice of the Supreme Court. A special prosecutor, a representative from either party, or even members of the public can request an investigation, although the Committee or the full House must agree to proceed with the inquiry.

At trial, the Senate acts as both jury and judge, with the power to subpoena witnesses, issue contempt rulings, dismiss charges, set trial procedures, and overturn rulings of the chief justice. Prosecutors appointed by the House present their case to the Senate, and the accused makes his choice of counsel for the defense. There is no requirement that the accused must appear in his own defense. At the end of the trial, the Senate has the power to convict and remove the president by a two-thirds vote of those present.

A president cannot pardon himself from impeachment, and if ousted by the Senate, he immediately sheds the protection of presidential immunity and becomes subject to arrest, prosecution, trial, and conviction under state or federal criminal law. By a separate vote, the Senate can bar a convicted president from holding any future federal office. Otherwise, an impeached president, if constitutionally eligible, could run again for White House. A president can run again if he was not elected twice or if elected once he did not serve for more than two years as an unelected president.

Decisions on whether to impeach a president turn on the wisdom of Congress and do not require proof of a specific indictable crime under either federal or state law. The verdict of the House and Senate is final. There is no right of appeal or judicial review of their decisions.[1]

Impeachment covers not just presidents, but other federal officials, notably judges appointed for life. Since America's founding, the House has impeached two presidents and fifteen judges. The Senate acquitted both presidents. It convicted eight of the judges.[2]

AMERICA'S FOUNDERS STRUGGLE WITH IMPEACHMENT

After what George Washington called the "standing miracle" of his victory over British arms, the general retired to his Mount Vernon plantation. Bouts of smallpox, tuberculosis, malaria, and dysentery and years of tense warfare had racked his body, leaving him prey to debilitating aches and fevers and a "rheumatic complaint" so severe at times that he was "hardly able to raise my hand to my head, or turn myself in bed." Yet in 1787, Washington donned his best breeches and frock coat, powdered his hair, and pushed his body to serve his country again: this time as the indispensable president of a constitutional convention in the sweltering Philadelphia summer.[3]

In the span of just over a hundred days, the delegates created a radically new frame of government powerful enough to protect and preserve their fledging republic, but one with enough checks and balances to safeguard against the tyranny that Americans had endured under British rule. These learned but pragmatic politicians adhered to the later warning of John Adams that: "Men are not only ambitious, but their ambition is unbounded: they are not only avaricious, but their avarice is insatiable." Therefore, "it is necessary to place checks upon them all."

The framers adopted impeachment as a necessary check against tyranny. "Shall any man be above justice?" asked the influential Virginia delegate George Mason. He warned that it is the president "who can commit the most extensive injustice."[4]

Although they agreed on the need for impeachment, the delegates struggled with defining the grounds for indicting and removing federal officials. During the convention debates, to specify the criteria for removing a president, delegates used such disparate terms as "great crimes," "malpractice or neglect of duty," "corruption," "incapacity," "negligence," and "maladministration." They finally cast their vote for "high crimes and misdemeanors against the state," then dropped the "state" qualifier, which both broadened and obfuscated the meaning of the impeachment.[5]

POLITICS WITHOUT CRIME

In the election of 1800, after one of the nastiest campaigns in U.S. history, the nation experienced its first political upheaval when the Democratic-Republican Thomas Jefferson defeated the Federalist incumbent president John Adams. Federalists attacked Jefferson for his alleged atheism, radicalism, and lack of moral standards. One propagandist warned that with Jefferson as president, "murder, robbery, rape, adultery, and incest will be openly taught and practiced, the air will be rent with the cries of the distressed, the soil will be soaked with blood, and the nation black with crimes."[6] The Jeffersonians fought back, charging Adams with scheming to extinguish the republic by marrying one of his sons to the daughter of the King of England and reestablishing British rule over America.

During this interregnum, John Adams pushed through the Judiciary Act of 1801, infuriating the victorious opponents. The act created sixteen new circuit court judgeships and reduced the size of the Supreme Court from six to five, thereby depriving Jefferson of an appointment. In the nineteen waning days of his presidency, Adams appointed so-called Midnight Judges to these new circuit court positions.

When Oliver Ellsworth, the chief justice of the Supreme Court and an Adams loyalist, conveniently retired, Adams was quick to appoint the staunch Federalist John Marshall as his replacement. Marshall served as chief justice for more than thirty years.[7]

Jefferson and his new partisan majority in Congress repealed the Judiciary Act and turned to impeachment for rectifying what they decried as the Federalists' packing of the courts. They carefully picked as their first target the elderly Federalist district court judge John Pickering, whose advanced dementia and alcoholism led to erratic and sometimes bizarre behavior on the bench. The impeachment of one of many federal trial judges may not amount to very much, but Jefferson and his allies in Congress targeted Pickering as part of a larger plan: to breach the separation of powers and place the constitutionally independent judiciary under the heel of the president and his party. Ironically, it was Thomas Jefferson, who famously had written in his "Notes on the State of Virginia" that concentration of power "in the same hands is precisely the definition of despotic government," who led this assault on the separation of powers.

Jefferson as party leader set in motion the House's proceedings against Pickering by transmitting to Congress "letters and affidavits exhibiting matter of complaint against John Pickering, district judge of New Hampshire, which is not within executive cognizance." Eventually, Jefferson's loyalists in the House drafted four dense articles of impeachment. None charged a specific violation of law, instead merely citing Pickering's poor judgment, intoxication, and rants from the bench as evidence that he lacked the "essential qualities in the character of a judge."[8]

The Senate convicted Pickering in a straight party vote, making him the first federal official removed from office under Article II, Section 4 of the Constitution. Senator William Giles of Virginia, the Jeffersonian leader in the Senate, said bluntly: "We want your offices, for the purpose of giving them to men who will fill them better." Lynn W. Turner, the pre-eminent historian of the Pickering impeachment, wrote, "By confusing insanity with criminal misbehavior they [the Jeffersonians] also wiped out the line between good administration and politics and made any word or deed which a political majority might think objectionable the excuse for impeachment and removal from office."[9]

Emboldened by Pickering's successful conviction, the Jeffersonians next targeted the United States Supreme Court by impeaching Federalist justice Samuel Chase. In 1804, the House voted along party lines to charge Chase with eight articles of impeachment; seven turned on his allegedly unjust and partisan judicial conduct and rulings. The final article cited "intemperate and inflammatory" and "indecent and unbecoming" remarks that Chase made while charging a Baltimore grand jury. None charged him with an indictable crime. The Senate acquitted Chase on all articles, which ended Jefferson's war on the judiciary but did nothing to clarify the grounds for an impeachable offense or stop similar maneuvers in the future.[10]

In his famed 1833 *Commentaries,* U.S. Supreme Court Justice Joseph Story reflected on the constitutional history of impeachment and the examples of Pickering and Chase. Impeachment, he concluded is "of a political character" and reaches beyond crimes to "gross neglect, or usurpation, or habitual disregard of the public interests, in the discharge of the duties of political office. These are so various in their character, and so indefinable in their actual involutions, that it is almost impossible to provide systematically for them by positive law." [11]

The first impeachment of an American president, Andrew Johnson in 1868, would show just how prophetic Story's words proved to be. Johnson's impeachment raises three major issues that are still lively and controversial today: 1. What are the grounds for impeachment, 2. What is the scope of presidential authority and, 3. What is the president's responsibility to obey the law?

THE MOST ACCIDENTAL OF PRESIDENTS

Like Donald Trump, hardly anyone expected Andrew Johnson to become president of the United States. If Trump seemed destined for stardom in business, young Andrew Johnson, born into poverty and apprenticed to a tailor at the age of ten, seemed destined to sew buttons and cut cloth for the rest of his days. What Johnson lacked in sophistication he compensated for in ambition, grit, and bravado. With help from his wife and customers at his shop, he first learned to read and eventually became a compelling speaker who had a say-anything style that confounded the conventional politicians of his time.

Johnson scratched his way up the sand hill of Tennessee politics as a Democrat in the early and middle years of the nineteenth century. He eventually became a United States senator in 1857. Johnson campaigned as the champion of the common people of America, who he said the political elites of his time had scorned and ignored.

Four years later, Johnson's political career seemed over when the nation plunged into civil war. Seven southern states, threatened by the election of Republican president Abraham Lincoln on a platform opposed to the expansion of slavery, seceded from the Union before his inauguration. The Civil War began when Confederate batteries fired on Fort Sumter on April 12, 1861, and in June, Tennessee seceded, becoming the last of the eleven states of the Confederacy.

As a slaveholder who upheld the sanctity of the federal union, Johnson was the maverick of his time, and he was the only senator in a seceding state who refused to resign his seat and join the Confederacy. Although Union predictions of a quick victory proved false and the war would grind on for four bloody years, Johnson's exile was short-lived. In February 1862, Union troops captured Nashville, Tennessee, making it the first Confederate state capital restored to the Union. Republican president Abraham Lincoln rewarded the loyal "war Democrat" Andrew Johnson by appointing him governor of Tennessee.

Two years later, Lincoln dumped his vice president, Hannibal Hamlin, and put his prized Democrat, Andrew Johnson, on his reelection ticket in a show of national unity. In his second inaugural address, Lincoln spoke of how the great and bloody war was a divine retribution for slavery, visited upon a guilty people both north and south. If the bloody war "continue until all the wealth piled by the bondsman's two hundred and fifty years of unrequited toil shall be sunk," he declared, "and until every drop of blood drawn with the lash shall be paid by another drawn with the sword, as was said three thousand years ago, so still it must be said, 'the judgments of the Lord are true and righteous altogether.'" His new vice president, Andrew Johnson, listened, but failed to comprehend the profound implications of Lincoln's words.[12]

THE WORST FATE THAT COULD BEFALL HIM

On April 15, 1865, just over a month after his inauguration, Lincoln died after the first presidential assassination in
American history, and Johnson became the most accidental
of presidents. In the wake of Lincoln's death, Johnson showed
a humility of the moment never seen in Donald Trump, com-
menting, "I feel incompetent to perform duties so important
and responsible as those which have been so unexpectedly
thrown upon me." But Johnson's humility did not last. His
more enduring character traits inclined him to stubbornness,
hasty action, disdain for cautious advice, and ill-tempered re-
torts against critics.[13]

Johnson loved the Union but not the black people it had
liberated from slavery. Although later in life a moderately
wealthy slaveholder, Johnson rose from the lower ranks of
white society, what some at the time called "mudsills," the
humble white farmers, laborers, tradesmen, and mechanics
that, like Trump, he had championed in his political campaigns. He saw mudsills as threatened both by aristocrats
from above and aspiring black people from below. At an out-
door rally, he told a crowd of cheering white men that he
was their Moses who would lead "the emancipation of the
white man" from their slavery under postwar Reconstruction.
Johnson, declared the former slave and abolitionist Frederick
Douglass euphemistically, is "no friend of our race."[14]

———

Johnson was an odd man in his time. He was an apostate Democrat assuming the incumbency of a Republican president. He lacked allies in either party and prided himself as an outsider untethered to a capital city that he called "12 square miles bordered by reality." By opposing efforts to reconstruct the nation and integrate newly freed slaves into American life, Johnson quickly fell afoul of a Congress controlled by Republicans with southern states still in limbo. He pardoned from the consequences of rebellion thousands of wealthy planters, some of whom with their wives had wined and dined him in Washington. With his humble roots and his penchant for spouting populism but privileging the rich, Johnson foreshadowed Trump.

Johnson pushed to restore southern states swiftly to the Union with no controls on race relations. He lambasted the "Radical Congress" for giving blacks privileges "torn from white men." In a comment eerily similar to Trump's denigration of a "so-called judge," Johnson decried Congress as "a body called or which assumes to be the Congress of the United States." He proclaimed to be protecting America, not from ex-Confederates, but from radical Republicans and their Negro allies. He forced Congress to override his vetoes on legislation aimed at protecting black rights and safety in the South and exploited his powers as president to evade and obstruct the enforcement of these laws.[15]

Johnson's conduct had tragic consequences for black people in the South. He restored to power, political and economic, much of the old slaveholding elite, who proceeded to keep their former slaves poor, controlled, and powerless. He forced his successor president and Congress to essentially begin anew much of the process of Reconstruction. Ultimately Reconstruction failed. The South remained mired in poverty, and the white supremacists who regained full control of southern governments imposed on African Americans the Jim Crow system of segregation and discrimination that endured for nearly a century. The failure of Reconstruction, "to a large degree," wrote the historian Michael Les Benedict, "could be blamed alone on President Johnson's abuse of his discretionary powers." [16]

In 1867, murmurings of impeachment began to circulate among exasperated, radical Republicans in Congress. In March, they had enacted over Johnson's veto the Tenure of Office Act, a law that cut into his powers by prohibiting the president from replacing without consent of the Senate any federal official who had previously won Senate approval. To bait an impeachment trap, Congress inserted a clause that said any violation constituted a "high crime and misdemeanor." And then, they waited. [17]

JOHNSON STANDS HIS GROUND

Johnson was at the defining moment of his presidency. His response to Congress's challenge would decide his own fate as president, with profound implications for every successor in the White House. He could battle Congress and risk impeachment or withdraw from the fray and count down passively the final days of his presidency. Or he could change his ways and reach an accord with the Reconstruction Congress.

Johnson stayed true to his notoriously pugnacious character and chose to fight. He taunted Congress by deliberately violating the Tenure of Office Act. "I have been advised by every member of my Cabinet that the entire Tenure-of-Office Act is unconstitutional," he later said.[18]

The House of Representatives struck back, by voting along party lines to approve articles of impeachment tied to Johnson's violation of the act. "He is not Napoleon," said Republican representative Tobias A. Plants of Ohio, "there will be no coup d'état!" To keep open all options for the Senate, members voted for eleven verbose and repetitive articles, totaling some forty-five hundred words.[19]

In the fixation on the dubious Tenure of Office violation, lost were the potentially more serious charges that Johnson had abused presidential power to obstruct Reconstruction and delegitimize another branch of government. Embedded within the garrulous articles was the charge that his conduct was "denying and intending to deny, that the legislation of said Congress was valid or obligatory." The articles charged him with saying that Congress was not a legitimate body "authorized by the Constitution to exercise legislative power." The articles further charged that he had willfully schemed to "prevent the execution" of legislation vital to congressional Reconstruction.[20]

Johnson's last chance to fight for his survival in the Senate had arrived. The Senate trial dragged on for nearly three months, with House prosecutors and defense lawyers clashing on issues that cut to the heart of the meaning of impeachment and the scope of presidential authority.

IMPEACHMENT'S BIG ISSUES

America's founders, insisted the prosecutors, placed no restrictions on what qualifies as an impeachable offense. Impeachment is not meant solely "for the *punishment of crime*," argued the chief prosecutor, Benjamin F. Butler of Massachusetts. A president should be impeached and convicted if he "imperils the public safety" and shows himself "unfit to occupy official position." Wrong, said Johnson's defense attorney Benjamin Curtis. Impeachment, he argued, requires a violation of law and not just of any law, but of "only *high* criminal offenses against the United States." The Senate cannot sit "as some nameless tribunal with unbounded and il-limitable jurisdiction."[21]

Prosecutors claimed that Johnson had no absolute au-thority to disobey the law, and that his discretion begins and ends with his veto power. The right "to judge upon any sup-posed conflict of an act of Congress with the Constitution is exhausted when he has examined a bill sent to him and returned it with his objections," Butler said. After that, he "must execute the law, whether in fact constitutional or not." Otherwise, "the government is the government of one man."[22]

The House's constriction of presidential power "does of-fend every principle of justice," responded another presiden-tial lawyer, William Evarts. "If an act be unconstitutional [the president] had a right to obey the Constitution," and "to raise a question between the Constitution and the law." The prosecutors, he warned, had proposed a subversive doc-trine that "constitutional laws and unconstitutional laws are all alike in this country," and the president must obey both equally.[23]

In their final bold argument against excessive presiden-tial authority, prosecutors said that the laws of Congress re-stricted the president's powers to remove federal officials. "If we concede such royal power to a president," said Represen-tative John A. Logan of Illinois, "he is henceforth the govern-ment." Americans must ask, "Will you have Andrew Johnson as President or King?" Johnson's attorney general, Henry

Stanbery, who rose from a sickbed to defend his president, argued that the Constitution granted the president absolute authority over removing administration officials. He fired Stanton "in the exercise of an undoubted power vested in him by the Constitution," performing "a strictly executive duty."[24]

Eventually, the Senate voted on three of the House's charges, only to fall one vote short of the two-thirds needed for conviction in each case. Seven Republicans joined all the minority Democrats in voting for Johnson's acquittal. "I knew he'd be acquitted; I knew it," declared Johnson's wife, Eliza, unsurprisingly his staunchest supporter.[25]

Yet defecting Republicans who saved Johnson's presidency may have been informed less by a quest for justice than by the rules of presidential succession at the time that would have elevated the controversial Speaker Pro-Tem of the Senate, Benjamin Wade of Ohio, to the presidency. The outspoken Senator had earned the nickname of "Bluff" and alienated many fellow Republicans with his radical views on Reconstruction and his support for paper money and protective tariffs. James Garfield, then a member of Congress, privately wrote that conservative Republicans feared "the Presidency of Ben Wade, a man of violent passions, extreme opinions, and narrow views."[26]

A WARNING FOR TRUMP

Johnson's acquittal may have pleased his wife, but it resolved none of the momentous issues debated at the trial. Johnson narrowly escaped removal, but a healthy majority of senators still had voted for his conviction. Although the Johnson precedent did not define the grounds for impeachment or disinfect the process from policy and politics, it showed how an impeachment and trial could benefit the nation. After his impeachment, Johnson tamed his invective and moderated his opposition to Republican Reconstruction. He served out quietly his last nine months in office without renewing his conflicts with Congress.[27]

To this day, impeachment remains subject only to the judgments of Congress. Too liberal use of impeachment could diminish the standing of Congress or unleash a chain reaction of uncontrolled partisan warfare. But too much restraint threatens to allow corruption and abuse to fester in the most powerful office in the world.

Andrew Johnson's *New York Times* obituary contains a warning for Donald Trump. The *Times* observed that "Undoubtedly the greatest misfortune that ever befell Andrew Johnson was the assassination of President Lincoln." Johnson's fatal flaw, it said, was that "he was always headstrong and 'sure he was right' even in his errors." The chapters to come will intimately acquaint you with Trump's arrogance and errors. Don't be fooled by the shifting decisions, policies, and pronouncements of a fast-moving presidency. May this be your guide to Trump's many vulnerabilities to the ultimate sanction of restraint on a president, and your foundation for building a case for his impeachment.[28]

CHAPTER 2

The Resignation of Richard Nixon: A Warning to Donald Trump

———

This is the operative statement. The others are inoperative.
                                    —*Richard Nixon press secretary*
                                    Ron Ziegler, April 17, 1973

You're saying it's a falsehood. And they're giving—Sean Spicer, our press secretary—gave alternative facts.
                                    —*Donald Trump senior advisor*
                                    Kellyanne Conway, January 22, 2017

In a retrospective on the Nixon scandals forty years after the Watergate break-in, Woodward and Bernstein conceded that "Nixon was far worse than we thought." Even early in his presidency, Donald Trump exhibits the same tendencies that led Nixon to violate the most basic standards of morality and threaten the foundations of our democracy. Both

———

Nixon and Trump exhibited a determination to never quit, to win at all costs, to attack and never back down, and to flout conventional rules and restraints. But as ambitious and headstrong as they were, they also shared a compulsion to deflect blame, and they were riddled with insecurities. They exploited the resentments of white working class Americans and split the world into enemies and loyalists. In the first month of his presidency Trump talked more about "enemies" than any other president in history. Neither man allowed the law, the truth, the free press, or the potential for collateral damage to others to impede their personal agendas. They cared little about ideology but very much about adulation and power. They had little use for checks and balances and stretched the reach of presidential authority to its outer limits. They obsessed over secrecy and thirsted for control without dissent.

The establishments in New York and Washington and at the elite universities viewed the two men with distaste throughout their long careers. In turn, these professed populists scorned a cultural elite of mainstream journalists, Hollywood celebrities, revered politicians, and Ivy League professors. When first elected president, Nixon had commanded his aides, "No one in Ivy League schools to be hired for a year—we need balance—trustworthy ones are the dumb ones." But "trustworthy" to whose benefit? Certainly not to the American people, who've put their welfare in the hands of that government meant to represent their—and not its own—best interests. So far, with few exceptions, Donald Trump has avoided Ivy League professors for cabinet or top staff positions in his administration.[1]

Long after he resigned the presidency, Richard Nixon confessed to an intense admiration of Donald Trump. To the magnate in 1987, he wrote: "Whenever you decide to run for office you will be a winner!" Trump proclaimed that he would hang Nixon's "amazing" letter in the Oval Office.[2]

In 1974, two years after winning a landslide reelection victory, Nixon avoided near certain impeachment and removal by becoming the only American president to resign the office. Nixon's story is *the* cautionary tale for Donald Trump.

WATERGATE: A CANCER ON THE PRESIDENCY

In 1972, Richard Nixon brilliantly orchestrated his reelection campaign, but he still feared that leaks of such illegal acts as a covert bombing war in Cambodia and the wiretapping of reporters and administration officials could sink his reelection and even lead to his impeachment. In 1971 he established in the White House a covert unit known as the Plumbers to plug leaks. Members of the unit doubled as dirty tricks specialists who would conduct the Watergate break-in and the burglary of the office of the psychiatrist of Daniel Ellsberg, the man who had leaked the Defense Department's secret history of the Vietnam War known as the "Pentagon Papers." "You can't let the Jew steal that stuff and get away with it," Nixon told his chief of staff, H. R. "Bob" Haldeman. "People don't trust these Eastern establishment people. He's Harvard. He's a Jew. You know, and he's an arrogant intellectual." [3]

In his campaign, Nixon set a model for Donald Trump by targeting the forgotten Americans: the so-called "Silent Majority, of white voters of modest means and education, ignored and scorned by Washington's elite." This Silent Majority of Americans believed that "as individuals they have lost control of a complicated and impersonal society which oppresses them with high taxes, spiraling inflation and enforced integration while rewarding the very poor and very rich." Nixon would woo the Silent Majority with the "old values of patriotism, hard work, morality, and respect for law and order." [4]

As for minorities, Nixon said that the administration would "pay attention" to blacks, "keep some around [to] avoid Goldwater problem." Earlier he had said, "I have the greatest affection for them, but I know they ain't gonna make it for five hundred years." As for Jews, they "won't get many, but don't write them off." Nixon advised that they should quietly woo Jewish and black support by meeting with leaders, but should "avoid speaking publicly to groups."[5]

This strategy worked so well that, by mid-1972, the polls showed Nixon some twenty points ahead of the presumptive Democratic nominee, South Dakota senator George McGovern.

Why then did Nixon or his top aides launch the break-in of the Democratic Party headquarters at the Watergate Building in June 1972? This foolishly bungled caper that the *Washington Post* labeled "Mission Incredible" could only upset Nixon's glide to reelection. The answer lies in a trait that Nixon and Trump share: a need for total control, combined with minimal self-awareness. Nixon still feared that somehow his enemies—the Kennedys, the press, the professors—would snatch from his hands the final victory he had worked so hard to earn. No loose end could be left unattended.[6]

What Nixon's press secretary Ron Ziegler dismissed as a "third-rate burglary attempt" would prove to be so much more. This was the hole in the dike that even Nixon's Plumbers could not plug. Eventually the dike would collapse and a flood of revelations about Nixon's corruption would wash away his presidency.

A month after the break-in, Nixon lectured his aide John Ehrlichman on what he had supposedly learned from his crusade as a young congressman that helped convict the alleged Communist spy Alger Hiss of perjury: "If you cover up, you're going to get caught. And if you lie you're going to be guilty of perjury. Now basically that was the whole story of the Hiss case. It is not the issue that will harm you; it is the cover-up that is damaging."[7]

Nixon's words to Ehrlichman may have been delivered with breezy assurance, but he was frantically working to cover up a trail that led from the break-in to the leadership of his administration and campaign. He relied on deception posing as candor and on preemptive sallies against anyone in the press who dared to dig into the story. In a press conference filled with lies, Nixon falsely claimed that he had personally investigated the matter and settled all concerns over Watergate. He said "categorically" that a White House investigation indicates "that no one in the White House staff, no one in this administration, presently employed, was involved in this very bizarre incident." Nixon added, "What really hurts is if you try to cover it up."[8]

When reporters Bob Woodward and Carl Bernstein began investigating the break-in and other dirty tricks for the *Washington Post*, Nixon trotted out Ziegler to assail the press, just as Donald Trump would do more than four decades later. Ziegler was a former Disneyland skipper and guide for its popular jungle cruise with no political experience other than with the Nixon team. In 1969 at the age of twenty-nine he became the youngest presidential press secretary in history. Nixon could always count on Ziegler to get out the administration's message of the day.

Ten days before the election he accused the now iconic Woodward and Bernstein of "shabby journalism," "character assassination," and "a vicious abuse of the journalistic process." He charged their employer, the *Post*, with a "political effort" to "discredit this administration and individuals within it." Earlier, Bernstein had told Nixon campaign manager John Mitchell, his former attorney general, that the *Post* would be publishing a story linking the Watergate burglary to a secret slush fund that Mitchell controlled. Mitchell responded with an unmistakable threat: "All that crap, you're putting in the paper? It's been denied. Jesus, Katie Graham [the *Post*'s publisher] is gonna get her tit caught in a big fat wringer if that's published."[9]

Nixon and Ziegler had set the precedent for Donald Trump and his aides when confronted with news reports of repeated contacts between Trump's campaign staff and Russian officials. Deny. Lie. Threaten. And blame the messengers in the press, not the message itself, for the scandal.

In 1973, the reelected president could not stanch the flood of revelations that poured out in the spring of 1973, indicating that high officials of the Nixon administration and CREEP had directed the break-in and pressured the defendants to remain silent. On March 21, White House counsel

John Dean warned Nixon that "We have a cancer within— close to the presidency, that's growing." A month later, Nixon's lies had become so tangled that Ron Ziegler had to declare all of the president's prior statements on Watergate "inoperative." "The Nixon Administration has developed a new language," commented *Time* magazine, "a kind of Nix-speak. Government officials are entitled to make flat statements one day, and the next day reverse field with the simple phrase, 'I misspoke myself.'" Surrogates would later find themselves caught in the same trap of struggling to explain away Trump-speak, often in the form of Trump-tweets.[10]

THE COVER-UP EXPOSED

By summer of 1973, as part of a deal with the Democratic Senate for his confirmation, Attorney General Elliot Richardson had appointed law professor Archibald Cox as a special prosecutor. This came as a stinging affront to Nixon, who had told his advisor Henry Kissinger six months earlier that "the professors are the enemy. Write that on a blackboard 100 times and never forget it." Worse still, Cox was from the Ivy League flagship of Harvard.[11]

With Democrats in control of the House and the Senate, a special Senate Watergate Committee headed by veteran Democratic senator Sam Ervin of North Carolina had begun holding spectacular televised hearings. The committee's investigation uncovered an iceberg of illegal and illicit activities that Nixon had desperately sought to keep hidden. The Watergate break-in, it suddenly became clear, was only the tip.

Not long after, in July 1973, Alexander P. Butterfield, an obscure former White House aide, launched a bombshell: the president had tape-recorded all conversations held in his White House offices. During a yearlong struggle over access to the tapes, Vice President Agnew became the first vice president since John C. Calhoun to resign the office. Investigators had found that as governor of Maryland, Agnew had accepted bribes and kickbacks from contractors doing business with the state. In December 1973, with the approval of both houses of Congress, Nixon appointed House Minority Leader Gerald Ford of Michigan, America's first unelected vice president.[12]

Even before the release of the tapes, though, another turn of events had already wounded Nixon beyond recovery. On Saturday evening October 20, 1973, in what would go down in history as the "Saturday Night Massacre," President Nixon ordered Attorney General Elliot Richardson to fire Cox; Richardson refused to obey what he believed to be an illegal order and resigned. Deputy Attorney General William D. Ruckelshaus also refused to carry out what he too believed was an illegal order and he resigned. Solicitor General Robert H. Bork then complied with the president's order and became the acting attorney general.

A *Time* magazine cover story called the massacre "one of the gravest constitutional crises," in presidential history. It spurred outrage in Congress across the aisles and for the first time, polls showed that a plurality of the American people favored the president's impeachment. On November 15, 1973, federal District Judge Gerhard A. Gesell ruled that, absent a showing of gross misconduct as required in the regulation establishing the special prosecutor's office, the dismissal of Cox was illegal. Two days later at a nationally televised press conference an increasingly desperate Nixon pleaded, "I'm not a crook. I've earned everything I've got." [13]

The firing proved to be of no avail to Nixon, though. Nixon ordered his compliant Acting Attorney General Robert Bork to replace Cox with Texas attorney Leon Jaworski—a former "Democrat for Nixon." Although neither a law professor nor an Ivy Leaguer, Jaworski wasn't dumb, corrupt, or compromised. He continued to investigate faithfully the Watergate scandal and pursue the tapes.

Who would be the Cox or Jaworski in an investigation of Donald Trump? Or the Ken Starr who later pursued Bill Clinton? Currently, the attorney general appoints a special prosecutor. But Trump has lost his security blanket in his loyalist Attorney General Jeff Sessions of Alabama. On March 2, 2017, Sessions recused himself from investigating the connections between Russia and the Trump team, after a Russia-related scandal of his own. Trump's nominee for Deputy Attorney

General, career prosecutor Rod Rosenstein, will take over the probe. Notably, in an Op Ed during the campaign co-authored with several other Trump backers, Sessions called for a special prosecutor to investigate Hillary Clinton.[14]

If a Special Prosecutor is appointed, even one seemingly sympathetic to the administration, the Jaworski example shows that she or he might respond in unpredictable ways. And members of Congress will be monitoring any investigation. Even the most self-assured of prosecutors may be loath to tangle with Senators Elizabeth Warren or John McCain.[15]

In fighting a subpoena to surrender the White House tapes to the Special Prosecutor, Nixon's attorneys argued for an absolutist interpretation of presidential power, just as Trump would in defending his travel ban. The courts, his attorneys argued, cannot review a presidential decision based on his "executive privilege" to withhold "confidential conversations between a President and his close advisors." The Supreme Court unanimously disagreed, pointing out that "Our system of government 'requires that federal courts on occasion interpret the Constitution in a manner at variance with the construction given the document by another branch.'"[16]

The release of the tape recordings—clearly showing that Nixon obstructed justice in covering-up the break-in and through other violations of law—made the most cut and dry case for impeachment in the history of the presidency. The depth and breadth of the scandal astonished even fellow Republicans. "The dread word 'Watergate,' is not just the stupid, unprofitable, break-in attempt," said Republican senator Ed Brooke. "It is perjury. Obstruction of justice. The solicitation and acceptance of hundreds of thousands of dollars in illegal campaign contributions. It is a pattern of arrogance, illegality and lies which ought to shock the conscience of every Republican." [17]

In July 1974, members of both parties in the Judiciary Committee voted three articles of impeachment against the president. Two of the articles indicted the president for the crimes of obstructing justice and ignoring subpoenas issued by the House Judiciary Commission. Another article charged the gross abuse of presidential power, a likely ground for an impeachment of President Trump.

A week after the Committee's vote, former GOP presidential nominee Barry Goldwater, Senate Minority Leader Hugh Scott, and House Minority Leader John Rhodes warned Nixon of an inevitable impeachment by the House and conviction by the Senate, where Republican support for acquittal had dwindled to a few diehards. Two days later, the ever-pragmatic Nixon resigned the presidency, the first and last president to do so. Ever the dissembler, Nixon said he resigned to put "the interest of America first" and although some of his judgments "were wrong, they were made in what I believed at the time to be the best interest of the Nation." [18]

In his later years, Nixon seemed to have learned nothing from Watergate, but continued to believe that his problems resulted not from his own misdeeds, but from the failure of his cover-up. In 1987, during the Iran-Contra scandal, Nixon privately advised President Ronald Reagan: "Don't *ever* comment on the Iran-Contra matter again. Have instructions issued to all White House staffers and Administration spokesman that they must *never* answer any question on or off the record about that issue in the future." [19]

THE 'UNWRITTEN' ARTICLES OF IMPEACHMENT: TREASON AND A CRIME AGAINST HUMANITY

The House Judiciary Committee, caught up in the events of Watergate and lacking full information, did not impeach Nixon for arguably his two most serious crimes: treason and a crime against humanity. During his campaign for the presidency in 1968, Nixon claimed that he had a "secret plan" to end the War in Vietnam. But like Trump's secret plan to defeat ISIS that he promoted in 2016, Nixon's plan was political rhetoric lacking in substance. What Nixon really feared was a peace deal before Election Day that would steal his thunder and snatch away his last chance for political redemption. Defeat was not an option, and in preemptive response, Nixon illegally meddled in the peace process as a still-private citizen, thereby committing a serious and impeachable offense.

Although peace in Vietnam may have been a long shot, Nixon had tried to sabotage negotiations, putting at risk for his own political ends the lives of many thousands of Americans and Asians. Nixon pressured the South Vietnamese government to stall the peace process and await a better deal under his presidency. Historian John A. Farrell said that Nixon's "apparently criminal behavior" during the campaign "may be more reprehensible than anything Nixon did in Watergate," because of "the human lives at stake and the decade of carnage that followed in Southeast Asia."[20]

President Lyndon B. Johnson, who had wiretapped Nixon's telephone, knew of Nixon's traitorous conduct. He overheard Nixon declare that "we're going to say to Hanoi, 'I [Nixon] can make a better deal than he [Johnson] has, because I'm fresh and new, and I don't have to demand as much as he does in the light of past positions.'" In a conversation with Republican Senate Minority Leader Everett Dirksen, Johnson said, "This is *treason* . . . that they're contacting a foreign power in the middle of a war."[21] Nixon had at worst committed treason and at best violated federal law. The Logan Act of 1799 forbid unauthorized citizens from contacting "any foreign government or any officer or agent thereof with intent to influence the measures or conduct of any foreign government." Violation of the law is a felony, punishable by fines and imprisonment. For the first time since the Nixon era, talk of possible treason and violations of the obscure Logan Act have arisen again with new revelations of contacts between members of the Trump team and Russian officials.[22]

The Judiciary Committee passed over another potential article charging Nixon with his worst offense, a "crime against humanity" for his illegal, secret war in Cambodia. The concept of a crime against humanity originated during the Nuremberg War trials of Nazi leaders in 1945–1946. As opposed to a specific war crime like torture, a crime against humanity is generally regarded as a widespread or systematic attack directed against any civilian population or an identifiable part of a population, with no exemption for heads of state. Nixon's covert bombing of Cambodia falls within that rubric.[23]

In 1965, the violence of America's war in Vietnam spilled into neighboring Cambodia when President Johnson began a secret but limited bombing campaign against sanctuaries in Cambodia for the Army of North Vietnam and the Communist Vietcong guerillas. President Nixon escalated the raids into an intense carpet-bombing of Cambodia over four years. "There is no limitation on mileage and there is no limitation on budget," he said. The U.S. dropped a greater tonnage of TNT on this small nation than on all its enemies during World War II.[24]

The carpet-bombing that devastated Cambodia did nothing to help the American war effort, but it killed some 50,000 to 150,000 civilians, and tragically pushed many young men and women into the camp of the Khmer Rouge Communist guerrillas led by the French-educated Pol Pot. During its brief reign from 1975 to 1979, the Khmer Rouge directly or indirectly killed some 1.5 million Cambodians in a population of just 8 million.[25]

Nixon's bombing of Cambodia was illegal in both its conception and execution. He lacked authorization from Congress to bomb Cambodia and kept the operation secret, covering it up with lies. "It's the best kept secret of the war!" Nixon told Senate hawk John Stennis of Mississippi in April 1970. Days later, Nixon lied to the American people at a press conference, saying that U.S. policy "has been to scrupulously respect the neutrality of the Cambodian people." Once the bombing became public, Nixon draped himself in the justification of "national security," even though he had earlier admitted that the cumulative impact of all his bombings in Southeast Asia was "zilch."[26]

One of the most consequential questions facing the Trump presidency is whether he will commit a crime against humanity by exacerbating climate change, and posing an existential threat to humanity. In 2016, the International Criminal Court announced that it would expand its focus to "crimes against the environment," which would include catastrophic climate change.[27]

THE ROAD TO IMPEACHMENT

Nixon's first political campaign, a successful run for Congress in 1946, would mirror in many ways Trump's first campaign—for president of the United States. Fighting for average Jane and John Doe against a corrupt and even treasonous Washington establishment, Nixon campaigned as the outsider. He exploited voter fear and resentment by smearing his opponent Jerry Voorhis, a middle-of-the road Democrat, as a Communist sympathizer.[28]

Nixon rode his anti-Communism all the way to a seat in the U.S. Senate in 1950, defeating former movie star Helen Gahagan Douglas, who he branded as a Communist sympathizer. He distributed literature, printed in black ink on pink paper, with the dark warning that Douglas voted in lockstep with the socialist member of Congress Vito Marcantonio. Douglas forever became known as the "Pink Lady," but

Nixon couldn't shake the name she had plastered on him: "Tricky Dick Nixon."[29]

Right-wing extremists rallied to Nixon's cause. Gerald L. K. Smith, the notorious anti-Semite, exhorted voters to reject a woman "who sleeps with a Jew," a reference to the fact that her husband, Melvyn Douglas, had a Jewish father and a Christian mother. Nixon repudiated Smith's support, but the damage was done.[30]

In 2016, the outpouring of support for Donald Trump by anti-Semites, neo-Nazis, and white nationalists far exceeded what Nixon experienced. For these extremists, the advent of Trump has "been an awakening," in the words of Richard B. Spencer, who some journalists credit with coining the term "alt-right" to describe his movement. Like Nixon, Trump belatedly and tepidly rejected such support, but he openly courted it by appointing Steve Bannon as his campaign manager and then his chief White House strategist.[31]

As the CEO of Breitbart News, Bannon bragged that "We're the platform for the alt-right." Under his watch, Breitbart belittled conservative editor Bill Kristol, as a "Renegade Jew." It warned that "Political Correctness Protects Muslim Rape Culture." It smeared the NAACP, saying, "NAACP Joins Soros Army Planning DC Disruptions, Civil Disobedience, Mass Arrests," and glorified the Confederacy saying, "Hoist It High and Proud: The Confederate Flag Proclaims a Glorious Heritage." It equated feminism with "cancer," and warned of a "Dangerous Faggot Tour" coming to college campuses.[32]

In 1952, after Eisenhower tapped him for the second spot on his presidential ticket, the press reported that Nixon's business backers had set up a secret slush fund for hm. "Tricky Dick" defused the scandal and demonstrated his mastery of showmanship and the media by delivering a brilliant televised speech that rather framed himself as a humble, uncorrupted man of still-modest means. The clincher came when Nixon admitted to receiving one gift, his little dog, Checkers. With this so-called "Checkers speech," the most-watched television event to date, Nixon pulled off his first political comeback and saved his place on Eisenhower's ticket. Donald Trump would later prove to be Nixon's equal and even his superior in exploiting free media.[33]

In 1960, Nixon easily won the Republican nomination for president, but lost narrowly to his former House colleague John F. Kennedy. Kennedy's narrow margins of victory in Illinois and Texas prompted Republicans to challenge the vote count in court despite an official disavowal from Nixon, who refused to disparage American democracy and was already planning his next political resurrection. Nevertheless, GOP Representative from Minnesota and former missionary Walter Judd preached a sermon on voter fraud that foreshadowed Donald Trump's cry against the same more than a half century later: "A party can still lose an election if it is not sufficiently alert and tough in policing registrations and voting booths and counting procedures to make certain that only legitimate votes are cast and all votes legitimately cast are honestly counted."[34]

After losing the presidency in 1960 Nixon lost again two years later when he ran for governor of California. In his post-election press conference, Nixon delivered a 15-minute self-absorbed, Trump-style harangue against his enemies in the press, whom he blamed for his loss. "You won't have Nixon to kick around anymore, because, gentlemen, this is my last press conference," he said before walking away.[35]

Yet the resilient Nixon won another presidential nomination in 1968, when Michigan Governor George Romney, his closest rival, and the father of Mitt, wrecked his campaign by attributing earlier support for the War in Vietnam to "brainwashing" by American generals and diplomats. In his winning general election campaign Nixon returned to the attack strategies that had served him well in his earlier campaigns for the U.S. House and Senate. Through his surrogate, vice presidential nominee Spiro Agnew, the governor of Maryland, he smeared his Democratic opponent Vice President Hubert Humphrey as "soft on inflation, soft on Communism, and soft on law and order." Agnew belittled anti-war demonstrators as "spoiled brats" who "take their tactics from Castro and their money from Daddy." Reprising the success of his "Checkers" speech Nixon expertly played the press, gaining widespread coverage often in carefully staged settings of his own choosing.[36]

Trump too is a creation of the media. He expertly played the media in his campaign as a show they could not ignore. According to a study by mediaQuant, in the year before the election, Trump received some $5 billion in free media coverage, compared to $3.2 billion for Hillary Clinton, an extraordinary edge of $1.8 billion.[37]

Once elected, Nixon's paranoia, his obsession with secrecy and control, and his penchant for punishing enemies guided the organization of his administration. He ran his presidency through the National Security Council (NSC) and his White House staff, led by chief of staff Bob Haldeman and his aide John Ehrlichman. Trump too would place importance on his NSC and centralize decision-making in the White House. Trump too would place great importance on his NSC and centralize decision-making within a tight corps of the White House.[38]

As President, Nixon's loathing of any independent check on his presidency led to a deep-seated animosity toward the media. "The press is your enemy." "Enemies," he un-

derscored. "Understand that? . . . Don't help the bastards.
Ever. Because they're trying to stick the knife right in our
groin." Nixon threatened journalists with banishment from
the White House. He went as far as to wiretap the phones
of his own aides suspected of disloyalty and journalists he
found particularly troublesome. His surrogate Agnew famously blasted the press as the "nattering nabobs of nega-
tivism." "Our real game plan," wrote political advisor Lyn
Nofziger, "[is] making our own point in our own time and
in our own ways that the press is liberal, pro-Democratic
and biased."[39]

IS THE LONG NIGHTMARE OVER?

Following Nixon's resignation, Gerald Ford was now president, even though he had never been elected to any position
higher than member of Congress from Grand Rapids, Michigan. In his most notable decision as president, Ford issued
a full and unconditional pardon to Nixon for any crimes he
may have committed against the United States. "Our long
national nightmare is over," he said. Ford was wrong. The
nightmare of Watergate lives on in America's collective
memory, and resonates as a loud and clear warning to President Trump.[40]

John Dean, Nixon's former White House counsel whose

testimony helped uncover the truths of Watergate, warned that Trump could be headed for a Nixonian crash. "The way the Trump presidency is beginning it is safe to say it will end in calamity," Dean said. "It is almost a certainty. Even Republicans know this!"[41]

CHAPTER 3

Flouting the Law

———

"I'm very confident he's not breaking any law."
—*Kellyanne Conway, November 21, 2016*

A SERIAL LAWBREAKER

Since his early days in business, Trump has elevated himself again and again above the laws that govern others. Andrew Johnson broke a law that he believed was unconstitutional; Donald Trump has broken many laws for personal gain. No other president comes close to matching his history of violations.

As a private citizen, Donald Trump has escaped serious retribution for his crimes and transgressions. He's settled civil lawsuits charging him with breaking racketeering and civil rights laws, paid fines that he could well afford, protracted litigation, and concealed lawbreaking for many years. There are two avenues of impeachment opened by Trump's practice

———

of disregarding the law. First, although unlikely, the House of Representatives could vote articles of impeachment and the Senate could convict Trump for illegal acts *that occurred prior to assuming office.* The Constitution specifies no time limits on any of its enumerated impeachable offenses. There is no statute of limitations and no judicial review of decisions made by either the House or the Senate. Past actions could also become part of a larger impeachment.

There are several laws that I believe Trump might break while in office. His expansive view of presidential authority echoes Richard Nixon's claim that "when the president does it, that means that it is not illegal." Nixon was wrong and paid a heavy price for his error. As the expression goes, history does not repeat itself, but it rhymes.

VIOLATION OF THE FAIR HOUSING ACT

Sheila Morse, an undercover real estate "tester" of housing discrimination for the Human Rights Commission in the early 1970s, still vividly remembers the work. When black people began to complain that building managers were denying them the chance to rent an apartment, the commission dispatched Morse, who is white, to see if she would receive a different response. Morse recalls, among other episodes, that the division dispatched her to a specific apartment building where a black man had complained that when he inquired about a FOR RENT sign posted outside the building, the superintendent had told him that the apartment was rented and the sign was still posted in error. When Morse arrived at the location, the sign was up, and the superintendent immediately welcomed her into the building, showed her the vacant apartment, and assured her that she could sign a lease the next day. "I guess I was the right color and the gentleman was the wrong color," Morse concluded.[1]

When Morse, an official of the commission, and the rejected black applicant confronted the superintendent, he said, "I'm only doing what my boss told me to do—I am not to rent to black tenants." The superintendent's "boss" was Trump Management, which owned and operated the building; Donald J. Trump was the president and his father, Fred Trump, was the chairman of the board. Thus marked the first of Trump's many clashes with the law.[2]

Based on the findings of testers like Sheila Morse, complaints from minorities, and evidence that the company "discouraged rental to blacks" and had secretly marked minority applications with codes such as "C" for colored, the United States Department of Justice sued Trump's company in 1973 for violating the Fair Housing Act of 1968. Rather than attempting to resolve the matter, Trump hired Senator Joseph McCarthy's former lawyer Roy Cohn to attack the Justice Department and obstruct their efforts to enforce the law. After two years of extraordinary obstruction and delay, which the head of Justice's Civil Rights Division said exceeded anything he had witnessed in seventeen years at the bar, Trump reached a settlement with the government in 1975.[3]

Trump spun the settlement into proof that his company had done nothing wrong, contrary to his two years of obstruction, his avowed reluctance to settle lawsuits, and the weight of the evidence. The government "had the [racial] coding, they had the testers, and had the testimony of people who worked there," said former Justice attorney Elyse Goldweber. "It was an important, significant step for enforcement of the Fair Housing Act. It was a big deal." It was clear to everyone except Trump that he had flagrantly broken the law.[4]

The government found that Trump's promise to correct the rental practices at his properties proved of little avail. A year later, the Justice Department dispatched white and black testers to Trump buildings and found *again* that his managers were denying black people apartments or steering them to selected properties. Justice officials concluded that "an underlying pattern of discrimination continues to exist in the Trump management organization." Justice reopened the case, but the matter was never fully resolved.[5]

THE FRAUDULENT CHARITY

A decade later, Trump broke the law once again, this time with his establishment of the Trump Foundation in New York

City to donate proceeds from his book *The Art of the Deal*. Trump contributed $5.5 million to the charity through 2008 and has not deposited a penny since. It has hauled in $9.3 million from outside donors—all of it raised without legally required registration.[6]

Under New York state law, "most organizations that hold property of any kind for charitable purposes or engage in charitable activities in New York State and/or solicit charitable contributions (including grants from foundations and government grants) in New York are required to register with the Attorney General's Charities Bureau." An investigation by the New York attorney general Eric Schneiderman discovered that Trump never registered his charity; it had been operating without legally required registration ever since it began trolling for donations.[7]

The failure to register a charity in New York is no minor, technical violation of law. By operating unregistered, the Trump Foundation avoided required audits that would likely have disclosed the many ways in which Trump has exploited the foundation for illegal self-dealing. Laws against self-dealing prohibit heads of nonprofit organizations from using their charity's funds to benefit themselves, their businesses, or their family members.

In drawing upon foundation funds solicited from others to settle personal and business debts, Trump has, in effect, laundered tax-free donations for his own gain. Donations to the "charity" included some $4.5 million from Vince and Linda McMahon of World Wrestling Entertainment. Trump has since appointed Linda McMahon to head the Small Business Administration. In 2007, the town of Palm Beach, Florida, fined Trump's Mar-a-Largo resort $120,000 for failing to take down a flagpole that soared thirty-eight feet above the legally authorized limit. When Trump proposed donating $100,000 to veterans' organizations, the city agreed to rescind the fine. He made the donation not with his own money, but with tax-free foundation funds donated by others, and thereby escaped paying the fine.[8]

Trump further flouted the law by diverting taxable personal and business income to the tax-free foundation. An investigation by the *Washington Post* found that Donald Trump's charitable foundation "has received approximately $2.3 million from companies that owed money to Trump or one of his businesses but were instructed to pay Trump's tax-exempt foundation instead." Because Trump has refused to release any of his tax returns, it is not possible to verify whether he paid taxes on these payments. If Trump did, indeed, fail to pay the required taxes, he could be guilty of the federal and state crimes of tax evasion—which may be just one of many reasons why he has not and will not release his tax returns.[9]

Trump's reportedly illegal use of his foundation does not end there. In 2007, and again in 2014, Trump used $30,000 of his foundation's funds to purchase two portraits of himself, which he reportedly displayed in his business properties. In 2012, his foundation spent $12,000 on a Tim Tebow football jersey and autographed helmet, whereabouts unknown. In 2013, the Trump Foundation made an illegal $25,000 campaign contribution to a political committee supporting Florida attorney general Pam Bondi while her office was examining allegations of fraud against Trump University. The IRS fined Trump $2,500 for this violation of law.[10]

In October of 2016, the New York attorney general ordered the foundation to cease soliciting donations, which it did shortly thereafter. Then, a month and a half after the presidential election, Trump announced that he was shuttering the foundation, "to avoid even the appearance of any conflict with my role as president." Not so fast, responded Attorney General Schneiderman. "The Trump Foundation is still under investigation by this office and cannot legally dissolve until that investigation is complete," Schneiderman's office confirmed.[11]

In its 2015 tax filings, the Trump Foundation admitted to having engaged in self-serving activities, including the transfer of "income or assets to a disqualified person." The filing did not, however, provide full details on the matter, and Trump has refused any comment. Louisiana State University law professor Philip Hackney, who formerly worked in Office of the Chief Counsel of the IRS, rightly asked, "What transactions led to the self-dealing that they're admitting to? Why weren't they able to recognize them in prior years?"[12]

CUBA AND CASINOS

Trump began expanding his enterprises abroad in the 1990s, and he looked to Cuba as a possible venue for casino operations, perhaps under the misguided belief that the Clinton administration might end the embargo against doing business there. According to documents found by Kurt Eichenwald of *Newsweek,* representatives of Trump Hotels & Casino Resorts Inc. spent $68,000 in Cuba in 1998 to explore investment opportunities, violating the federal government's strict embargo against spending any money for commercial purposes in the country. Exceptions to the embargo did not cover casinos, and the company did not apply for a federal license in advance of travel. The documents further indicate that rather than directly fund the Cuban venture, Trump's company sought to cover up their crime by funneling the cash through an American consulting firm, and then falsely attempting to link the spending to a charitable group.[13]

The U.S. Government Accountability Office reports that "the embargo on Cuba is the most comprehensive set of U.S. sanctions on any country, including the other countries designated by the U.S. government to be state sponsors of terrorism." Violation of the Cuban embargo is a federal crime punishable by up to ten years in prison, $1 million in corporate fines, and $250,000 in individual fines. Trump can no longer be charged with violating the Cuban embargo only because the statute of limitations has long run its course.[14]

The Cuba venture was not the only time that Trump's casino operations violated the law. State officials in New Jersey and New York repeatedly fined his enterprises in amounts ranging from tens to hundreds of thousands of dollars. One of the violations in particular showed just how little Trump had learned from the housing discrimination litigation. New Jersey regulators fined the Trump Plaza casino $200,000 for removing African American and female employees from the craps tables when a favored high roller who objected to the presence of minorities and women was playing there. "There are, or ought to be, certain things that a casino hotel cannot sell or provide to a customer in order to assure his continued patronage," said Steven Perskie, then a casino commissioner who had helped Trump win his licenses. "These things include honor and decency and simple human courtesy and an unwavering commitment to statutory obligations, including the law against discrimination."[15]

When Trump's Atlantic City casinos collapsed, in typical fashion he passed the buck, blaming the economy. While other Atlantic City casinos thrived in the same economy, Trump's enterprises bled red ink in the amount of $1.5 billion—not of his money, but of investor money. Yet somehow Trump managed to deduct $916 million in paper losses on his 1995 taxes, which could have enabled him to avoid paying taxes for nearly two decades. In the first presidential debate, Trump said that not paying taxes "makes me smart." If he ever builds his vanity "Trump Wall" on the Mexican border, it probably won't be Mexico that funds it, but the many Americans who weren't smart enough to avoid paying their taxes.[16]

TRUMP'S FRAUDULENT UNIVERSITY

In 2004, Trump hit upon a new way to make money and extend the reach and renown of his brand when he entered the lucrative, for-profit education business. For-profit colleges and universities had proliferated across America in the 1990s and the early twenty-first century and Trump saw his chance to get a slice of the pie. He launched the for-profit Trump University, which promised to impart his lucrative real estate secrets to anyone willing to pay. The university began with online instruction before moving into live seminars and allegedly long-term mentoring.[17]

Can a university exist if it offers no course credit, confers no degrees, does not grade students, and submits to no outside review? The answer under the law is no. Like the Trump Foundation, Trump University was illegal from its inception;

it failed to fulfill the most basic requirements for a university under New York state law. New York state officials were not fooled and ordered Trump to cease using the word "university." Unsurprisingly, Trump delayed complying, and it was five years before he changed the name of his operation to the Trump Entrepreneur Initiative and then soon after closed its doors. Trump claimed that running a bogus university was "not like a big deal," and then deflected by blaming the project's director, Michael Sexton, for violating the law: "I thought [Sexton] had it all worked out." [18]

Lawsuits filed on behalf of thousands of former students charged that Trump University "violated federal law across the country and state law (in California, Florida, and New York) by promising, but not delivering, access to Trump's real estate techniques taught by 'handpicked' professors at an elite 'university.'" This fraud, the lawsuits charged, had swindled students out of fees allegedly of up to $50,000. [19]

In 2006, well before disgruntled students began filing lawsuits or Trump University became front-page news, journalist Kelly Roesler detailed the efforts by Trump and his marketers to sign her up for expensive real estate instruction. She received by e-mail "a personal invitation from Donald Trump." Follow-up callers told her that she was chosen out of "thousands upon thousands of people" for a chance to make untold riches through enrollment at Trump University, where "the coaches and mentors have been hand-selected by

Donald J. Trump"—"$100,000 your first year." But "it takes money to make money," some $15,000 a year in tuition and fees. "Do you trust Donald Trump?" they pressed. "[He] has billions riding on this." "Probably the most important thing I've learned," she said, "is that $15,000 means a great deal more in my pocket than in Donald's."[20]

The allegations against Trump's bogus "university" were serious enough to justify a federal class-action lawsuit, charging that Trump violated the Racketeer Influenced and Corrupt Organizations Act (RICO), an act usually directed against organized crime. In his deposition, Trump claimed that "hand-picking" meant telling Sexton to find "very good people." He could not identify any instructors and did not know whether they had "presented any of [Trump's] actual real estate strategies," and was unaware "of the exact details" of the seminars. He didn't know "whether the instructors for these seminars ever bought and sold real estate." He conceded that the secrets presented in pricey seminars could be found in his published books. Former instructor Ronald Schnackenberg testified by affidavit that "I never saw Donald Trump at Trump University." Based on personal experience, he said, "I believe Trump University was a fraudulent scheme, and that it preyed upon the elderly and uneducated to separate them from their money."[21]

In 2016, Trump settled the lawsuits for $25 million pending final judicial approval. And again, he claimed victory instead of defeat: "The ONLY bad thing about winning the Presidency" he tweeted, "is that I did not have the time to go through a long but winning trial on Trump U. Too bad!"[22]

The settlement means that there will not be a final judicial verdict on whether Trump's operation violated the RICO statute and other laws. But the miserly tycoon would not have shelled out $25 million to settle what he had called an "easy win." Contrary to Trump's dismissal, running an illegal university was a "big deal," and he paid dearly to avoid a racketeering verdict that he knew might lead to calls for his impeachment.

EXPLOITATION OF UNDOCUMENTED IMMIGRANTS

In his everlasting quest for an edge in business, Trump exploited undocumented immigrant workers, men and women who dared not protest low wages or dreadful working conditions out of fear of arrest and deportation. Under 8 U.S. Code Section 1324a, it is a federal crime, punishable by fines and imprisonment, to recruit or hire undocumented immigrants. Ironically, Donald Trump made opposition to illegal immigration the centerpiece of his presidential campaign. To build his iconic Trump Tower in Manhattan in 1980, he hired undocumented Polish immigrants to take down the existing structure on the property. Aware of his leverage over them, Trump reportedly paid the workers substandard wages, kept them working long hours in unsafe conditions, and avoided paying them overtime or benefits.

For decades, Trump insisted that he had no involvement in hiring undocumented workers; he blamed his contractors and subcontractors. After combing through thirteen boxes of court testimony and sworn depositions, investigators from *Time* magazine found that "Trump sought out the Polish workers when he saw them on another job, instigated the creation of the company that paid them and negotiated the hours they would work." Trump often toured the site himself, talking with the workers and meeting with them outside the job to haggle over wages. The workers ultimately sued Trump, who, true to form, dragged out the case for fifteen years and then settled for undisclosed terms.[23]

Some twenty-four years after the Polish workers cleared the Trump Tower site, charges by Canadian-born fashion model Rachel Blais indicate that his exploitation of illegal foreign workers may well have persisted through recent times and was not confined to manual laborers. For six months in 2004, Blais worked for the profitable Trump Model Management before obtaining a legally required work visa. During that time, she modeled outfits on Trump's reality TV series, *The Apprentice*, while Trump looked on from the front row of the audience. She told a reporter for *Mother Jones* that she arrived in New York City by bus in April 2004. Like "the majority of models who are young, [and have] never been to NYC, and don't have papers, I was just put in Trump's models' apartment."[24]

The models lived in small dormitories. As young foreign women working illegally, they were in no position to protest their conditions. Blais provided *Mother Jones* a detailed financial statement showing that Trump's agency charged her as much as $1,600 a month for a room she shared with five other girls.

Blais said she only had a tourist visa, not a work visa, and that "most of the girls in the apartment that were not American didn't have a work visa." Blais said that Trump's company docked her not just for rent, but also for trainers, beauty treatments, travel, administrative costs, and eventually the cost of her work visa itself. Her financial statement shows that despite making tens of thousands of dollars for the company during her three years of employment, she netted precisely $8,427.35. That's when she left the agency. "This is a system where they actually end up making money on the back of these foreign workers," Blais said. His agency, she said, didn't bother getting work visas for all their models; those who couldn't cut it were sent back to their homelands. "Honestly, they are the most crooked agency I've ever worked for, and I've worked for quite a few. It is like modern-day slavery." The penalties for a "pattern and practice" of hiring unauthorized foreign workers includes fines and possible imprisonment. Trump did not respond to these charges. Ronald Lieberman, executive vice president for management and development at the Trump Organization, however, said that the allegations refer to events from "many, many years ago," He said he couldn't verify what might have happened 10 or more years ago without combing through company records, but as of now, "everything is being done perfectly."[25]

IMPEACHMENT—BREAKING THE LAW

These examples demonstrate Trump has also already arguably violated a staggering number of federal and state laws: The Fair Housing Act, New York charity law, tax laws, the Cuban embargo, casino regulations, the RICO statute, and laws against employing illegal immigrants. And any number of these laws could, if resurrected through an investigation, trigger impeachment while in office.

The most likely targets of an impeachment inquiry are the illegal operations of his foundation and his alleged exploitation of undocumented immigrants at his modeling agencies. Both violations are recent and significant. The employment of undocumented immigrants also contradicts one of Trump's fundamental appeals, to a fundamental theme of the Trump campaign and presidency: to keep American jobs for Americans.

Shortly before retiring from the Senate in 2017, Democrat Barbara Boxer of California called for an investigation into Trump's modeling agency by the U.S. Citizenship and Immigration Services, writing that "firsthand accounts by several former Trump models, coupled with a thorough review of financial and immigration records by *Mother Jones,* indicate widespread noncompliance with immigration and labor laws by Trump Model Management."[26]

Impeachment, as I've stressed, need not be limited to violations that occur during the president's term of office. In 2010, the House impeached and the Senate convicted Louisiana district court judge G. Thomas Porteous, at least in part for transgressions committed prior to his assuming the federal judgeship. The Senate convicted Porteous on all four articles that included charges of misconduct while he served as a state court judge and of having lied to the Senate and the FBI during his confirmation process for the federal bench.

After Porteous's conviction, one senator, who had previously served as a U.S. attorney and state attorney general, unequivocally stated that grounds for impeachment and conviction are not limited to offenses committed while in office:

As a former federal prosecutor and state attorney general, I have reviewed and drafted a number of indictments. I do not believe that evidence of acts committed *before confirmation should be withheld from consideration in the impeachment process* . . . The Constitution does not require that all conduct be committed post federal appointment nor does it stipulate at all when the conduct must occur. Whether treason or bribery occurs before or after confirmation is not the question, but whether or not it occurred. If this were not so, individuals like Judge Porteous, who are very capable of practicing the art of deception and are confirmed, could not be removed from office.[27]

Senator Jeff Sessions of Alabama, now the attorney general of the United States under President Donald J. Trump.

Not only can a president be impeached for prior conduct, but also for conduct unrelated to his official duties. See Bill Clinton. Against the strenuous objections of Democrats, the Republican-controlled House in 1998 impeached Bill Clinton for perjury and obstruction of justice related to his private, consensual affair with White House intern Monica Lewinsky. Republican representative Steve Buyer, a leader of the movement to impeach Clinton, said, "Personal misconduct, violations of trust and other charges of a more private nature can be impeachable offenses." Nearly every Republican in Congress issued their agreement by voting to impeach the president. The Republicans who now control Congress should held be held to the same standard when it comes to Donald Trump.[28]

As president, it is not just past offenses but also any future violation that can become grounds for impeachment as a "high crime" or "misdemeanor," or lead to civil lawsuits. For example, Trump said during his first week that "torture or waterboarding or however you want to define it," in his opinion "does work."

This could lead to violating anti-torture laws, and America's international treaty commitments. Trump also said that he would defer to his defense secretary, James Mattis, who opposes torture. Ultimately, though, Trump, not Mattis, is the boss, and the deference lasts only as long as Trump wants it to.[29]

Besides, as America witnessed during the presidency of George W. Bush, when Justice Department officials tried to exclude waterboarding from the meaning of torture, there emerged alternative ways to construe the word. If, for Trump, sales can be nonsales and developing, nondeveloping, then torture could be redefined as nontorture.

If Trump were to leak highly classified information from America's intelligence agencies, he could be in violation of federal secrecy laws. Trump has already waged war against the intelligence community, calling their work "catastrophic." Like National Security Advisor retired general Michael Flynn did before resigning less than three weeks into Trump's term, Trump might regard secrecy rules as a ruse for covering up the "corrupt" establishment's misdeeds. In defiance of "corrupt" authority, General Flynn has in the past leaked highly classified information to Pakistan without permission and had technicians secretly install an illegal Internet connection in his Pentagon office.[30]

The administration has also edged close to breaking the law protecting federal whistleblowers. You can't wiretap cell phones today like Nixon did with landlines decades ago, but press secretary Sean Spicer came close when he ordered staffers to hand over their cell phones so he could check for traces of leaks. Spicer warned that the initial search would be "recess" compared to what he would do if he didn't uncover the sources of leaks.[31]

Even more ominously, President Trump has implied that he might enlist the military for domestic crime control except under special circumstances, according to 18 U.S. Code Section 1385. Trump called his stepped-up deportations "a military operation because what has been allowed to come into our country." He said this operation is getting "really bad dudes out of this country." Like Mattis, Homeland Security

Secretary John Kelly backtracked on Trump's comments. But Trump is his boss, too.[32]

So far in his presidency, Trump has shown signs that he will follow his history of not letting laws and regulations get in the way of his goals. We must keep a close eye on Trump and look to hold him accountable to the law.

CHAPTER 4

Conflicts of Interest

––––––––

Prior to the election, it was well known that I have interests in properties all over the world. Only the crooked media makes this a big deal!
—*Donald J. Trump, November 21, 2016*

The law's totally on my side, meaning, the president can't have a conflict of interest.
—*Donald J. Trump, November 22, 2016*

THE BUSINESS OF THE PRESIDENCY IS BUSINESS

In private business, Trump used lawsuits to his advantage more than any other magnate of his time. Now, as president, he has at his disposal the much greater discretionary power of the presidency. If that strikes you as ominous, you're not alone. Luckily, though, the law and the constitution limit presidential conflicts of interest. While, unlike his employees,

––––––––

a president cannot be punished under the strict federal ethics rules, he certainly can be impeached.

President Trump has obstinately failed to follow the practice of past presidents and divest himself from his many private business interests. He will still personally profit from every transaction by the many hundreds of Trump businesses in the United States and in twenty or more foreign lands. Trump's financial empire includes owned or party-owned enterprises and numerous licensing agreements from which Trump profits. Trump's private ventures have clashed with his public duties as president.

THE PROHIBITION OF FOREIGN "EMOLUMENTS"

To guard against foreign leverage on a president, the founders placed in the Constitution a provision known as the "Emoluments Clause," which covers all federal officials, presidents included. The "Emoluments Clause" says that "No Title of Nobility shall be granted by the United States; And no Person holding any Office of Profit or Trust under them, shall, with the Consent of the Congress, accept of any present, Emolument, Office, or Title, of any kind whatever, from any King, Prince, or foreign State."

Delegates to the Constitutional Convention of 1787 unanimously adopted the Emoluments Clause to prohibit—absent specific congressional authorization—all federal officials, including the president, from receiving anything of value from foreign governments and their agents. The prohibition is absolute; no amount is specified, and a quid pro quo from a foreign government, agent, or entity is *not* required to trigger a violation. "Foreign influence," Alexander Hamilton said, "is truly the Grecian horse to a republic."[1]

The Emoluments Clause, writes Zephyr Teachout, Fordham law professor and author of *Corruption in America,* was no mere afterthought. It expressed "the animating spirit of the Constitutional Convention" that "goes to the heart of the fears at the Convention"—fears that have no less relevance today, several centuries later.[2]

Among Donald Trump's callers a few weeks after his election was the notorious president of the Philippines, Rodrigo Duterte. He is a tough-talking politician who rails against the elites of his country and claims to represent the ordinary Filipino. He purports to be defending his nation from all enemies, internal and external, and has blasted his nation's press, saying, "As Trump said, they are dishonest." Sound familiar? Duterte, it was reported, said that he and the American president-elect had "very engaging, animated" conversation during which Trump commended him for conducting the war against drugs "the right way," and invited him to the United States as the president's guest. Trump's team did not contest this report.[3]

The French daily *Liberation* labeled Duterte the "serial

killer president" in a headline story about how death squads of police and vigilantes had killed thousands of suspects without arrests or charges in Duterte's "war on drugs." UN officials have accused Duterte of "incitement to violence and killing, a crime under international law." Beyond demeaning journalists, he has threatened their lives: "Just because you're a journalist you are not exempted from assassination." He has compared himself to Hitler. "Hitler massacred three million Jews . . . Now there are three million drug addicts. There are. I'd be happy to slaughter them," Duterte said. In early 2017, after Philippine police murdered a Korean businessman, Duterte claimed to suspend his drug war while investigating police corruption, a move that Human Rights Watch condemned as a diversion from his crimes.[4]

Trump has millions of reasons for dealing respectfully with Duterte, and those reasons can be measured in dollars. The Trump Company has licensed its name to the $150 million Trump Tower at Century City in Manila, the Philippines' capital. President Duterte has appointed Jose E. B. Antonio, the head of Century Properties Group, which owns the Trump Tower, as Special Envoy to the United States. This means that Trump's profits depend on the good faith of Duterte's agent in the United States. Antonio denies any conflict of interest, but indicates that his "role is to enlarge the relationship between the two countries." As for his partnership with Trump, he allowed that, "it would be an asset. We interact with everyone—Donald, the kids."[5]

This potential conflict of interest looms at a particularly sensitive moment in relations between the United States and the Philippines. Trump will have to consider sensitive questions of American aid to the Philippines, trade—especially after he withdrew from the Trans-Pacific Partnership—and America's military arrangements there. Any financial arrangement between Trump's and Duterte's supporters, "will have an adverse impact on our policy and our ability to figure out how to deal with Duterte and try to put back together our relationship with the Philippines," said University of Minnesota law professor Richard Painter, formerly George W. Bush's ethics lawyer.[6]

Trump's business ventures in China also raise bright red flags. On February 14, 2017, the Chinese government granted the president a valuable trademark right for the use of the Trump name in the construction industry. It came as a lucrative coup for Trump, as he had ostensibly spent hundreds of thousands of dollars seeking this very trademark in the Chinese courts for a decade, without success. After granting preliminary approval following the election, the Chinese gave final approval for the trademark just a few days after Trump abandoned his earlier flirtation with a "two China" policy. He indicated instead that the U.S. would continue its "one China" policy of recognizing the People's Republic as the sole representative of the Chinese people.[7]

At the time of this development, Trump had in China nearly fifty trademark applications still pending and seventy-seven existing trademarks, many of which will require renewal during this term. But Trump has yet—if ever—to fulfil his campaign promise actually to punish China as a "currency manipulator"—which he had vowed to make a priority on his first day in office.

Then, in late February, the Chinese gave preliminary approval to 38 of his pending trademarks, which he had applied for less than a year previously, in April 2016. The trademarks cover a wide range of enterprises, "including branded spas, massage parlors, golf clubs, hotels, insurance, finance and real estate companies, restaurants, bars, and bodyguard and a class of trademarks called 'social escort and concierge services,'" the Associated Press reported. Dan Plane, a Hong Kong intellectual property consultant said he had never seen this many trademarks sail through the Chinese approval process so rapidly. "Boy, it's weird," he said.[8]

All this begs the question of whether there's a quid pro quo between Trump and the Chinese government. Did China corrupt an American president? Has Trump allowed his personal business ventures—and the Chinese manipulation thereof—to intrude on his foreign policy? The American people should not have to guess at the answers to such questions. That's why framers made the Emoluments Clause absolute. It does not require a quid pro quo or proof of corruption and includes no exemption for financial dealings initiated by a federal official before assuming office. Any economic benefit from a foreign government triggers a constitutional violation, punishable by impeachment.

Conflicts of interest in the Philippines and China ripple across at least twenty nations or more in which Trump has business connections. The danger to every American is that Trump even unconsciously fails to distinguish between his economic interests and the interests of the United States. I would say that it would be impossible even for someone far more selfless and introspective than Donald Trump to disentangle public policy from private gain.

GUTTING THE EMOLUMENTS CLAUSE

To avoid constitutional scrutiny, Trump's lawyer Sheri Dillon tried to gut the Emoluments Clause. Her distortion of this clause would have the founders turning in their graves. She claimed that the clause exempted so-called "fair market exchanges" arises in the normal course of business.

However, the framers made it clear that the Emoluments Clause has unlimited coverage over anything of value received by a president from foreign entities. Governor Edmund Randolph of Virginia, a delegate to the Constitutional Convention, told his state's ratifying convention, that the Constitution guarded against "the president receiving emoluments from foreign powers. If discovered, he may be impeached . . . I consider, therefore, that he is restrained from receiving any present or emoluments whatever. It is impossible to guard better against corruption."[9]

The Trump team never clarified the meaning of "fair value exchange." Trump branded properties have commanded a premium above market, and the brute fact of his presidency, not just market forces, will undoubtedly increase the value of all economic exchanges involving Trump branded properties and enterprises. "No question, in the last twelve months, his brand became stronger and more global," said Hussain Sajwani, Trump's partner on golf courses and residential developments in Dubai. A few days before Trump's inauguration, *Politico* reported that "the value of Trump's name has risen to all-time highs, coinciding with a surge in demand for everything from his condominiums and hotel rooms to his golf courses and men's suits." Even more concerning? The very real risk that foreign governments may also decide to patronize Trump properties not for their fair market value, but to curry favor with the president.[10]

Trump has pledged to donate the profits from foreign governments that use his hotels to the U.S. Treasury. The pledge omits golf courses, along with office, apartment, and condominium properties; it wouldn't even cover most "Trump" hotels, where Trump has a licensing agreement with the owners but no equity stake. He didn't explain how he would calculate profits on a hotel room.

DANGEROUS DEBTS

Portending another potential constitutional clash, Trump businesses are laden with debts that give lenders leverage over his presidency. Per an analysis by the *Wall Street Journal*, Trump owes more than a billion dollars to some 150 financial institutions. "The problem with any of this debt is if something goes wrong and there is a situation where the president is suddenly personally beholden or vulnerable to threats from the lenders," said Trevor Potter, a former general counsel to the presidential campaigns of Republicans George H. W. Bush and John McCain. Take a moment to let that sink in.[11]

Trump and his appointees will also be making policy and regulatory decisions that impact their lenders. For example, federal regulators have sanctioned two of Trump's largest creditors, Wells Fargo and German-based Deutsche Bank, for fraud and the laundering of money from Russia. Trump also has debts in China. He has a 30 percent stake in a partnership that owes about $950 million to lenders that include the state-owned Bank of China. A high-paying tenant at

Trump Tower is the Industrial & Commercial Bank of China, also owned by the state.[12]

Investigative reporters Rosalind S. Helderman and Tom Hamburger, who analyzed Trump's foreign holdings, warned that "Trump's election may usher in a world in which his stature as the U.S. president, the status of his private ventures across the globe, and his relationships with foreign business partners and the leaders of their governments could all become intertwined." Trump has promised that his companies would eschew new foreign deals during his presidency, a positive if not also very limited maneuver to avoid a collision with the Emoluments Clause.[13]

For both America's framers and contemporary authorities, impeachment is the appropriate remedy for a breach of the Emoluments Clause. Already, there is a lawsuit, brought by a bipartisan group called Citizens for Responsibility and Ethics in Washington (CREW), which accuses Trump of having violated the clause.[14]

THE LAW SAYS NO CONFLICTS OF INTEREST AT HOME

Trump's business interests, not just foreign but also domestic, could subject him to a violation of two federal laws. The Stop Trading on Congressional Knowledge ("STOCK") Act mirrors the laws prohibiting securities trading on inside information, which you'll recall snared domestic goddess Martha Stewart for a stretch in prison. A Republican Congress enacted the law in 2012, to prevent members of Congress and other federal employees from reaping private economic benefits through access to nonpublic governmental information.

Violators of the STOCK Act are subject to a fine or imprisonment of up to fifteen years, or both. The law restricts members of Congress and all employees in the executive and judicial branches of the federal government. Contrary to the assertion of the Trump team, STOCK Act prohibitions do apply to the president of the United States. Section 18 of the law "Extends the meaning of 'covered government person' . . . to include the President . . ." Ironically, it was Republicans in Congress during Barack Obama's term that insisted on including the president among the Act's covered federal officials. A companion law, 18 U.S. Code Section 227, forbids members of Congress, federal employees, and the president, from influencing "solely on the basis of partisan political affiliation, an employment decision or employment practice of any private entity." [15]

Larry Noble, former general counsel for the Federal Elections Commission, said that "If he [Trump] continues to own his businesses and he uses insider information or information he has as president, then arguably it's a violation of the STOCK Act." The act would apply to any nonpublic information that Trump may provide to family members, Noble confirmed. If Trump continues to withhold his tax returns, which White House Counselor Kellyanne Conway said he would, it will be difficult to distinguish between benefits flowing to him personally, versus those flowing to members of his family.[16]

"All of this emanates from the problem with Donald J. Trump, the president, who simply rejects the notion that he can't effectively have his business enterprises and be president at same time," said Thomas Mann, a senior fellow at the Brookings Institution. "The conflicts of interest between the president and Trump enterprises has no precedent in American history."[17]

Even as she remains in New York, some 220 miles from the White House, Melania Trump has already signaled her intention to profit from her position as first lady. On February 6, 2017, Melania refiled a $150 million lawsuit against the corporation that publishes the *Daily Mail* newspaper, for allegedly damaging her brand by printing unsubstantiated rumors that she once worked as a high-priced escort in the 1990s. The new complaint charges that the newspaper had harmed "the unique, once-in-a-lifetime opportunity, as an extremely famous and well-known person, as well as a former professional model, brand spokesperson and successful businesswoman, to launch a broad-based commercial brand in multiple product categories, each of which could have garnered multimillion-dollar business relationships for a multi-year term during which the plaintiff is one of the most photographed women in the world. Those product categories would have included, among other things, apparel, accessories, shoes, jewelry, cosmetics, hair care, skin care and fragrance."[18]

The terms "unique," "once-in-a-lifetime," and "one of the most photographed women" can only refer to Melania's elevation to First Lady of the United States; she has accomplished nothing else of consequence recently. Melania seems to have signaled her intention to profit as First Lady through the many lucrative product lines detailed in her complaint, which means that her husband profits as well. She would profit, even if that litany of branded enterprises was only for the purpose of extracting riches from the *Daily Mail*'s parent company. Despite the plain language of her complaint, Melania's lawyer said counterintuitively that "the First Lady has no intention of using her position for profit and will not do so. It is not a possibility." With typical Trumpian doublethink, Melania wants to pocket a cool $150 million from harm to her brand as First Lady, while insisting that she doesn't intend to make any money from that brand.[19]

Melania has since amended her complaint on February 17, scrubbing the details of her business opportunities as First Lady that had apparently become 'inoperative' in ten days. But she's still asking for $150 million and claiming damage "to her business interests and prospective economic opportunities."

Her words may have changed, but their import has not. Melania may not be expecting to profit from insider information, but rather from her *insider position*. She may not be violating the letter of the STOCK Act, but she is surely violating its spirit. A president's family should not be profiting from his public office, whether through a lawsuit or a branded enterprise. It's impossible to disentangle Trump's financial interests from those of his family.[20]

Public position and private gain for the Trumps clashed again in early February 2017, when the luxury retailer Nordstrom's dropped Ivanka Trump's fashion products after its sales of her line declined. In response to this routine business decision, President Trump crossed the red line he had vowed to honor between the presidency and his personal and family enterprises. He tweeted, and then retweeted on the official POTUS account: "My daughter Ivanka has been treated so unfairly by @Nordstrom. She is a great person—always pushing me to do the right thing! Terrible!" His press secretary, Sean Spicer, added in his briefing—though, typically, without evidence—that, *there's clearly efforts to undermine that name based on her father's positions on particular policies that he's taken.*[21]

Trump's counselor Kellyanne Conway put more official weight behind Ivanka's cause by telling viewers of *FOX & Friends* to "Go buy Ivanka's stuff." She said, "Go buy it today, everybody. You can find it online." "I got this suit from the

Ivanka Trump men's collection at Nordstrom's," quipped Alec Baldwin. "Big sale right now—95 percent off." [22]

Aside from its satiric richness, Conway's infomercial for Ivanka Trump violated federal ethics regulations that prohibit a government employee from "the endorsement of any product, service or enterprise." Conway's violation for the first time awakened Republicans in Congress to the treacherous conflicts of interests within the Trump administration. Jason Chaffetz, Republican and House Oversight Chairman, said Conway's infomercial for Ivanka was "wrong, wrong, wrong, clearly over the line, unacceptable." In a joint letter to the White House, Chaffetz and Elijah Cummings, the ranking Democrat on his committee, urged that Conway's actions "clearly" violated ethical standards, and that disciplinary action should be taken against her. [23]

But to focus on Conway is to miss the forest for the trees. It was the president and not his aide who began the Nordstrom dust-up, which shows just how fiercely economics and politics collide in the Trump administration. Although Trump promised to blind himself to all operations of the Trump enterprises, here, already, we see him unable to resist intervening on a minor matter involving just one of the dozens of outlets that carry Ivanka's products. Texas A&M law professor Milan Markovic says Trump is likely in violation of 18 U.S. Code Section 227, because he "is not allowed to misuse his authority to put pressure on private companies or influence who they hire or do business with." He said that the law is broad enough to cover decisions by companies regarding private contractors or vendors like Ivanka Trump.[24]

Ivanka is not just a private citizen. Her husband, Jared Kushner, is a senior advisor to the president, and Ivanka is an informal advisor with real sway in the White House. Soon after the incident over Nordstrom's, Ivanka tweeted a photo of herself at a desk in the Oval Office, sitting between the president and Prime Minister Justin Trudeau of Canada. She called it "having a seat at the Table!" Since she is not on the government payroll, Ivanka does not have to disclose the extent to which she has divested herself of private economic ventures.[25]

Through the Nordstrom's matter, the president has sent a strong message to companies in America and throughout the world: that Big Brother is watching you.

TRUMP REFUSES TO DIVEST

There is a way to avoid trouble in this area, but Trump has resisted it, thereby turning his conflicts of interest into one of the easiest grounds for impeachment. Trump supporters and opponents have urged him to sell his interests in all properties, both owned and licensed, to liquidate his debts, and to put the remaining assets in a blind trust, administered by a third party who would not report to the president or his family any details of financial transactions. Instead, Trump handed over management of his enterprises to his two sons, Eric and Donald Jr.

Trump has already delegated much decision-making authority over his businesses to his children. In a recent deposition, Trump said, "I think as they've become older and wiser, I give them more and more decision-making ability. But—but they have the right to make a decision, yes."[26]

Critically, Trump's arrangement is neither blind nor meets the specifications of a trust. Trump retains all ownership and licensing rights to his enterprises, which means he will continue to personally profit from all existing businesses. And whether he talks business with his sons or not, he will still know how his decisions and appointments will impact his bottom line. He has also, disturbingly, not pledged to erect a wall of silence between himself and the many hundreds of partners in his enterprises.

The list of potentially conflict-making presidential decisions cuts across virtually the entire range of national policies, including taxation, regulation, infrastructure spending, government contracts, trade, military operations, relations with foreign leaders, and so on. Profits at Trump's enterprises will rise and fall with decisions made by many hundreds of Trump appointees at virtually every federal agency,

Trump has appointed an ethics advisor and compliance counsel to review family business decisions, but it is unlikely that these individuals will have the power to veto Trump family deals, and he's kept it a closed, inside operation. The ethics advisor, Bobby Burchfield, is chairman of Karl Rove's Crossroads GPS, a dark-money, pro-Republican political operation that need not disclose the identity of its donors. The chief compliance counsel, George Sorial, is a Trump insider who serves as Executive Vice President of the Trump Organization and has worked with Donald Trump on several business deals, including Trump University. When it comes to Trump and his family, self-policing has never been a strong point.[27]

Trump may have pledged that his companies would initiate no new foreign deals, but that doesn't apply to ventures in the United States. Eric Danziger, the CEO of Trump Hotels, said that the company plans an aggressive program to expand its American properties. "There are twenty-six major metropolitan areas in the U.S., and we're in five," Danziger said. "I don't see any reason that we couldn't be in all of them eventually." The expansion could benefit from Trump's actions or nonactions as president. And after the Nordstrom intervention, partners may be reluctant to call off a bad Trump deal—think Fort Lauderdale and Tampa—or stand up for the most favorable terms.[28]

His attorney Dillon called divestment a "fire sale" that would destroy Trump's business empire. Maybe so. But no one forced Trump to run for president, and he has a net worth of close to $4 billion—much more, even, per his own calculation. He could lose most of his wealth and yet still remain a billionaire in retirement. The trade-off? Retaining the most important position in the world.[29]

In a 1974 memo, the famous "strict constructionist" Supreme Court Justice Antonin Scalia, Trump's model jurist, then serving in the Justice Department, warned that presidents should strive to adhere to the same rigid conflict of interest laws and regulations that bind other federal officials, even if they are technically exempt.

"Notwithstanding the conclusion that neither the Executive Order nor the regulations pursuant to it legally bind the President or Vice President, it would obviously be undesirable as a matter of policy for the President or Vice President to engage in conduct proscribed by the Order or regulations, where no special reason for exemption from the generally applicable standards exists. Failure to observe these standards will furnish a simple basis for damaging criticism, whether or not they technically apply."[30]

A *technical violation* of the law, as we have learned, is not necessary to trigger impeachment. Any subordination of America's national interests to Trump's financial interests should suffice.

Professor Matthew Stephenson of Harvard, who studies

international corruption, remarks that he's seen conflicts of interest like President Trump's before, but in foreign lands where rulers have used their power to extend their personal wealth. "Over and over again, you see this pattern of populist leaders, often democratically elected, who use the power of office to enrich themselves, their families and their cronies."[31]

CHAPTER 5

Lies, Lies, and More Lies

If falsehood, like truth, had only one face, we would be in better shape. For we would take as certain the opposite of what the liar said. But the reverse of truth has a hundred thousand shapes and a limitless field.

—*Michel de Montaigne, 1580*

A HISTORY OF LIES

Lying is treacherous for a president for many reasons. Lying can itself get a president impeached if done under oath, like Bill Clinton's false testimony to a Grand Jury in 1998. But lying opens the gates to other grounds for impeachment as well. Lies can become embedded in a Nixon-style effort to cover up a scandal. Or lying can jeopardize the national security of the United States. Some believe that George W. Bush should have suffered impeachment for pushing America into war through falsehoods about the threat of weapons of mass

---

destruction in Iraq. One Bush critic said, "For the war! He lied! He got us into the war with lies!" He was surprised that Democratic leader Nancy Pelosi didn't look to impeach Bush and get him out of office. "Which personally I think would have been a wonderful thing." That critic was none other than Donald J. Trump.[1]

Despite condemning Bush's lies, Donald Trump has his own history of lying as an ingrained way of life. Trump's lies have profited him in business, burnished his image, and helped him fight thousands of lawsuits, and, ultimately, it could be argued, it was lying that won him the White House. Over time, Trump's lying escalated in frequency and severity and became his reflex response to any challenge or opportunity.

It's unlikely that Trump will cease his lying or his hypocritical justifications for his lies. Legally, Trump *can* lie while in office, but what could be his downfall is a lie made under oath. To lie intentionally on a material matter in sworn testimony is known as perjury, and if part of a consequential deception or cover-up of scandal, doing so can quickly become grounds for impeachment. There is also the related crime of lying to Congress or to federal officials. It is possible of course that Trump may not even know anymore whether he is lying or not, but just thinks that whatever he believes at the moment must be true.

Before we dive into a discussion of where Trump's lying *could* land him, though, let's take a look back at where it already has. Because, regardless of whether the hypothetical of Trump's lying under oath is realized, the loss of presidential credibility through the mere habit of day-to-day deception will impede his defense of *any* potentially impeachable conduct.

THE ART OF DECEPTION

In his 1987 book *The Art of the Deal,* Trump hinted at his affection for the malleability of truth, writing, "People want to believe that something is the biggest and the greatest and the most spectacular. I call it truthful hyperbole. It's an innocent form of exaggeration—and a very effective form of promotion." Trump alone decides where "truthful" ends and falsehood begins. When asked under oath in a 2007 deposition if he ever "inflated the value of his properties," Trump responded, "Not beyond reason." When probed to explain what "beyond reason" meant, Trump said, "I don't know . . . It's very subjective."[2]

In 2007, Trump sued reporter Timothy L. O'Brien for over $2 billion, more than the journalist could earn in thousands of years. The suit alleged that in his book *TrumpNation*, O'Brien made false and reckless statements about Trump's net worth and business operations. "I didn't read [the book], to be honest with you," Trump later admitted. "I never read it. I saw some of the things they said. I said: 'Go sue him. It will cost him a lot of money.'" In their analysis of Trump's deposition in this one lawsuit, *Washington Post* reporters David A. Fahrenthold and Robert O'Harrow Jr. found that O'Brien's lawyers caught Trump in no less than thirty lies.[3]

Two independent Trump profiles in the respected business publication *Fortune* found that even in the world of real estate puffery, Trump is first among his peers in the art of deception. Jerry Useem, writing in 2000, made special note of Trump's "astonishing ability to prevaricate." Trump, he proposed, ought not to "be held to the same standards of truthfulness as everyone else; he is, after all, Donald Trump. But when Trump says he owns 10% of the Plaza hotel, understand that what he actually means is that he has the right to 10% of the profit if it's ever sold. When he says he's building a '90-story building' next to the U.N., he means a 72-story building that has extra-high ceilings. And when he says his casino company is the 'largest employer in the state of New Jersey,' he actually means to say it is the eighth-largest."[4]

"Trump is the Reality Tycoon," said Daniel Roth four years later when Trump had become a reality TV star on *The Apprentice*. "He lives his life straight out of the *Survivor* handbook: Start with the truth, then add enough drama, celebrity, sex, and what might very charitably be called creative editing to make something entirely outlandish."[5]

These profiles, it's worth noting, came *before* Trump's most notorious deceptions. By the early twenty-first century,

Trump had transformed himself from a builder to a brand. Why brave the perils of development as an owner when you can trademark your name and sell it to other developers for a riskless fee and a cut of the profits? The allure of the Trump name soared when he began hosting *The Apprentice* in 2004. His name would, I suspect, carry much less allure if people knew that he was not developing the projects of which he boasted, and the fact that he began to actively conceal his participation in name only leads me to believe that he suspected the same.

TRUMP TOWERS BECOME VACANT LOTS

Trump became a marketer of lies for Trump-branded projects, reeling in buyers with the allure of luxury and prestige that his personal involvement in such a project would ensure. If a project succeeded, everyone benefited, and the deception could be written off as "innocent" exaggeration. If it failed, only the investors and buyers who put in real money would suffer; Trump could walk away. This is precisely what happened with overly ambitious Trump-branded ventures in Tampa and Fort Lauderdale.

In 2004, five small-time developers in Tampa incorporated under the anonymous name of SimDag/Robel and began to think big. After buying some property in downtown Tampa, they hit on the idea of developing a grandiose con-

dominium building. The name SimDag Tower would not at-
tract well-heeled buyers, but the name Trump Tower Tampa
would. The developers reached out to the Trump organization, traveled to Trump Tower Manhattan, and cut a deal
with the orange tycoon. Trump agreed to license his name to
the developers in return for a fee of $2 million and a share
of profits from condominium sales. As part of the deal, Sim-
Dag and Trump agreed that the public would never learn
that Trump had given his name to the project but nothing
more: "Licensor and Licensee covenant and agree that . . .
they will not under any circumstances disclose or permit to
be disclosed the existence of this agreement." As far as buyers knew, Trump Tower meant Trump development, management, and ownership.[6]

Trump aggressively marketed the condos in the planned
fifty-two-story tower. On January 10, 2005, he announced
that he would "partner" with SimDag on a property "so spectacular that it will redefine both Tampa's skyline and the
market's expectations of luxury." Five weeks later, when the
celebrity "developer" and his new bride, Melania, arrived for
the sales launch at an upscale champagne reception for six
hundred potential buyers, he boasted to reporters that he had
a "substantial stake" in the project, which he would have increased if the condos were not already selling out.

Trump's bogus stake in the project attracted buyers willing to pay a premium for Trump luxury and they quickly

plunked down deposits for all 190 imaginary units, priced at $700,000 to $6 million. "The marketing pretty much reflected the Trump brand, it was exquisite," said one of the SimDag partners. "We sold out in a week." "The main reason we went into this was Trump," said Jay McLaughlin, a physical therapist from Connecticut who hoped to move to Florida. He put a significant amount of his savings down on a Trump condo.[7]

The actual Trump Tower was far less exquisite than the marketed dream. Structural problems, cost overruns, and a lack of financing doomed the project, leaving buyers gaping at nothing more than a vacant lot. When difficulties first arose, Trump renegotiated his deal, upping his flat fee to $4 million in return for concessions to SimDag on profits. When SimDag stopped paying in 2007, Trump sued for unpaid fees. SimDag countersued, claiming that Trump had breached their confidentiality agreement. The cases were eventually settled and SimDag declared bankruptcy, pleading that it had nothing left but a few Trump Tower mock-ups worth $3,500.

The buyers who had invested in mythical luxury lost the half of their deposits that the developers had not escrowed, in some cases to the tune of more than $250,000. Some of the buyers sued Trump, claiming that he misled them about his participation in the project. Other buyers just swallowed their losses; McLaughlin said he lost $90,000. Only Trump, who had put up nothing, walked away unharmed, even after a settlement of the lawsuit cut into his fee payments. "In Tampa I was not involved in the job," he later admitted.[8]

The fiasco in Tampa was reprised in 2005 with Trump Tower Fort Lauderdale. Glossy marketing brochures featured a signed letter from Donald Trump, saying, "It is with great pleasure that I present my latest *development,* Trump International Hotel & Tower, Fort Lauderdale. This magnificent oceanfront resort offers the finest and most luxurious experience I have *created*." Trump sent personal letters to buyers congratulating them on buying into his development.[9]

As was the case in Tampa, the Trump name and endorsement enticed buyers to put down deposits on pricey unbuilt units, and the project similarly fell apart, taking investor deposits along with it. "The word 'developing,'" Trump later tried to explain, "it doesn't mean that we're the developers." With plain common sense, Joseph Altschul, attorney for some of the buyers, said, "How were they supposed to know he wasn't the developer? He said this is 'my development.' I was representing them, and I even thought he was the developer."[10]

During seven years of the protracted litigation against Trump by condo buyers, a federal judge sanctioned Trump for failing to disclose that his organization had had a $5 million insurance policy in place that could have potentially covered a settlement. Eventually Trump escaped major liability because unlike the marketing materials, the property report and fine print of the documents that buyers signed did not identify Trump as the developer.[11]

THE TRUMP INSTITUTE AND THE
INDIAN CASINO LAWSUIT

Always on the prowl for new ventures, Donald Trump saw an opportunity to profit by selling his name to a real estate instructional program known as the Trump Institute. Trump marketed the institute with what had become his standard practice of lying bravado. "I put all of my concepts that have worked so well for me, new and old, into our seminar," Trump said in a 2005 video. "I'm teaching what I've learned," he said. "People are really doing well with it, and they're loving it." Of course, none of this was true.[12]

Trump sold his name to the institute and made an info-mercial, but he didn't provide the institute with any special insights or talk to any instructors or students, hundreds of whom eventually filed complaints with their state attorneys general or Better Business Bureaus. The book of Trump real estate secrets that students received after paying their seminar fees had his picture and signature plastered on the cover. It imparted not a snippet of Trump's hidden wisdom, but did include some twenty pages of material plagiarized from a 1995 real estate manual published by *Success* magazine.[13]

In yet another suspect Florida venture, Trump filed suit to

gain ownership of recently developed, profitable casinos in the state. Trump Hotels and Casino Resorts sued the developer of two Indian casinos in Florida in January 2005, charging that the developers had cheated Trump out of participation in the deal and that they should turn over the casinos to him. Lawyers for the company retorted that Trump had known about the deal since 1999, and that the four-year statute of limitations had expired. Trump counterclaimed that he only had learned of it two years later, in 2001.

Under court order, lawyers for the opposition sought discovery of e-mails and other records that might prove that Trump knew about the casino deal before 2000. Trump responded that he had no e-mails or other digital documents for review, because he had no computer server until 2001. Depositions of Trump's information technology specialists exposed this lie, by revealing that *a server for e-mails had in fact been installed in 1999,* the year that the lawyers claimed Trump had first learned of the deal. Ironically for a future presidential candidate who would excoriate his opponent for allegedly wiping out e-mails, Trump had no e-mails or other electronic records to turn over to defendants, because *they had been destroyed.* Eventually, Trump dropped the lawsuit and cut a deal with the opposition.[14]

LYING HIS WAY TO THE PRESIDENCY

When Trump turned to politics, his lies ballooned to proportions matched only in the fictional tall tales of the infamous Baron Munchausen, who claimed to have defeated a forty-foot crocodile and flown to the moon. Trump first made the transition from businessman and reality-TV host to political stardom by propagating the biggest and most sustained lie in the history of American politics: The so-called birther fantasy that Barack Obama, the nation's first African American president, was born in Africa and had defrauded America as an illegitimate president.

"Birtherism" shows that the lying engrained in Trump's business life had become the same technique he would later use as candidate and president. He deployed the "Big Lie," a favored propaganda technique of history's dictators. Repeat a lie loudly, over and over, until people come to believe it. He relied on unnamed sources, ignored debunking, and used the shock value of his claims to keep the media lights on himself. Trump's birther lies had nothing to do with Obama and everything to do with Trump and they paid off. Trump rose to the top of the polls among potential candidates for the Republican presidential nomination in 2012.[15]

Trump declined to run against Obama in 2012, but three years later he announced that he was ready to leave the private sector and run for president. On June 16, 2015, alone—

his first day as an announced candidate—Trump told enough jaw-dropping lies to keep battalions of debunkers fully employed. Fact-checkers for the *Washington Post* wrote the next day that Trump's announcement speech was "a fact checker's dream . . . and nightmare. He spouts off so many 'facts,' often twisted or wrong, that it takes a lot of time to hack through the weeds." A couple of examples prove the point.[16]

Trump told voters not to believe the official unemployment rate of 5.6 percent issued by the Obama administration. "Our real unemployment is anywhere from 18 to 20 percent," he said. A few months later, he more than doubled the "real rate" to 42 percent. Trump conjured up this outlandish percentage by counting as "unemployed" most or all the approximately 85 *million* Americans of working age who aren't working because they are students, homemakers, retirees, or persons too disabled to work.[17]

The real unemployment rate is so high, Trump claimed, because people "can't get jobs . . . there are no jobs." Yet the Bureau of Labor Statistics had, in its most current analysis at the time of Trump's statement, reported that the number of job openings had hit 5.4 million, the largest bounty of jobs since the Bureau began calculating this statistic in December 2000.[18]

The mass debunking of his debut speech by professional fact-checkers and experts didn't deter Trump from lying thereafter. In just six months, Trump's many falsehoods earned him the independent fact-checker PolitiFact's annual "Lie of the Year" award for 2015. "In considering our annual Lie of the Year, we found our only real contenders were Trump's," the PolitiFact staff wrote of his misstatements. "But it was hard to single one out from the others. So we have rolled them into one big trophy." In evaluating all presidential candidates of both parties at the end of the nominating process, PolitiFact found that Trump had more Pants on Fire ratings *than all twenty-one other candidates combined.* Pants on Fire is the fact-checker's rock-bottom designation, reserved for the most outrageous of calls.[19]

These findings show that Trump is an outlier, that his lying far exceeds the normal tendency of politicians to stretch and sometimes even break the truth. It is this extreme, nearly automatic propensity to lie that shreds his credibility and makes him more vulnerable to impeachment and removal than any American president since Richard Nixon.

It mattered not to Trump that fact-checkers could so easily disprove his lies, and it only served to further incense his followers, who shared his belief that the "dishonest" and "disgusting" media was out to sink his campaign. In November 2015, to bolster his call for banning Muslim immigrants to the United States, Trump recounted how, on 9/11, "I watched in Jersey City, N.J., where thousands and thousands of people were cheering . . . in a heavy Arab population," as the World Trade Center collapsed. "It was on television. I saw it." He didn't; it never happened. To validate his "tough on crime" approach, he claimed to have met with "a top police officer in Chicago" who said that he could stop the city's violence "in a week." A spokesman for the Chicago Police Department, however, has said that "no one in the senior command . . . has ever met with Donald Trump."[20]

To resurrect the myth that Barack Obama might be a Muslim, Trump said that the president wears a ring with an "Arabic inscription." The ring in question has no inscription of any kind. To frighten Americans about illegal immigrants, Trump's first campaign ad showed dozens of dark-skinned persons swarming across a border, with a narrator saying, "He'll stop illegal immigration by building a wall on our southern border that Mexico will pay for." That footage, though, was incredibly misleading, as what it depicted was actually migrants flooding into a town in Morocco, five thousand miles from Mexico.[21]

Many of Trump's claims during the campaign were so absurd that they required no debunking. To explain why he alone could save a failing nation, Trump had to be "the biggest and the greatest and the most spectacular," a larger-than-life figure just as he had been in business. Trump said that he knows "more about ISIS than the generals," more about renewable energy "than any human being on Earth," and more about taxes than anyone, "maybe in the history of the world."

Throughout his campaign and beyond, Trump also reprised the Big Lie technique that he had used to propagate the birther lie. One chilling example was his repeated fabricated claim that the election was "rigged" against him by voter fraud. Trump proclaimed that voter fraud is "very, very common." He warned that "we are competing in a rigged election. They even want to try and rig the election at the polling booths, where so many cities are corrupt and voter fraud is all too common."[22]

Every study, including one by the Republican National Lawyers' Association that set out to find as much fraud as possible, has shown that voter fraud is vanishingly small. Trump contended that Philadelphia is a hotbed of voter fraud. State Judge Bernard McGinley, in his opinion on litigation challenging the Pennsylvania voter identification law, noted that in its defense the state could cite *no specific incidents of voter fraud.*[23]

Trump's Big Lie took hold. A *Politico/Morning Consult* poll taken before the election found that 41 percent of all voters believed that the election could be "stolen" from Trump through widespread voter fraud.[24]

WINNING DOESN'T STOP THE LIES

Trump's "astonishing ability to prevaricate" did not end with his successful campaign. After winning the Electoral College, but losing the popular vote, President-elect Trump bragged, "In addition to winning the Electoral College in a landslide, I won the popular vote if you deduct the millions of people who voted illegally." Trump not only claimed to be victimized by a conspiracy of fraud far beyond anything ever seen in American politics, but every analysis of the 2016 election found that illegal votes were a vanishingly small fraction of the votes cast.[25]

Despite such alleged fraud, Trump asserted, "We had a massive landslide victory, as you know, in the Electoral College." Trump lost the popular vote by a record number for a winning candidate, and his Electoral College margin of victory ranked 46th out of 58 presidential elections.[26]

To substantiate his claim of biased press coverage, Trump said that "the *New York Times* sent a letter to their readers apologizing for their BAD coverage of me." Yet the letter he referred to contained nothing approaching an apology and never mentioned any bad coverage of Donald Trump. At his January 11, 2017, press conference on conflicts of interest, Trump displayed piles of folders that he said represented "just some of the many documents that I've signed turning over complete and total control to my sons." Trump staffers blocked members of the press from viewing their contents, but photographs indicate that they may well have been filled with blank paper.[27]

TRUMP'S "1984" WHITE HOUSE

As president, Trump has pushed back the clock to the Watergate era of "Nix-speak" lying, or worse yet to the world of George Orwell's novel *1984*, where falsehood and truth are one. After the election, prominent Trump surrogate Scottie Nell Hughes began the Trumpian assault on truth by declaring that facts are dead and that anything is true if people believe it or when Trump says it:

> "People that say facts are facts—they're not really facts. Everybody has a way—it's kind of like looking at ratings, or looking at a glass of half-full water. . . . *Everybody has a way of interpreting them to be the truth, or not truth. There's no such thing, unfortunately, anymore as facts.* And so Mr. Trump's tweet, amongst a certain crowd—a large part of the population—are truth. When he says that millions of people illegally voted, he has some—amongst him and his supporters, and people believe they have facts to back that up." [28]

If there are no facts, then Trump can project his own deceptions on others. Even though independent fact-checkers found that Trump out-lied Hillary Clinton by more than 5 to 1, she is "Crooked Hillary," while he is a George Washington who "will never lie to you." What Trump says about himself and Clinton must be true, because he and his followers want it to be true, an updated version of the lying Nix-speak that journalists wrote about during the Watergate investigation.[29]

The torrent of Trump's "nonfacts" continued unabated from the White House after his inauguration. Trump said that his inauguration crowd was so large that it "went all the way back to the Washington Monument." Aerial photos of the event show that it didn't come close. Trump blamed the "dishonest media" for inventing a "feud" between himself and the intelligence community, even though Trump had repeatedly blasted the intelligence community in tweet after tweet, going so far as to draw a comparison with Nazi Germany. To bolster his "law and order" theme he told a group of county sheriffs that he had invited to the White House that "the murder rate in our country is the highest it's been in forty-seven years, right? . . . I'd say that in a speech and everybody was surprised, because the press doesn't tell it like it is." Yet the murder rate peaked in 1980, when it was *twice as high* as in 2015, the last year for data when Trump made his claims.[30]

At a news conference in mid-February, Trump repeated a version of an earlier lie, bragging that he had scored "the biggest Electoral College win since Ronald Reagan." Yet five other candidates since Reagan garnered more Electoral College votes than Trump. George H. W. Bush in 1988, Bill Clinton in 1992 and 1996, and Barack Obama in 2008 and

2012. When confronted with his lie, the shameless Trump deflected, "I was given that information." He said, "Actually, I've seen that information around," just as he had seen the information around that Obama was born in Kenya or that Muslims in New Jersey cheered the 9/11 attacks.[31]

In early March 2017 Trump tweeted, "122 vicious prisoners, released by the Obama Administration from Gitmo, have returned to the battlefield. Just another terrible decision!" But according to the Office of the Director of National Intelligence, 93 percent of these detainees were released during the administration of George W. Bush. Trump also charged without evidence that Barack Obama had tapped his phone during the campaign, an issue that I'll examine when we get to Trump's abuse of power.[32]

There exist many more examples, but there are bigger points to be made. Trump can toss out a lie in a sentence or two, forcing fact-checkers to research and report the truth. And by then, Trump has moved on to new lies, hoping to leave the old ones fixed in people's minds. Trump can't be shamed into telling the truth, because as his history of lying proves, Trump has no shame.

Early in the Trump administration, Kellyanne Conway confirmed that lies are not lies, but rather "alternative facts" that can be whatever best serves Trump's interests. In an interview on NBC's *Meet the Press* three days after the inauguration, she brushed aside host Chuck Todd's astonished response to her defense of Sean Spicer's false statements about the size of the Inauguration Day crowd: "Look, alternative facts are not facts. They're falsehoods," he said. If the press failed to accept the White House's "alternative facts," she replied, "I think we're going to have to rethink our relationship here."[33]

The hashtag #AlternativeFacts immediately took hold, but the assassination of truth is no laughing matter. It recalls George Orwell's world of doublethink, where reality dissolves and the totalitarian Big Brother holds sway by telling deliberate lies that he simultaneously believes to be true. Orwell's *1984* rocketed to the top of the bestseller list after Trump's inauguration.[34]

FALLING INTO CLINTON'S IMPEACHMENT TRAP

Trump's disregard for lying in sworn testimony, examined in context of the Bill Clinton precedent, shows how Trump's opponents could set an impeachment trap for him through a civil lawsuit. In the sexual harassment case against Clinton brought by former Arkansas employee Paula Jones, the U.S. Supreme Court ruled that a president cannot be sued for his or her official duties but is otherwise not immune from lawsuits involving unofficial conduct, whether before or after assuming office. Only on a case-by-case basis may judges consider whether a lawsuit merits postponement when balancing the litigant's interest in a prompt resolution against the burdens placed upon the president.[35]

By forcing Clinton to testify under oath in a deposition, the Jones case led directly to his impeachment. During an August 1998 grand jury hearing, Clinton was asked how he could have claimed that an affidavit statement made by Monica Lewinsky, that "there is absolutely no sex of any kind in any manner, shape or form, with President Clinton," was "absolutely true." Clinton responded by saying that since the two were not having sex at the moment of the statement, then it must be true. "It depends upon what the meaning of the word 'is' is," he said. "If the—if he—if 'is' means is and never has been, that is not—that is one thing. If it means there is none, that was a completely true statement."[36]

Clinton further insisted that he had accurately testified that he never had sexual relations with Ms. Lewinsky because they did not engage in intercourse, which in his mind and in the minds of ordinary Americans was a necessary condition. "Oral sex," he said, "didn't count." A *Time*/CNN poll taken at the time found that 87 percent of Americans disagreed.[37]

Such verbal contortions cost Bill Clinton his credibility and opened the door for his impeachment. Trump's own propensity to lie under oath and then offer similar, logic-defying justifications will very likely get him into the same mess. Anti-Clinton conservative groups set Clinton's trap by encouraging Jones's lawsuit and giving her legal assistance and financial support. I would not be surprised to see Democrats, disgruntled Republicans, and liberal or feminist activists follow this strategy for persons wronged by Trump.

Trump has unofficially been involved in more than 3,500 lawsuits on his tab. A study by *USA Today* found that Trump was a plaintiff 1,900 times, a defendant 1,450 times, and was involved in bankruptcy or third-party suits 150 times. Trump has been sued by businesses claiming that he failed to pay their bills, by individuals alleging fraud, personal injury, sexual harassment, or discrimination, and by government agencies. He has sued gamblers at his casinos who didn't pay their debts, critical journalists, business associates, and government agencies.[38]

The *USA Today* study found that Trump has been a plaintiff or defendant in more lawsuits than the nation's five other leading real estate executives combined. Trump still has unresolved civil cases pending, and new cases have already been filed or contemplated; any one of these could force Trump to testify under oath.

OTHER PATHS TO IMPEACHMENT, PAVED IN LIES

Retired lieutenant general Patrick M. Hughes, the former director of the Defense Intelligence Agency, has warned that lies propagated by the president could threaten the national security of the United States in many ways. "When you're talking about intelligence that involves military or intelligence operations, or when you're talking about international relations—relations between the United States and other countries, or between other countries themselves and groups and subnational entities . . . of course, there will be consequences. And that's a reason why you should be absolutely factual," he explains.[39]

Trump could persuade Congress to lift the sanctions against Russia by lying about Vladimir Putin's commitment to withdraw from the Ukraine. Or he might start an economically devastating trade war with China by lying about their currency manipulation. He might also lie to cover up a scandal, that might emerge, for example, over alleged ties between his campaign and the Russians.

There is another avenue to impeachment if Trump corrupts the government information upon which an informed citizenry depends. He has repeatedly disparaged the official unemployment statistics that for many decades has provided comparable data to judge the performance of presidential administrations. On January 23, 2017, in response to a simple question about the rate, Trump's press secretary Sean Spicer said, "No, no, it's not a question of what I accept. There are ways you can put out full employment—right, there's a reason we put out several versions of that. . . . But there's a reason that you put out several of these statistics, so that economists can view them and decide—look at different landscapes on, on how to make economic policy." President Trump, he went on, is "not focused on statistics as much as he is on whether or not the American people are doing better as a whole," thereby opening the door to the distortion of statistics "within reason," as Trump has so subjectively defined it.[40]

The combustible mixture of lost credibility and presidential misdeeds could ignite a crisis that consumes the Trump presidency. Lies shred the credibility of a president and chip away at the political capital he would need to draw upon in response to *any* impeachment investigation that may arise during his term. "Your most important job, in my view," George W. Bush's close advisor Karen Hughes told incoming press secretary Scott McClellan in 2003, "will be to make sure the president maintains his credibility with the American people." Drawing on his own experience with Bush, McClellan has warned the Trump White House that "there will be tough times ahead—there are for every White House—and that's when that credibility and trust is most important."[41]

CHAPTER 6

Trump's War on Women

———

People want me to [run for president] all the time . . .
I don't like it, can you imagine how controversial I'd
be? You think about him [Clinton] and the women.
How about me with the women? Can you imagine?
—*Donald J. Trump,* New York Post, *July 12, 1999*

AN ADDICTION TO SEX

A decade before the release of his infamous *Access Hollywood* tape, just before wedding his current wife Melania in
2005, Trump said that he could not have a bachelor party
with strippers because "that would be like putting a glass of
whisky in front of an alcoholic." Donald Trump's need for
gratification, attention, and adoration leads to a lack of respect for the dignity and autonomy of women. He craves the
public company of glamorous women, disdains women who
don't measure up to his standards of beauty, and cannot con-

———

trol his impulse for sexual contact with women, consensual or not.[1]

Can Donald Trump really be impeached for his predatory behavior towards women? The answer, of course, is yes. First, amped up with the star power of the presidency, it wouldn't be a stretch to say that he might sexually harass or grope a woman. Second, the feminist lawyer Gloria Allred has already filed a civil lawsuit against Trump. The suit charges that he had defamed former *Apprentice* contestant Summer Zervos by using his bully pulpit to denounce her for charging that he had committed sexual assault against her. If the courts authorize the suit to move ahead, Trump would be compelled to testify under oath, potentially opening him up to perjury.

FINDING THE "NO-MAINTENANCE" WIFE

Despite seeking gratification from women, Trump has tried to avoid any deep emotional commitments, even to his wives. In what may be the ultimate "no maintenance" move for Trump, Melania became the only first lady in history who didn't move with her husband to the White House.

In 1977, at the age of thirty-one, Donald Trump married his first wife, Ivana. For more than a decade, the media lavishly covered the glittering couple as royalty—America's version of Diana and Prince Charles. Trump was a rich and handsome titan of business, Ivana a glamorous former model and socialite. They had three children between 1977 and 1984 and graced society magazines in New York and across the world. Ivana was eye-catching, but she was much more than a trophy wife. As vice president of interior design for the Trump Organization, she led the team that designed Trump Tower in New York. She served as president of the Trump Castle Hotel and Casino in Atlantic City and presided over the renovation of the once-iconic Plaza Hotel in Manhattan. The press dubbed her the "Queen of Trump."[2]

The couple separated in February 1990 and began a battle so contentious over their impending divorce that the New York tabloids dubbed it "the war of the Trumps." Ivana's lawyer said they planned to challenge the couple's prenuptial agreement, which he termed "unconscionable and fraudulent." Donald said that such agreements were "sealed in gold."[3]

Ivana and Donald divorced in December, less than a year after separating. Donald's excruciatingly public affair with former beauty queen Marla Maples—seventeen years his junior—which he did not deny, was ruled "cruel and inhuman" treatment of his wife by the New York court. Trump said that he had "even thought briefly about approaching Ivana with the idea of an 'open marriage,'" but decided against it. Ivana didn't get all she wanted from the settlement, but even with Trump's casino empire collapsing, she reportedly still pocketed $14 million in cash, along with $650,000 per year in alimony and child support, and a forty-five-room mansion in Connecticut.[4]

After the divorce, in late June 1991, Trump extolled the virtues of his new single life, saying, "I want more room. I want more time. I don't want to make a decision right now." The press reported his unceremonious dumping of Maples for the Italian model Carla Bruni, who had famously dated rock stars and would later marry the president of France, Nicolas Sarkozy. "Your 15 Minutes Are Up, Marla," headlined the *Boston Globe*. But then, less than a week later, in what the *Las Vegas Review* called "the greatest reversal of fortune since Claus von Bulow's," Donald proposed marriage to Maples—on the television show *Live With Regis and Kathie Lee*. "I spent one week being single, and single life isn't what it used to be," he told the hosts.[5]

Trump's stormy on-again, off-again relationship with Maples would sputter along for another two years. Trump never did manage to fully extricate himself from Maples, though, and the two finally agreed to wed after she became pregnant with their child. Their daughter, Tiffany Trump, was born on October 13, 1993, two months before the couple's wedding. One guest, Trump's friend and shock radio jockey Howard Stern, said, "It's probably in poor taste to say it won't last, but I give it four months." The marriage lasted for four years before ending in separation in 1997 and divorce in 1999. According to a Trump biographer, Trump let Maples know that he wanted a divorce by first telling the *New York Post*, and then putting a copy in front of her door.[6] Trump made certain that Ivana's and maybe Marla's divorce settlements included a gag clause that prohibited the ex-wives from talking about his business ventures or their relationships with him. In 1999, when Trump first contemplated running for the presidency, Marla almost lost the remainder of her divorce settlement by saying, "I will feel it is my duty to tell the American people what he is really like. But I can't imagine that they would really elect him, would they? His drug is attention."[7]

In 1994, Donald Trump mused on the loss of his life in the 1980s, when he'd had it all: "My life was so great in so many ways. The business was so great . . . a beautiful girl-friend, a beautiful wife, a beautiful everything. Life was just a bowl of cherries." Then it collapsed in divorce, a second likely unwanted marriage, and a cascade of bankruptcies.[8]

After his divorce from Maples, Trump explained why his two marriages had failed. "My big mistake with Ivana," he said, "was taking her out of the role of wife and allowing her to run one of my casinos in Atlantic City, then the Plaza Hotel. . . . I will never again give a wife responsibility within my business. Ivana worked very hard, and I appreciated the effort, but I soon began to realize that I was married to a businessperson rather than a wife." With Marla, his problem was just the opposite. She wanted to be too much of a wife. "Marla was always wanting me to spend more time with her," he said. "'Why can't you be home at five o'clock like other husbands?' . . . One thing I have learned: There is high maintenance. There is low maintenance. *I want no maintenance.*"[9]

If you're thinking, *dream on,* think again. It took several years, but eventually, Trump did find his "no-maintenance" spouse. The Slovenian-born model Melania, whom he married in 2005, would neither stick her nose into Trump's businesses nor demand much of his time, attention, or emotion. As one of Melania's friends anonymously told the *Washington Post* at the time of her marriage to Trump, "For Melania it's never, ask what the Donald can do for you. It's, ask what you can do for the Donald."[10]

THE WOMAN PROBLEM EXPLODES

Trump's lack of respect for the dignity and integrity of women as true equals was clear in his denigration of Hillary Clinton. It was tweeted from his account, if she "can't satisfy her husband, what makes her think she can satisfy America?" And he scoffed that she lacked "a presidential look" and the "stamina" to be president.[11]

As we all know, Trump's mistreatment of women exploded into a catastrophe when, a month before the election, a videotape, which inadvertently captured a conversation about Trump's sex life between himself and Billy Bush, the host of *Access Hollywood,* was leaked to the public. In this tape, Trump admitted that his exploitation of women extended far beyond extramarital affairs and out-of-wedlock pregnancies. He provided a detailed blueprint of how and why he sexually assaulted women.

Trump was recorded claiming that he could sexually assault women with impunity because he was a "star." "And when you're a star, they let you do it," Trump says. "You can do anything . . . Grab them by the pussy. You can do anything." He also bragged in the tape about attempting to seduce a married woman. He said, "I moved on her, and I failed. I'll admit it, I did try and fuck her . . . I moved on her like a bitch, but I couldn't get there. And she was married." When Trump noticed the presence of Arianne Zucker, the actress who was waiting to escort him onto the television set, he said, "I've got to use some Tic Tacs, just in case I start kissing her. You know I'm automatically attracted to beautiful—I just start kissing them. It's like a magnet. Just kiss. I don't even wait." Trump was fifty-nine years old at the time and married to Melania.[12]

This was not the first time that Trump had boasted of relationships with married women. In *The Art of the Comeback,* Trump wrote, "If I told the real stories of my experiences with women, often seemingly very happily married and important women, this book would be a guaranteed bestseller (which it will be anyway!). I'd love to tell all, using names and places, but I just don't think it's right." [13]

A DOZEN CHARGES, A DOZEN DENIALS

The release of the *Access Hollywood* tape empowered more than a dozen women to come forth with their personal stories of sexual assault by Donald Trump. Many of the charges are credible because of their specific details, the naming of times and places, and contemporaneous conversations with friends, relatives, and associates.

To give you an idea of what these women suffered, consider the story related by *People* magazine reporter Natasha Stoynoff. In December 2005, Natasha was on assignment to write about Trump and his then-pregnant wife, Melania. Stoynoff said that when she and Trump walked into a room alone, "Trump shut the door behind us. I turned around, and within seconds he was pushing me against the wall and forcing his tongue down my throat." She added that Trump took the opportunity before Melania entered the room to tell her, "You know we're going to have an affair, don't you? Have you ever been to Peter Luger's for steaks? I'll take you. We're going to have an affair, I'm telling you." [14]

Five independent persons have corroborated Stoynoff's charge based on what she told them around the time of the 2005 attack. Marina Grasic, a longtime friend of Stoynoff's, said that Stoynoff had called her the day after the assault and described in detail what Trump had done to her. She said that Stoynoff considered reporting the incident but was embarrassed and concerned about Trump's pregnant wife: "Natasha was struggling about not hurting pregnant Melania if the story came out." Also, "character assassination by a powerful man was of great concern to her." Paul McLaughlin, Stoynoff's former journalism professor and a mentor, said that she called him in tears on the night of the assault. "She wasn't sure what she should do," McLaughlin recalls. "I advised her not to say anything, because I believed Trump would deny it and try to destroy her." [15]

Trump vehemently denied every single one of his dozen accusers' charges. He promised to present evidence debunking *all* their stories of sexual assault, but he never delivered. Trump has also pleaded, as a form of defense, that some of his accusers were not good-looking enough to merit his kissing, groping, and grabbing—and so the claims must be false. [16]

At a Florida rally, he sought to discredit charges of sexual assault by Stoynoff, saying, "Take a look. You take a look. Look at her. Look at her words. Tell me what you think." Much earlier, in a 1999 interview, he said, "I go out with the most beautiful women in the world. Certain guys tell me they want women of substance, not beautiful models. It just means they can't get beautiful models." About President's Clinton affair with Monica Lewinsky, he commented, "People would have been more forgiving if he'd had an affair with a really beautiful woman of sophistication."[17]

As not just a "star," but also an "owner" of beauty pageants, Trump has deemed himself entitled to voyeurism as well as to sexual assault. In a recorded interview on the Howard Stern show, Trump bragged of walking in on naked women backstage at the 2000 Miss USA Pageant. "I'm allowed to go in," Trump said, "because I'm the owner of the pageant . . . You know, they're standing there with no clothes. 'Is everybody OK?' And you see these incredible looking women, and so I sort of get away with things like that." One of the spied-on women, Bridget Sullivan, former Miss New Hampshire, confirmed this story.[18]

The day after Trump's inauguration, in the largest single day of protest in American history, more than three million women and male backers across America and the world demonstrated against his mistreatment of women and anti-woman policies. On *Saturday Night Live*, comedian Aziz Ansari said, "Today, an entire gender protested against him." The singer Katy Perry said from the march, "We should all be guardians for each other. I march today because I am not afraid anymore and I hope I can be an example of fearlessness and resilience. I will not let anyone suppress me, silence me, or clip my wings."[19]

Ironically, at this same time, Russia, whose leader Vladimir Putin, Trump has praised and defended, was finalizing a new law to decriminalize domestic violence against women and children. Trump has not gone nearly this far, but his crackdown on illegal immigrants will make life less safe for undocumented women who will now hesitate to report domestic abuse for fear of detention and deportation. The funding and enforcement of the Violence Against Women Act is also problematic in the Trump administration.[20]

GLORIA ALLRED'S IMPEACHMENT TRAP

How long will Donald Trump, as president, be able to get away with his treatment of women as objects for his own satisfaction? If one canny and determined foe has anything to do with it, he might not have long. Just three days before President Trump's inauguration, accuser Zervos filed a defamation suit against him. Zervos's complaint said that "Mr. Trump suddenly, and without her consent, kissed her on her mouth repeatedly; he touched her breast; and he pressed his genitals up against her. Ms. Zervos never consented to any of this disgusting touching." Zervos charged that Trump knew that his denial of her sexual assault claims was false, and that he had used his bully pulpit to broadcast his defamatory remarks to millions of Americans. He thus irreparably harmed Zervos and other Trump accusers by subjecting them to "threats of violence, economic harm, and reputational damage."[21]

Gloria Allred, Zervos's celebrity attorney, is a fierce feminist, and an abiding critic of Trump from his business days. Allred has said that her client is "willing to dismiss her lawsuit if he will retract his false statements about her" and admit that she was telling the truth. The likelihood of that happening is about as small as Trump nominating Allred to the Supreme Court. More recently, Allred said, "The time is up" for a retraction. "It is time for Trump to answer the allegations in a court of law, rather than in his bedroom by tweeting in the middle of the night."[22]

Whether lost or won, Allred's lawsuit, and others like it, pose a dangerous impeachment risk for the president. "If President Trump decides not to testify truthfully under oath in this case, should he be required to provide his deposition and/or testify at trial, then I think Congress will have a very important decision to make," she said. "I would hope that [Republicans who supported Clinton's impeachment] would put partisanship aside and do the right thing, apply the same standard to President Trump as was applied to President Clinton."[23]

CHAPTER 7

A Crime Against Humanity

———

"The climate change disinformation campaign is equal in destructive power to many human activities that are classified as crimes against humanity."
—*Donald A. Brown, Scholar in Residence, Sustainability Ethics & Law, Widener University Commonwealth Law School, January 30, 2013*

HUMAN SURVIVAL IS AT RISK
FROM CLIMATE CHANGE

Richard Nixon escaped retribution for his crimes against humanity in Cambodia. Donald Trump may not be so lucky if he reverses efforts to combat catastrophic climate change. In today's world, crimes against humanity crimes are not limited to the violence of genocide and wartime atrocities, like Nixon's bombing of civilians in Cambodia. The International Criminal Court has recently announced that it will

———

give priority attention to "crimes against the environment" that threaten people's well-being and survival.[1]

Humanity's survival is likely at stake with catastrophic climate change. Without fast action to reduce greenhouse gas emissions, the chance of cataclysmic results increases exponentially. "Let's face up to calling climate change an issue of human survival," says Ruth Greenspan Bell, a public policy scholar at the Woodrow Wilson International Center for Scholars. "Warming to this level changes everything . . . there really is no precedent in human history of what we're going through right now."[2]

On December 6, 2009, on the eve of UN Climate Talks in Copenhagen, a coalition of business leaders openly wrote to President Barack Obama:

> We support your efforts to ensure meaningful and effective measures to control climate change, an immediate challenge facing the United States and the world today. Please don't postpone the earth. If we fail to act now, it is scientifically irrefutable that there will be catastrophic and irreversible consequences for humanity and our planet. . . . Investing in a Clean Energy Economy will drive state-of-the-art technologies that will spur economic growth, create new energy jobs, and increase our energy security, all the while reducing the harmful emissions that are putting our planet at risk.

Signatories to that letter, which ran as an ad in the *New York Times*, included Donald J. Trump, Chairman and President, Donald J. Trump Jr., EVP, Eric F. Trump, EVP, Ivanka M. Trump, EVP, The Trump Organization.[3]

What has changed since 2009 is not the "irrefutable" science of climate change, its "catastrophic and irreversible consequences," or the job-creating power of a green energy economy, but Donald Trump's own political calculations. As a peerless manipulator of reality, as a businessman and television star, Trump knew that he could not win the Republican nomination unless he changed gears on climate change. So, Trump joined the discredited ranks of the self-interested deniers of science who would throw themselves into thwarting efforts to combat catastrophic climate change.

If Trump reverses efforts to reduce greenhouse gas emissions experts indicate that it would likely exacerbate weather extremes of all sorts: floods that kill and wash away homes; droughts that wither crops and lead to starvation; wildfires that scorch the earth and consume lives and property; superstorms that cause chaos and subsume entire towns; sea-level rises that engulf coastal areas and island nations; heatwaves that take tens of thousands of lives; snowstorms that bury regions; and infectious diseases that deform and destroy lives.

Trump's switch on climate change may have helped him win the presidency, but it could also cost him through impeachment. The impeachment of a president for crimes against humanity related to climate change may seem the most far-fetched of all impeachment scenarios, but I will explain how it could become a reality. Critics will argue that the alleged crime is really a matter of policy dispute and that it is not possible to prove a link between Trump's policies and changes in earth's climate. Yet Congress impeached and nearly convicted President Johnson for what was essentially a policy dispute over Reconstruction.

Scientists have established that any reversal of progress against the emission of greenhouse gases would wreak irreversible damage on our planet. According to an Institute of Electrical and Electronic Engineers posting, "Climate scientists have definitively shown that the buildup of carbon dioxide in the atmosphere poses a looming danger. Whether measured in dollars or human suffering, climate change threatens to take a terrible toll on civilization over the next century. To radically cut the emission of greenhouse gases, the obvious first target is the energy sector, the largest single source of global emissions." A statement by seventy-two Nobel Laureates in 2015 warned that failure to act decisively to reduce greenhouse gas emissions "will subject future generations of humanity to unconscionable and unacceptable risk."[4]

DENIER IN CHIEF

Trump embraced the flat earthers of climate change denial in 2012 when he tweeted that "the concept of global warming was created by and for the Chinese in order to make U.S. manufacturing non-competitive." He has continued to mock climate change as a "hoax." On January 25, 2014, he tweeted, "Is our country still spending money on the GLOBAL WARMING HOAX?" Then in December 2015, in his "alternative facts" universe, he told a cheering crowd at a campaign rally, "Obama's talking about all of this with the global warming and . . . a lot of it's a hoax. It's a hoax. I mean, it's a money-making industry, okay? It's a hoax, a lot of it."[5]

Most critically for policy he still insists that climate change is not a serious problem, regardless of where he stands on the science. On September 17, 2016, he said on *Morning Joe*, "I consider climate change to be not one of our big problems. I consider it to be not a big problem at all." "I think it's weather. I think it's weather changes." Trump is "very much for clean air and clean water," said Kathleen Hartnett-White, a member of the Trump campaign's economic advisory board. But "carbon dioxide has no adverse impact in the air we breathe at all. It's a harmless trace gas that is actually an essential nutrient for plants."[6]

THERE IS AN OVERWHELMING SCIENTIFIC CONSENSUS THAT HUMANS ARE CAUSING CLIMATE CHANGE

The debate over human-induced climate change as Trump recognized in 2009 is political, not scientific. Per a 2016 report by IOPscience, "The consensus that humans are causing recent global warming is shared by 90%–100% of publishing climate scientists according to six independent studies." A 2013 study of more than eleven thousand scientific papers published in *Environmental Research Letters* found that among those taking a position on human-induced climate change, "97.1% endorsed the consensus position that humans are causing global warming." Eighty National Academies of Science worldwide, including those in the United States, Russia, Britain, and China have officially endorsed the consensus view.[7]

The study of scientific papers found that the doubters have diminished over time, becoming "a vanishingly small proportion of the published research." With work that is too shoddy for scientific publication, deniers and skeptics, funded by fossil-fuel companies like ExxonMobil, have created their own world of "alternative facts" propagated through institutes, websites, opinion pieces, and propaganda campaigns.[8]

TRUMP'S POLICIES AND APPOINTMENTS POSE AN EXISTENTIAL THREAT TO HUMANITY

Michael Mann, Distinguished Professor of Atmospheric Science at Penn State University, said bluntly, "A Trump presidency might be *game over for the climate*. In other words, it might make it impossible to stabilize planetary warming below dangerous (i.e. greater than 2°C) levels." Scientists have moved the doomsday clock, a symbolic countdown to the end of the world, from 3 minutes to 2 and ½ minutes before midnight. Donald Trump's climate change denial, appointees, and dangerous policies have pushed the world closer to doomsday than at any time since 1953. The keepers of the doomsday clock said, "Never before has the Bulletin decided to advance the clock largely because of the statements of a single person. But when that person is the new president of the United States, his words matter."[9]

Now that he's in office, Trump appears to be preparing to gut current U.S. efforts to combat climate change. He has doubled down on denial through the policies he has proposed and the appointments that he has made to key energy and environmental posts.

To slow climate change we need to get off fossil fuels and switch to clean, renewable sources of energy. Trump's "An America First Energy Plan" ignores climate change, and says, "President Trump is committed to eliminating harmful and unnecessary policies such as the Climate Action Plan and the Waters of the U.S. rule." We cannot even burn the oil reserves that we have or we overshoot extremely dangerous levels of warming. We certainly cannot continue with business as usual on the fossil-fuel economy.

New Trump policy promises show that Trump would encourage "the production of 50 trillion dollars' worth of job-producing American energy reserves, including shale, oil, natural gas and clean coal." In late January Trump signed executive memos to revive the Keystone XL and Dakota access pipelines, and open onshore and offshore leasing on federal lands and waters for energy development. He also plans to end a ban on new federal coal leases and abolish the current regulations aimed at limiting greenhouse gas emissions from power plants.[10]

The Environmental Protection Agency (EPA) regulates greenhouse gases under the Clean Air Act's 2009 endangerment finding, which determined that CO_2 and other greenhouse gases pose a threat to human health. Fuel economy rules for cars and trucks and the Clean Power Plan for the nation's power plants, originate from the endangerment findings, without which the EPA could not regulate greenhouse gas emissions. In 2012, Scott Pruitt, now the director of the EPA, joined about a dozen conservative attorneys general to strike down the endangerment finding in federal court. The court rejected his challenge, but it clearly demonstrated where Scott Pruitt stands on the underpinnings of all EPA regulations of greenhouse gases.[11]

Trump could also unravel formally or in practice the international Paris accords on climate change agreed to by nearly two hundred countries. If the United States abrogates Paris by backtracking on measures to mitigate climate change, other nations may no longer feel obligated to control carbon emissions in their own lands. Trump would likely eliminate or weaken regulations aimed at limiting methane emissions from the oil and gas industry's operations. He is unraveling regulations on vehicle emissions of carbon dioxide and his proposed budget would slash by 70 percent the EPA's climate change program, in effect shuting it down.[12]

Trump believes that the answer to the world's refugee calamity is to keep people bottled up in their dangerous homelands. A far better solution is to deal with the global warming that is rapidly surpassing war and violence as the world's most prolific driver of refugees. The tragic picture of the dead three-year-old Syrian boy, Alan, washed up on a Turkish beach, is forever burned into our consciousness. It symbolizes the impact of climate change on the refugee crisis, in particular the severe drought in Syria.[13]

Richard Seager, a climate scientist at Columbia University's Lamont-Doherty Earth Observatory, and the co-author of a study on the Syrian drought, said the drought when "added to all the other stressors, it helped kick things over the threshold into open conflict. And a drought of that severity was made much more likely by the ongoing human-driven drying of that region." "That drought, in addition to its mismanagement by the Assad regime, contributed to the displacement of two million in Syria," said Francesco Femia of the Center for Climate and Security. "That internal displacement may have contributed to the social unrest that precipitated the civil war. Which generated the refugee flows into Europe." [14]

Femia warned that the events in Syria could be repeated elsewhere and the U.S. military agrees. The Department of Defense has assessed climate change as a "threat multiplier" that threatens wars over water and other resources and a massive displacement of refugees. It warned in a 2015 report that "climate change is an urgent and growing threat to our national security, contributing to increased natural disasters, refugee flows, and conflicts over basic resources such as food and water. These impacts are already occurring, and the scope, scale, and intensity of these impacts are projected to increase over time." Imagine a world with many millions of climate refugees seeking new homes. [15]

Although Trump's policies, like his net worth, are known to mutate from day to day, his appointments to critical energy and environmental posts are not good news for the planet. Former Oklahoma Attorney General Scott Pruitt, now Trump's EPA administrator, is a fossil fuel advocate and climate change denier, who is best known for his efforts to weaken or outright destroy the agency he now heads. He has sued the EPA numerous times, and received more than $300,000 in contributions from the oil and gas industries. Three weeks after taking office, Pruitt contradicted the consensus of scientists on climate change, saying, "No, I would not agree that it's [human activity] a primary contributor to the global warming that we see." [16]

Emails from Pruitt's time as attorney general, released under court order, show how he has worked fist and glove with the fossil-fuel industry. Pruitt allowed the Oklahoma oil and gas company Devon Energy to write a complaint to the EPA on his letterhead that objected to regulations that would limit planet-warming methane emissions. The lobby group American Fuel & Petrochemical Manufacturers gave Pruitt "template language" in 2013 for an Oklahoma petition objecting to both the Renewable Fuel Standard Program and ozone limits. It said that this argument "is more credible coming from a state." Pruitt complied by filing opposition to both these regulations. He also coordinated with industry lobbyists on a "clearinghouse" for efforts to topple environmental regulations, all the while soliciting fossil-fuel contributions as head of the Republican Attorneys General Association. Upon taking office, Pruitt recused himself from his lawsuit challenging the EPA over the Clean Power Act. As one commentator tweeted it, it's "hard to sue yourself." [17]

Rick Perry, a former governor of Texas and Trump's Energy Secretary, is best known as the politician who tried to say that he wanted to abolish the Department of Energy but couldn't remember its name. While Texas is the largest emitter of carbon dioxide (CO_2) in the country, Rick Perry took a classic denier position of saying the "science is not settled" and claiming that climate change has always existed, while dismissing the historically high CO_2 levels that scientists attribute to the burning of fossil fuels. He has vehemently opposed EPA attempts to regulate carbon dioxide and led more than a dozen states in suing the agency to halt the program. His idea of an energy policy is more drilling and digging.[18]

Donald Trump's secretary of state, Rex Tillerson, was the CEO of ExxonMobil, the world's largest publicy traded oil and gas company. As early as 1977, an internal memo revealed that Exxon's own scientists and managers knew that carbon dioxide emissions from fossil-fuel use contribute to global warming and would eventually endanger humanity, but Exxon concealed this information for decades, including during Tillerson's tenure as CEO. Tillerson publicly claims that he and ExxonMobil believe in anthropogenic climate change and support a carbon tax. But under his watch the company has lavishly financed denier groups and politicians. His company has pursued oil and gas deals across the globe and among fossil-fuel corporations is a laggard in exploring the transition to clean and renewable sources of energy.[19]

Ryan Zinke, a former Republican congressman from Montana and now secretary of the interior, will control some five hundred million acres of federal land, about one-fifth of the nation. He has spoken moderately about climate change. But in his confirmation hearing, Zinke said that "there's debate" on the extent of human influence. In responding to a question about fossil-fuel development on public land, he said "we need an economy"—remember, not that long ago Trump thought that a green economy would create jobs. Zinke's position is consistent with his support for fossil-fuel development on public lands during his campaign for Congress. In Congress, he voted both to cut funding for renewable energy and to shift money away from renewable energy to fossil fuels. He voted to overturn or undermine Obama Administration orders and EPA regulations concerning the environment.[20]

Trump's opposition to climate change comes at a critical moment. In 2016, scientists reported that the levels of carbon dioxide in our atmosphere have passed the "safe" point for humanity, reaching levels not seen on this earth for some 15 million years. The last time CO_2 was this high, humans did not exist on planet Earth. On January 18, 2017, two days before Trump's inauguration as president of the United States, NASA and the National Oceanic and Atmospheric Administration (NOAA) reported that 2016 was the hottest year since they began keeping records in 1880. The record-breaking year continues a long-term warming trend—sixteen of the seventeen warmest years on record have now occurred since

2001. Scientists have found that melting artic sea ice is entering a "death spiral" with potentially disastrous consequences around the globe.[21]

An analysis by Climate Central, an independent organization of climate scientists and journalists reporting on climate change, explains the implications of a failure to continue U.S. efforts to combat climate change: "Climate scientists have been outspoken about what Trump's 'brighter future' might look like if climate change is ignored and carbon emissions are not cut: Weather will become more extreme, heat waves will become more common, Earth's polar ice caps will melt and America's coastal cities could be underwater within the lifetimes of today's youngest children."[22]

Scientists report that climate change advances the spread of tropical diseases into new climes, and that it reduces and contaminates our supply of drinkable water. The Centers for Disease Control and Prevention reports that the mosquito that carries the Zika virus, which causes horrible birth defects, is already in the United States. Other diseases that could become much more widespread if climate change is unchecked include cholera, malaria, and Lyme disease.[23]

AN UNLIKELY IMPEACHMENT HAS
BECOME MORE LIKELY

There is a twist on impeachment law that makes the "crimes against humanity" scenario in this category less remote than it may seem. Impeachment for a crime against humanity could be triggered not from within the United States but from the international community. The International Criminal Court (ICC) in The Hague, Netherlands, recently expanded its priorities to include the prosecution of *governments and individuals* for crimes against humanity through "destruction of the environment," *which could include catastrophic climate change.* Although the United States is not a party to the Rome Statute that created the ICC, the court can still initiate prosecutions for crimes in some 120 signatory countries, all of which would be harmed by an American reversal on fighting climate change.[24]

The ICC could have an incentive to target President Trump for one of its first prosecutions for crimes against the environment. Some African nations recently withdrew from the ICC to protest what they believe is a prejudicial focus on crimes in Africa over the world's major (nonblack) nations. Prosecution of the world's most powerful leader, especially one with low approval ratings across most of the world, would refute this criticism and do much to restore the court's prestige and integrity.[25]

As perhaps a prelude to criminal charges, plaintiffs have successfully pursued civil climate-change litigation against governments in places such as Austria, The Netherlands, and Pakistan. In the United States, a federal judge refused to dismiss a lawsuit that 21 children filed, first against then-President Obama and against now President Trump. It claims that inadequate efforts to curb climate change violate their constitutional rights. These "young citizens," the complaint says, "will disproportionately experience the destabilized climate system in our country."[26]

An ICC prosecution would not have legal standing in the United States, but it would have the moral force to raise calls for President Trump's impeachment. Any information uncovered by international authorities could be used for an impeachment in the United States. Even under international pressure, it may seem unlikely for a Republican House of Representatives filled with climate change deniers to initiate such hearings. But any member of the U.S. House, including a Democrat, could introduce a resolution calling for impeachment hearings, which the House could then vote up or down. It would only take about two dozen Republicans to side with the Democrats to begin the hearing process. A study by the Center for American Progress found that 59 percent of House Republicans were climate change deniers. That leaves 41 percent or nearly one hundred members who are skeptics or even adherents of established science. The impeachment could also be led by Democrats if the 2018 midterm elections produce a reversal of party fortunes in the House.[27]

In another world, if a president of the United States denied the "scientifically irrefutable" evidence of climate change and exposed the next generation of Trump business interests to *"catastrophic and irreversible consequences,"* then perhaps, in that other world, Trump himself would be the one calling most loudly for impeachment.

CHAPTER 8

The Russian Connections

"We assess Russian President Vladimir Putin ordered an influence campaign in 2016 aimed at the US presidential election. Russia's goals were to undermine public faith in the US democratic process, denigrate Secretary Clinton, and harm her electability and potential presidency. We further assess Putin and the Russian Government developed a clear preference for President-elect Trump."

—Unclassified Report of Office of the Director of National Intelligence, January 6, 2017

IS DONALD TRUMP A TRAITOR?

Treason is among the most serious and yet the least common of crimes. The last non-dual American citizen convicted of treason was Mildred Gillars, the infamous "Axis Sally," whom the Nazis paid to broadcast anti-American propaganda during

World War II. Prosecutors have never charged an incumbent official of the United States government with treason, not even Richard Nixon, who resigned and was pardoned long before hard proof emerged about his efforts to stall the peace process in Vietnam during his 1968 campaign. But Trump at least stands a chance of becoming the first American president charged with treason or the failure to report treason by agents and associates.

If suspicions prove true, there may have been some level of collusion between Trump or his agents and a foreign power to manipulate directly the results of an American election. Trump could be charged with treason if in the most extreme case investigations reveal that, at his direction, members of his campaign conspired with Russian leaders. He could be charged with misprision of treason (failure to report treasonous conduct) if it's discovered that he knew about such complicity but failed to report the crime. He also could be charged with treason again in the extreme case that the Russians are found to have blackmailed him with compromising information. And we mustn't forget the Logan Act, which forbids private citizens from meddling in America's international relations. These are now only questions, not answers, pending the results of ongoing investigations. But the lack of honesty and disclosure by Trump and his team raises the suspicion that they have much to hide when it comes to their Russian connections.

Regardless of the outcome of ongoing investigation, with a big assist from Donald Trump, Vladimir Putin has already achieved his primary aim of disrupting American democracy and the solidarity of the free world. He has cast doubt on the legitimacy of America's presidential election and provoked Americans into questioning their nation's democratic practices and its free press. He has weakened the common values and alliances that have sustained and protected freedom across the world since World War II. Foreign policy expert Molly K. McKew, whose years as an advisor to Mikheil Saakashvili, the former president of Georgia, offered her deep insight into Putin's Russia, says that Putin aims to create "an unstable new world order of 'all against all'" and "to replace Western-style democratic regimes with illiberal, populist, or nationalist ones." After nearly bankrupting his own country while amassing corrupt riches in the billions for himself, Putin has no choice but to remake the world outside Russia into his own image.[1]

AN INVITATION TO INTERFERE

Following the warnings of the nation's founders, American leaders have, throughout history, categorically opposed any foreign interference in our politics. "Foreign powers" would seize "the opportunity to mix their intrigues & influence with the Election," warned James Madison at the Constitutional

Convention. "It will be an object of great moment with the great rival powers of Europe who have American possessions, to have at the head of our Government a man attached to their respective politics & interests." A few years later, when the French ambassador meddled in American politics, President George Washington and even his political opponents agreed that France must recall the ambassador.[2]

Washington's precedent held until July 27, 2016, when, regarding Hillary Clinton's much fixated-on correspondences, Donald Trump said, "Russia, if you're listening, I hope you're able to find the 30,000 emails that are missing . . . They probably have them. I'd like to have them released." And with that—a casually spouted yet nonetheless completely inappropriate invitation to a foreign power to meddle in an American election—Trump reversed nearly two hundred and thirty years of American tradition, and encouraged Russia to engage in criminal conduct. Federal law prohibits, under penalty of imprisonment and fines, hacking into a private email server.[3]

Trump's appeal to Russia's hackers coincides with campaign commitments that reverse long-standing bipartisan opposition to Russian aggression. Although otherwise indifferent to the content of the Republican platform, Trump's team strong-armed his party into jettisoning a plank that would commit the party to arming Ukraine in its fight with Russia and pro-Russian rebels. Trump suggested the possibility of ending the sanctions that America had imposed on Russia. On top of that, he also indicated that NATO may be obsolete, and he has suggested joining Russia in a common campaign against ISIS.[4]

Trump repeatedly praised Putin during the campaign, calling him a leader "far more" than Barack Obama, the first time a presidential candidate had unfavorably compared an American president to a foreign authoritarian. A shocking statement, but Trump's pandering to Putin isn't new. In 2013, when Trump held the Miss Universe pageant, which he co-owned, in Moscow, he tweeted, "Do you think Putin will be going to The Miss Universe Pageant in November in Moscow—if so, will he become my new best friend?" The *Washington Post* reported that the deal to bring the pageant to Russia was "financed in part by the development company of a Russian billionaire Aras Agalarov . . . a Putin ally who is sometimes called the "Trump of Russia" because of his tendency to put his own name on his buildings."[5]

Trump did not meet with Putin in Moscow after all, but he did meet with Russian oligarchs who had close ties to Putin, including Herman Gref, the chief executive officer of state-controlled Sberbank PJSC, Russia's largest bank. "The Russian market is attracted to me," Trump said. "Almost all of the oligarchs were in the room. "TRUMP-TOWER-MOSCOW is next," Trump tweeted.[6]

BUSINESSMAN TRUMP'S RUSSIAN CONNECTIONS

Despite his undisclosed tax returns, we still know for certain that Trump has tried to launch real estate ventures in Russia through the Bayrock Group, a shady Russian-connected outfit and Trump's partner on at least four proposed American projects: the Fort Lauderdale Trump Tower, the Trump Ocean Club in Fort Lauderdale, the SoHo condominium-hotel in New York, and a resort in Phoenix. Bayrock had its office on the 24th floor of Trump Tower, and its 2007 glossy brochure features a photo of Trump and Tevfik Arif, a principle Bayrock partner. It calls the Trump Organization a "strategic partner," and lists Donald Trump as their primary reference.[7]

Felix Sater, the Russian-born managing director and majority shareholder in Bayrock, was convicted of assault in 1991. He served a year in prison for a barroom fight, in which he stabbed another man with the stem of a margarita glass, breaking his cheek and jaw, lacerating his face and neck, and severing nerves. He lost his license to sell securities in the United States. Then, in 1998, federal prosecutors brought a complaint against Sater for running a $40 million bogus penny stock scheme in collaboration with the New York and Russian mafia. In return for a guilty plea, Sater reportedly agreed to work as a government informant, and to avoid the stigma of his past, unofficially changed his last name to Satter.[8]

The other principle Bayrock partner, Tevfik Arif, had worked for seventeen years for the Soviet government before becoming an independent entrepreneur, eventually becoming backed by the so-called Kazakh Trio of billionaire oligarchs—Alexander Machkevitch, Patokh Chodiev, and Alijan Ibragimov. In 2010, Turkish police raided a luxury yacht where, according to press reports, they found on board with Arif nine young Russian and Ukranian women, and the three oligarchs of the Kazakh trio. Prosecutors charged Arif with human trafficking and the running of a prostitute ring. A Turkish court acquitted him of these charges.[9]

After learning of Sater's sordid past, Trump claimed, under oath in a 2007 deposition, that he barely knew the man. He said that he had "not very much contact with Sater. I dealt mostly with Tevfik [Arif]. I would say that my interaction with Felix Sater was you know, not—was very little." Trump persisted in this denial under oath even though it was obvious that he had worked with Sater on several developments, had corresponded with him, and was even photographed sharing the podium with a smiling Sater when Trump announced the unveiling of the SoHo Condominium-Hotel. In 2016, Sater contributed the maximum $5,400 to Donald Trump's campaign.[10]

Trump testified that Bayrock was working with contacts in Russia and Eastern Europe to complete Trump/Bayrock deals in Russia, Ukraine, and Poland. "Bayrock knew the investors, and in some cases, I believe they were friends of Mr. Arif. And this was going to be the Trump International Hotel and Tower in Moscow, Kiev, Istanbul, et cetera, and Warsaw, Poland." Trump said that Arif "brought the people up from Moscow to meet with me," and that the two were planning other ventures in Moscow. The only Russians who likely had the resources and political connections to sponsor such ambitious international ventures were the "oligarchs" allied with President Vladimir Putin. Trump claimed Arif "thought the deal was going to happen," but later told him that negative publicity about Trump had killed it. Still, Trump insisted that "we are actually going to be [in Russia] fairly soon." When asked if he had "concerns about investing in Russia," Trump said "no."[11]

In a later 2013 deposition, after learning of Arif's arrest in Turkey, Trump backtracked, saying that he barely knew the man: "I mean, I've seen him a couple of times; I have met him." It must have been the ghost of Bayrock, then, who Trump worked with on his many deals.[12]

As usual, Trump's selective amnesia worked in his favor. In 2015, New York State filed a massive tax evasion, money laundering, and racketeering civil case against Bayrock, Sater, Arif, and another Bayrock principal, Julius Schwarz. Private parties Jody Kriss and Michael Ejekam, former Bayrock associates, filed the initial lawsuit. However, the State of New York gave its imprimatur to the lawsuit under the state's "qui tam" law; this law authorizes the Attorney General, after an investigation, to have the state's claims litigated by the private attorneys who filed the action. The state's complaint incorporated virtually all the allegations in the private lawsuit's complaint. Trump was not among the accused, but the state cited his joint Bayrock ventures as one avenue for laundering money and evading taxes.[13]

The state, through the private complaint, alleges that, although "Bayrock does conduct legitimate real estate business, but for most of its existence it was substantially and covertly mob-owned and operated. Arif, Satter, and Schwarz operated it for years through a pattern of continuous, related crimes, including mail, wire, and bank fraud; tax evasion; money laundering; conspiracy; bribery; extortion; and embezzlement." It cited as a "Concrete example of their crime," the Trump SoHo property in New York.[14]

Although Bayrock used its partnerships with Trump to execute their schemes, the complaint says that there "is no evidence Trump took any part in, or knew of, their racketeering." Through his lawyer, Alan Garten, Trump denied having consented to a Bayrock swindle in the Fort Lauderdale Trump Tower project that evaded taxes by switching a $50 million investment to a $50 million loan. However, newly uncovered evidence—including the discovery by the *Telegraph* in Britain of documents signed by Trump—shows that Trump did, indeed, give his consent.

A damning document exists, in the form of a letter from Bayrock to Trump, dated May 16, 2007, relabeling the investment as loan. At the bottom of the letter is the notation, "Acknowledged without objection by," with Trump's distinctive signature underneath, as clear a consent as one gets in the usually murky real estate business. Does Trump have any economic ties to Russia today? Only his accountants know for sure.[15]

During the campaign, Trump said, "I have no business there and no loans from Russia. I have a great balance sheet." He has since continued such denials. However, in September 2008, Donald Jr. gave the following statement to Cityscape USA's "Bridging U.S. and Emerging Markets Real Estate" conference in Manhattan: "[I]n terms of high-end product influx into the United States, Russians make up a pretty disproportionate cross-section of a lot of our assets; say in Dubai, and certainly with our project in SoHo and anywhere in New York. We see a lot of money pouring in from Russia."[16]

Trump's many deals with Bayrock helps unravel Donald Jr.'s comments. He refers specifically to the Soho venture in which Trump partnered with Bayrock. Although the sources of Bayrock's financing are mysterious they were likely getting money from the Russian-affiliated nation of Kazakhstan and possibly Russia. The New York State complaint against Bayrock refers several times to its sources of funding from Russia and Kazakhstan. A 2007 Bayrock investor presentation cites the Kazakh oligarch Alexander Machkevitch's "Eurasia Group" as one of its partners for Bayrock's equity financing. One of Trump's first, post-election conversations with foreign leaders was a congratulatory call to the authoritarian president of Kazakhstan, Nursultan Nazarbayev, a backer of Putin's imperial ambitions.[17]

Billionaire Wilbur Ross, Trump's Secretary of Commerce, and a long-time Trump associate and former Trump business partner, has financial ties to Russia. In 2014, an investment group that Ross heads took a controlling share in the Bank of Cyprus. Close to half of the bank's assets come from Russia. "Cyprus banks have a long and painful history of laundering dirty money from Russians involved with corruption and criminality," said Elise Bean, an authority on money laundering. She added, "Buying a Cypress bank necessarily raises red flags about suspect deposits, high-risk clients, and hidden activities." Bean has made the *International Tax Review*'s list of the top 50 authorities on tax policy worldwide.[18]

Russian oligarchs have major stakes in the bank, among them Viktor Vekselberg, a close Putin ally, and Vladimir Strzhalkovsky, a former KGB agent who also is closely tied to Putin. Another stakeholder is led is Dmitry Rybolovlev. In 2008, during the real estate bust, Donald Trump sold his Palm Beach mansion to Rybolovlev for some $95 to $100 million. Four years earlier, during the real estate boom, Trump had bought the property for just over $41 million. Ross selected as bank chairman Josef Ackermann, the retired CEO of Germany's Deutsche Bank, one of Trump's largest creditors. U.S. and British regulators fined Deutsche Bank $630 million for laundering $10 billion from Russia. Although the Senate confirmed Ross for Commerce Secretary, the White House has refused to release his written answers to questions about his ties to the bank of Cyprus and Russian oligarchs.[19]

TRUMP'S CAMPAIGN AND THE RUSSIANS

Trump's Russian connections have reach, extending beyond his own person to campaign officials and advisors. His one-time campaign manager, political consultant Paul Manafort, worked closely for many years with the corrupt and pro-Russian, former President of Ukraine Viktor F. Yanukovych. Manafort was the master strategist behind Yanukovych's election as president and worked to restore his pro-Russian Party of Regions to power after Yanukovych fled to Russia. Manafort and two partners, Rick Gates and Rick Davis, struck questionable business deals with Russian oligarch Oleg Deripaska, a close ally of President Putin. Manafort and Gates also covertly routed $2.2 million to two Washington lobbying firms whose work they had enlisted on behalf of their Ukrainian clients.[20]

An investigation by the *New York Times* uncovered handwritten ledgers that include 22 notations of undisclosed cash payments to Manafort from Yanukovych's party, totaling $12.7

million. Manafort's lawyers have denied that he received any such payments. The validity of their statement, however, remains unknown, because Manafort did not register as the agent of a foreign government, which shielded him from disclosing any foreign payments. In August, Manafort resigned as campaign manager, and Trump replaced him with Steve Bannon and Kellyanne Conway. Gates left the campaign in September.[21]

The saga of Manafort, the Ukrainians, and the Russians took another bizarre turn in late February, when hacked emails from the iPhone of Manafort's daughter Andrea revealed a blackmail attempt against him by Ukrainian parliamentarian Serhiy Leshchenko. The Ukrainian claimed that he had "bulletproof" evidence of Manafort's financial arrangements with Yanukovych. Manafort confirmed the authenticity of the emails. He said he had received similar communications, but that he did not respond and turned the material over to his lawyer.[22]

In the hacked communications, Andrea and her sister Jessica expressed their qualms over their father's work for the pro-Russian Ukrainians. "Don't fool yourself," Andrea said, "That money we have is blood money." She further said that her father's "work and payment in Ukraine is legally questionable." She called Manafort and his new employer Trump "a perfect pair" of "power-hungry egomaniacs." [23]

And still there are even more individuals involved in the

Trump campaign who have verifiable connections to Russia or Wikileaks. Carter Page, who Trump identified as an adviser on foreign policy, worked in Russia for several years for Merrill Lynch and had investments there. An opponent of U.S. sanctions against Russia, Page spoke at the New Economic School's commencement ceremony in Moscow. Blasting the "hypocrisy" of America's foreign policy, he said to the Russians, "Washington and other Western powers have impeded potential progress through their often-hypocritical focus on ideas such as democratization, inequality, corruption and regime change." Roger Stone, a long-time Trump ally and advisor, said during the campaign that he was in contact with Julian Assange of Wikileaks. "I do have a back-channel communication with Assange," he said, "because we have a good mutual friend." [24]

MANIPULATING THE ELECTION

On October 7, 2016, the Department of Homeland Security and Office of the Director of National Intelligence issued a joint statement concluding that "the U.S. Intelligence Community (USIC) is confident that the Russian Government directed the recent compromises of e-mails from US persons and institutions, including from US political organizations. . . . These thefts and disclosures are intended to interfere with the US election process." [25]

Although the October report did not charge Russia with

intervening on his behalf, Trump still made a point of disparaging its findings. In the second presidential debate, after Hillary Clinton raised the issue of Russian hacking, Trump said, "But I notice, anytime anything wrong happens, they like to say the Russians are—she doesn't know if it's the Russians doing the hacking. Maybe there is no hacking. But they always blame Russia. And the reason they blame Russia because they think they're trying to tarnish me with Russia." In the third presidential debate, when asked whether he condemns Russian hacking by moderator Chris Wallace of FOX News, Trump equivocated, saying, "By Russia or anybody else." When Wallace then pressed him to condemn their interference, Trump responded in the passive voice, "Of course I condemn," then added, "Of course I—I don't know Putin. I have no idea."[26]

Not until January 6, 2017, did the U.S. intelligence agencies released a second and more comprehensive report concluding at the direction of President Putin Russia had meddled in the American presidential election with the express purpose of aiding in the election of Donald Trump. The president-elect also received the classified briefing on the report, with corroborating evidence and analysis.[27]

In anticipation of the public release of this second intelligence report, Trump resorted to blaming the victim, saying that careless Democratic party online security accounted for their hacked emails. On January 4, 2017, he tweeted "Julian

Assange said 'a 14-year-old could have hacked Podesta'—why was DNC so careless? Also said Russians did not give him the info!" The Russians, it turned out, *did* have Republican party information; they just chose not to release it. Russian manipulation included not only stolen emails, but the propagation of false news stories and the use of state-controlled media to undermine Clinton.[28]

Even as he disparaged America's intelligence agencies, Trump referred to their report as proof that foreign meddling "had absolutely no effect on the outcome of this election." Once again, we have Trump attempting to mislead Americans. Only as far as the intelligence community's report concluded that Russian did not hack the election's voting machines did the claim have any merit. The report reached no conclusion as to whether Russia's release of negative information and stories about Clinton tilted the election in Trump's favor.[29]

During the campaign, from October through the election, Trump mentioned Wikileaks, the outlet for Russian-hacked Democratic emails, 164 times; that's an average of five references per day. He enthused "We love Wikileaks," and said that Wikileaks proves that Clinton should not "be able to run for president." Trump even credited the word of Wikileaks founder Assange, when he said that Russia did not give him information on the Democrats. Lest we forget: In 2010, Trump, the master of reversing position when it serves his interests, had called Wikileaks "disgraceful," and said "there should be like death penalty or something."[30]

Despite buying into Assange's self-serving claims, Trump dismissed the findings from the seventeen American intelligence agencies. Comparing their reports about Russian interference in the election to an alleged false assessment they had made, that Iraqi dictator Saddam Hussein possessed weapons of mass destruction, Trump said, "if you look at the weapons of mass destruction, that was a disaster and they [the intelligence community] were wrong."[31]

Yet being wrong once, and fifteen years ago at that, does not mean that American intelligence is wrong on Russian meddling today. What Trump fails to recognize is that the CIA learned from its 2002 mistake about Hussein's Weapons of Mass Destruction (WMD). Former CIA director John Brennan, who had served in the intelligence community under both Presidents Obama and Bush, said, "A number of steps . . . were taken to make sure that we're going to be as accurate as possible, so it's been light years since that Iraq WMD report." The evidence for Russian interference is not circumstantial, as it was in the case of the WMD report; it is based on hard evidence, including the "digital footprints" of Russian hacking, the monitoring of Russian-controlled propaganda, and analysis of the origins of anti-Clinton propaganda.[32]

CHARGES OF RUSSIAN COLLUSION
AND BLACKMAIL

A few days after the intelligence community released its findings, the press reported that the community had briefed both President Obama and President-elect Trump on an unverified and unproven dossier filled with explosive accusations. The dossier was compiled as opposition research by Christopher Steele, a former operative for Britain's MI6 intelligence agency and a Russian specialist who spent two years in the country. Steele's dossier charged that Russia had gathered compromising sexual information on Trump during his 2013 visit to Moscow for the Miss Universe pageant. It claimed that Trump had struck a deal with Putin, agreeing to adopt pro-Russian policies in return for Russian assistance in winning the election. Buzzfeed published in full the unredacted version of the dossier on January 10, 2017.[33]

Beginning with a jolt—that the "Russian regime has been cultivating, supporting and assisting Trump for at least 5 years"—the dossier goes on to claim that Putin was using Trump "to sow discord and disunity both within the US itself, but more especially within the Transatlantic alliance which was viewed as inimical to Russia's interests." Ultimately, Putin wanted to discard "the ideals-based international order established after World War II," and return to the "Nineteenth Century 'Great Power' politics."

Steele said that Putin had gathered enough dirt on Trump's allegedly "perverted" sexual conduct in Moscow to "blackmail" him as president. He had also offered Trump "lucrative real estate" deals in Russia, which "for reasons unknown" Trump had declined. The dossier also said that Russia had a robust cyber-crime operation targeting western governments as its first priority.

Steele charged that "there was a well-developed conspiracy of cooperation between them [the Trump campaign] and Russian leadership," led on the Trump side primarily by Manafort, Page, and others. Trump and the Russians shared "a mutual interest in defeating Democratic presidential candidate Hillary CLINTON, whom President PUTIN apparently both hated and feared." The quid pro quo from Trump was "to sideline Russian intervention in Ukraine as a campaign issue and to raise US/NATO defence commitments in the Baltics and Eastern Europe to deflect attention away from Ukraine, a priority for Putin who needed to cauterise the subject."

The dossier said that Putin valued Trump because he "was viewed as divisive in disrupting the whole US political system; anti-Establishment; and a pragmatist with whom they could do business." In addition, "Trump also supposedly provided Putin with intelligence regarding "business and otherwise, in the US of leading Russian oligarchs and their families." In an especially scandalous quid pro quo, Igor Sechin, the head of the Russian oil giant Rosneft, is purported by Steele to have offered Trump via his then-adviser Carter Page, "the brokerage of up to a 19 per cent (privatised) stake in Rosneft" in return for lifting the sanctions against Russia.

Steele said that the subject of payments to Manafort arose at a meeting between former Ukrainian leader Yanukovych and Putin, where Yanukovych admitted to ordering the payments but insisted that he had left "no documentary trail" that "could provide clear evidence of this." Putin was reportedly skeptical of any reassurance from Yanukovych.

Trump's reaction to the release of the dossier was ferocious. He again employed the epithet of "fake news" to slam not just the publication of the dossier itself, but any reporting about its existence and inclusion in presidential intelligence briefings. Trump may be right that the dossier concocts a pack of lies; after all, Trump's opponents first hired Steele to dig for dirt on the candidate. Critics have told tall tales about presidents before, like the one claiming that Obama had scammed America into believing that he was born in Hawaii, not Africa. And Steele seemed to have made some factual errors in his compilation of information. Trump had better hope he's right this time, because even if some of the dossier's damning allegations are true, Congress would have a near-airtight case for impeaching and convicting him on the grounds of treason or misprision of treason.

NEW EVIDENCE PILES UP

Trump's insistence about the dossier's incredibility aside, there is strong reason to take the dossier cautiously but seriously, especially where it alleges collusion between the Trump campaign and the Russians. The American intelligence community respected Steele as a reliable enough source to present his dossier in presidential briefing, something nearly unheard of for an unverified report.

As president, Trump has continued to serve as Vladimir Putin's apologist. Asked in a pre-Super Bowl interview on February 5, 2017, by FOX news host Bill O'Reilly, if he respects Putin, Trump responded, "I do." When O'Reilly pressed on to say, "Putin is a killer," Trump responded, "There are a lot of killers. We have a lot of killers. Well, you think our country is so innocent?" During the campaign Trump had defended Putin after a British inquiry concluded that Putin had probably sanctioned the assassination of Russian dissident Alexander Litvinenko in London. Trump said that he had seen "no evidence" of Putin's complicity and that "They say a lot of things about me that are untrue too."[34]

President Trump has reacted assertively and speedily to provocative conduct by other nations, but has stayed silent as Russia has tested America's resolve. One such incident involved Russia's dispatching of a spy ship to within 30 miles of the U.S. Naval Submarine Base in Groton, Connecticut.

It deployed a nuclear armed cruise missile capable of striking our NATO allies in Europe, it violated Ronald Reagan's Intermediate-Range Nuclear Forces Treaty. Candidate Trump threatened to "blow out of the water" any Iranian vessels that came too close to American warships, but President Trump said and did nothing after Russian aircraft buzzed an American destroyer in a way that the Pentagon described as "unsafe and unprofessional."[35]

A Trump insider has also provided some corroboration for one of the dossier's important allegations. It alleges that "The reason for using Wikileaks" to release hacked Clinton emails "was 'plausible deniability' and the operation had been conducted with the full knowledge of Trump and senior members of his campaign team." It added that "In return the TRUMP team has agreed to sideline Russian intervention in Ukraine as a campaign issue." Consistent with this claim was the blocking of a GOP platform plank advocating the arming of anti-Russian resisters in Ukraine.

Trump and his then campaign manager Paul Manafort adamantly denied any campaign involvement in omitting that plank. "I wasn't involved in that," Trump said, shortly after the convention. "Honestly, I was not involved." When asked if anyone from the Trump campaign was involved, Manafort said, "No one, zero."[36]

Then in early March 2017, J. D. Gordon, the Trump campaign's national-security policy representative for the Republican National Convention, contradicted these denials. Consistent with the claims in the Steele dossier, Gordon said that at Trump's behest he had "advocated for the GOP platform to include language against arming Ukrainians against pro-Russian rebels." The press discovered that both Gordon and Carter Page had a previously undisclosed conversation with the Russian ambassador Kislyak at the convention. On July 22, 2016, the day after the Republican convention, WikiLeaks released its first trove of hacked Democratic Party emails, nearly 20,000 in all.[37]

Shortly after the publication of his dossier, Steele disappeared for two months, fearful for his life, sources close to the former intelligence operative said. Such fear may well be justified. In mid-January, a former Russian FSB General, Oleg Erovinkin, who worked closely with Rosneft chief Sechin, was found dead in his car in Moscow. Christo Grozev, an authority on Russian security issues, confirmed that Erovinkin was likely Steele's source for information about Sechin. Erovinkin joins a long list of Putin's enemies who have died under mysterious circumstances.[38]

A CNN report stated that intelligence officials had corroborated some of the material in the dossier involving Russian conversations—but not necessarily any compromising material—intercepted by the National Security Agency and analysts have since begun to take the dossier more seriously. Various news outlets reported from leaked sources, some de-

gree of contact during the campaign between Russian officials and Trump's inner circle.[39]

When asked at a press conference about contacts between
his campaign and Russian officials, Trump typically deflected,
saying, "Russia is a ruse . . . I have nothing to do with Russia."
When pressed about whether members of his campaign had
contacted the Russians, Trump said, "nobody that I know of."
We now know that at least five Trump insiders had contact
with the Russian ambassador during the campaign and the
transition: Attorney General Jeff Sessions, former National
Security Advisor Michael Flynn, White House advisor and
Trump son-in-law Jared Kushner, former campaign advisor
J. D. Gordon, and former campaign advisor Carter Page.
Trump's denial was one of about 20 times that he or a mem-
ber of his team had denied any contacts with the Russians.[40]

The communications between Attorney General Sessions and Kislyak at the GOP Convention in July and again
in Session's office in September are especially disturbing, because Sessions was not truthful about them under oath at his
confirmation hearing in early January. Democratic Senator
Al Franken of Minnesota asked Sessions "If there is any evidence that anyone affiliated with the Trump campaign com-
municated with the Russian government in the course of this
campaign, what will you do?" "I'm not aware of any of those
activities," Sessions responded. "I have been called a surrogate at a time or two in that campaign and I did not have

communications with the Russians." Senator Patrick Leahy of Vermont asked Sessions in writing whether he had "been in contact with anyone connected to any part of the Russian government about the 2016 election, either before or after election day." Sessions answered with an unequivocal, unqualified "No."[41]

In a news conference and a written "supplement" to his testimony, Sessions issued a medley of excuses, which would have made even Richard Nixon blush. He said he met with Kislyak not as part of the campaign, but as a member of the Senate Armed Services Committee, somehow implying that he could cleave himself in half. Sessions didn't disclose that when he met with Kislyak at the Republican National Convention in July, he was not there in his official capacity as a senator, but as a representative of the Trump campaign. He paid for his travel with campaign funds, not funds from his official legislative account.[42]

Sessions added that "I did not mention communications I had had with the Russian ambassador over the years because the question did not ask about them." But the questions by Franken and Leahy and Session's answers referenced only the campaign period. Sessions conceded that he didn't have any meetings with the Russian ambassador "over the years," but only during the campaign. It is not routine for members of Session's committee, which deals with military matters, not diplomacy, to meet with the Russian ambassador. The *Wash-*

ington Post contacted all 26 members of the Senate Armed Services Committee, not one of whom, except for Sessions, had met with the Russian ambassador during the past year.[43]

Sessions further tried to explain that he was "taken aback" by Franken's question at his hearings, which involved "brand-new information" and that he should have "slowed down" and disclosed his contacts with the ambassador. Yet questions about contacts with the Russians had beset the Trump campaign since the Manafort scandal exploded in July 2016 and were a sore spot in confirmation hearings. Sessions had some seven weeks following his hearing to "slow down" and clarify his testimony. He did so only after the press unmasked his deception. This excuse also fails to explain his response to Leahy's question in writing, when he had ample time to "slow down" and answer with care. He also said that because the Russian ambassador was "gossipy" he couldn't be certain that nothing came up about the campaign in their meetings.

In his explanations, Session resorted to the failed Bill Clinton defense of trying to twist the plain meaning of words. In 1999, Sessions voted to convict Clinton of perjury, saying that he wasn't buying the president's excuses. "It has been proven beyond a reasonable doubt and to a moral certainty that President William Jefferson Clinton perjured himself before a Federal grand jury," he said. He added, "It is crucial to our system of justice that we demand the truth. I fear that an acquittal of this President will weaken the legal system for those who consider being less than truthful in court."[44]

President Trump insisted that Sessions "did not say anything wrong," and as usual tried to deflect blame elsewhere. "The Democrats are overplaying their hand. They lost the election and now, they have lost their grip on reality," Trump said. "The real story is all of the illegal leaks of classified and other information. It is a total witch hunt!" The president added that Sessions should not recuse himself from investigations of the 2016 campaign and the Russians, just shortly before Sessions announced his recusal. However, Sessions said he was recusing himself not because of his Russian contacts, but because "I had involvement with the campaign," something that he knew from the day he became attorney general. Trump's claim of a "witch hunt" was backed by none other than Putin's foreign minister Sergey Lavrov, who said, "all of this looks very much like a witch hunt or the days of McCarthyism, which we long thought have passed in the US, a civilized country."[45]

There are instructive precedents for punishing attorneys general for lying under oath. One of Nixon's attorneys general, Richard Kleindienst, as part of a plea deal, pleaded guilty to a misdemeanor charge of failing to testify truthfully to the U.S. Senate. Even if Sessions did not commit perjury which is hard to prove, like Kleindienst, he certainly did not testify truthfully to the Senate.

Another Nixon attorney general, John Mitchell, who had resigned his post to run the president's 1972 campaign, was sent to prison for perjury and obstruction of justice. Mitchell's justification for committing perjury and encouraging others to do so casts a light on the political calculations of the Trump administration. He said that his decision "was a very expedient one," that "so close to the elections, we certainly were not volunteering any information."[46]

The response of Trump and his team to allegations of communications with Russian officials fits the classic pattern of a cover-up. First conceal and deny, then when outed by press claim that the communications were routine, innocuous, or incidental—kind of like a "third-rate burglary."

THE MICHAEL FLYNN SCANDAL AND THE ONGOING WAR ON THE PRESS

The first revelations about contacts between Trump's inner circle and the Russians involved retired General Michael Flynn, Trump's National Security Advisor. Flynn resigned in disgrace after just three weeks on the job, because he had lied about discussing Russian sanctions on a telephone call with ambassador Kislyak during the transition. After the press disclosed that Flynn had made this call, Press Secretary Sean

Spicer said that Flynn had only exchanged pleasantries with Kislyak and talked about arranging a conversation between Trump and Putin. Vice President Mike Pence vouched for this innocent account of the conversation. Pence also promised—falsely—that there had been no contact between any member of the Trump team and the Russians during the campaign. To believe otherwise, he said, "is to give credence to some of these bizarre rumors that have swirled around the candidacy."[47]

Flynn had lied to Pence and the American people when the *Washington Post* reported that according to nine sources, the FBI had intercepted and recorded what was a not-so-innocent call. Flynn and Kislyak were recorded discussing the sanctions imposed by the Obama administration for Russian meddling in the election. These measures included the expulsion of some suspected Russian spies from the United States. Per former federal officials who had reviewed the recording, Flynn had intimated that the new administration might take a fresh look at the sanctions and that Russia should not respond in kind. Five decades earlier, Nixon's agent had told the South Vietnamese leadership that they should do nothing about peace negotiations and wait until they got a better deal from his administration.[48]

President Putin apparently got the message. The next day, he said that he would not retaliate, but would await developments in relations with the Trump administration. He refrained from expelling American diplomats, and went so far as to invite their children to attend "the New Year and Christmas children's parties in the Kremlin." Trump responded by heaping more praise on the Russian leader: "Great move on delay (by V. Putin)—I always knew he was very smart!"[49]

Yes, this is a story about Flynn, but on a much more consequential level, what it's really about is Trump and a potential impeachment. In speaking about Flynn's resignation/firing, Trump followed the Nixonian model for a cover-up. Rather than dealing with the facts of Flynn's severe and possibly illegal transgression, Trump lambasted the media for uncovering the facts. A day after Press Secretary Sean Spicer shared that the president had "an eroding level of trust" in Flynn, Trump made a statement that calls to mind Ron Ziegler's disparagement of Woodward and Bernstein after they began unearthing facts about Watergate. "I think he's [Flynn] been treated very, very unfairly by the media—as I call it, the 'fake media,' in many cases," Trump said. "I think it's really a sad thing that he was treated so badly. . . . People are trying to cover up for a terrible loss that the Democrats had under Hillary Clinton."[50]

Trump tried to deflect attention away from the substance of the Flynn matter with an equally Nixonian emphasis on the way the information had been obtained. "I think it's very, very unfair what's happened to General Flynn, the way he was treated, and the documents and papers that were illegally—I stress that—illegally leaked. Very, very unfair." He later added, that the press "shouldn't be allowed to use sources unless they use somebody's name." Never mind that Trump had once been the anonymous leaker-in-chief to the New York media or that he had reveled in the illegal leaks of hacked Clinton emails during the campaign. The truth is that most leaks are not explicitly criminal unless they disclose certain classified information or grand jury testimony. Leaks helped break open the Watergate scandal. Without them we would know only what the administration wanted us to know and nothing more—and that's a frightening prospect.[51]

When Trump continued to slam the *Washington Post*'s story about Flynn's conversation with Kislyak as "fake news" based on phony sources that they just "make up," the *Post* struck back "Everything we published regarding Gen. Flynn was true, as confirmed by subsequent events and on-the-record statements from administration officials themselves," said executive editor Marty Baron. "The story led directly to the general's dismissal as national security advisor. Calling press reports fake doesn't make them so."[52]

What makes this attack on the media so bizarre is that two weeks before the press broke the Flynn story, Acting Attorney General Sally Yates—who Trump later fired for refusing to defend his first travel ban—informed him that Flynn has discussed sanctions with Kislyak. Apparently, neither this improper contact with a Russian official. She warned that

Flynn could be blackmailed by the Russians who of course knew about his deception. Apparently, Flynn's improper contacts with Kislyak, his deceiving of the vice president and the American people, and the possibility that he could be subject to blackmail, troubled Trump not at all.[53]

But the Flynn saga does not end there. According to a report in the *New York Times*, "A week before Flynn resigned as national security advisor, a sealed proposal was hand-delivered to his office, outlining a way for President Trump to lift sanctions against Russia." The *Times* said that three men were responsible for developing the plan. The first two were: Andrii V. Artemenko, a pro-Russian member of the Ukrainian parliament, and Michael Cohen, Trump's personal lawyer who was cited in the Steele dossier as one of the contacts between the Trump campaign and the Russians. The third man was none other than the convicted fraudster Felix Sater, who had connections with the Russian mafia.[54]

This is the same man who had teamed with Trump on major real estate ventures, and is charged by the New York State Attorney General with perpetrating a massive tax evasion and money laundering scheme. He's the man that Trump conveniently forgot about when asked about him in a deposition. How and why Sater became involved with a key member of the Trump administration in the most sensitive of diplomatic transactions between the United States and Russia remains a mystery to be resolved by investigators.

Cohen subsequently admitted meeting with the other two men, but has denied any role in developing or delivering a peace plan. But we've seen what denials from the Trump team are worth.[55]

There are now multiple investigations underway—by Congress and by law enforcement and intelligence agencies—into ties between the Trump campaign and the Russians. Here's what every American should demand of the investigators: that they search for all evidence of possible collusion between the campaign and the Russians. That they probe any direction by Trump or knowledge of contacts between his campaign and the Russians. That they examine all evidence of a possible quid quo pro on policy between Trump or members of his team and the Russians.

A Russian sword of Damocles hangs over Trump's head, and it's suspended by a slowly unravelling thread. If it falls, his presidency is over. Neither Republicans nor Democrats in Congress will tolerate a compromised or treasonous president. Impeachment and trial will be quick and decisive.

put himself above the law . . . and that they are mortally true.

CHAPTER 9

Abuse of Power

"The essence of Government is power; and power, lodged as it must be in human hands, will ever be liable to abuse."

—*James Madison, December 1, 1829*

NIXON REDUX?

Trump may be destined for impeachment for egregious abuses of power. Former Democratic representative Elizabeth Holtzman, who served on the House Judiciary Committee and voted for the articles of impeachment against Richard Nixon in 1974, said that "while there's not an exact similarity here" between Nixon and Trump, "what we have is the same mentality of abusing power, of taking power into your own hands and saying, 'I'm first'—not 'America First.'" Trump has "put himself above the law. . . . And that's the mentality that will bring this president down."[1]

Early in his tenure, President Trump established a Nixonian pattern of wielding power with little regard for the law, the Constitution, or America's traditions and ideals. Using as a case study President Trump's exploitation of presidential power through his executive order of January 27, 2017, on immigrants and refugees, I predict that he will continue to operate as a rogue president, basing the case for impeachment on the Nixon model of abused power. However, it took over five years for Nixon to accumulate the sins that are now collectively known as Watergate.

Through the drafting, implementation, and defense of his first travel ban, Trump trampled on core American traditions and principles. He has effectively claimed absolute presidential authority and breached the separation of powers that the framers established as a check against tyranny. He has tried to crush the independent press, another crucial safeguard of a flourishing democracy. As sad as it is unsurprising, the result of Trump's ban has been to make America less, not more safe. The president has already sounded an alarm bell for the world, and he cannot unsound it with a more carefully drafted and executed travel ban.

As a candidate, not as a president, Trump exhibited a far more restrained view of presidential power. He pledged to "cancel every *unconstitutional* executive action, memorandum and order issued by President Obama." During the campaign, to rein in Obama, Republicans in the House passed the Separation of Powers Restoration Act of 2016. Republican representative John Ratcliffe of Texas, one of the act's sponsors, wrote that it was "key to rebalancing government" by protecting the judicial review of executive actions. He said that "since the days of our founding fathers, we've witnessed a drastic shift away from the original separation of powers established by the Constitution and the emergence of an almighty administrative state filled with unelected bureaucrats who have the ability to effectively implement, interpret, and create laws."[2]

I will not explore Trump's second travel ban except to note that he has preserved the core of the initial ban with some exceptions. He has excluded Iraq; suspended refugee admission from Syria for 120 days, not indefinitely; removed the preference for religious minorities, and excepted legal permanent residents and current visa holders. Despite claiming that he had to rush out the first ban to keep "bad dudes" from flooding into America, he waited nearly a month after courts enjoined his initial ban before issuing the second ban and then delayed its implementation for ten days. Trump signed his Executive Order on the revised ban in secret, with no reporters present.[3]

DIMMING THE TORCH OF LIBERTY

On the one-week anniversary of his inauguration, Trump issued an executive order that banned, for ninety days, immigration from seven Muslim-majority nations: Iran, Iraq, Syria, Libya, Somalia, Sudan, and Yemen. It prohibits refugees from entering America for 120 days and suspends indefinitely refugee admissions from Syria. In its lawsuit challenging the legality of this order, the state of Washington contends that the ban undermines its "sovereign interest in remaining a welcoming place for immigrants and refugees."[4]

This claim has deep historical resonance. With one stroke of the pen, Donald Trump dimmed America's beacon of freedom, prompting cries of anguish from allies, and censure from independent voices and both Republicans and Democrats at home. His travel ban has alienated Americans from one another and has had a chilling effect on the estimated 3.3 million Muslims in our country. It has inspired angry grassroots demonstrations at airports across America, which are perhaps the largest spontaneous protests in the history of the nation. It has led to kindred demonstrations erupting across the world.

Trump's travel ban fed into terrorist propaganda that America has declared a religious war against Islam. "The [ISIS] chatrooms have been abuzz about how [the travel ban] shows that there is a clash of civilizations, that Muslims are not welcome in America, et cetera," said Mia Bloom, an authority on terrorism at Georgia State University.[5]

The ban further risked the radicalization of America's Muslims. It betrayed the trust of Muslims in the Middle East, North Africa, and Pakistan on whom America relies in the fight against terrorism. It has entrapped, for example, Iraqis who risk their lives by working with the American military as interpreters or informants and who were promised safe haven in America. The ban left untouched terrorists operating within targeted nations as trainers of bomb makers and likely solidifies their support and protection by local peoples.

The ban has provoked an international backlash from nations that America counts on for cooperation in the war on terror and other global challenges. Before the election, retired general James Mattis, now Trump's secretary of defense, warned that even talk of a Muslim ban "is causing us great damage right now, and it's sending shock waves through this international system." The Foreign Ministry of Iraq, whose armies are critical for the defeat of ISIS, expressed its "regret and astonishment" over the ban and insisted that "it is necessary that the new American administration reconsider this wrong decision." The Iraqi Parliament voted symbolically to impose a reciprocal ban on American travelers to Iraq.[6]

Trump issued his executive order on January 27, 2017,

a day that is memorialized and observed internationally as Holocaust Remembrance Day. The commemorative statement that his administration issued deliberately omitted explicit mention of the slaughter of Jews. The Nazis murdered many diverse peoples, but their Final Solution only targeted Jews for total annihilation. Submergence of the Final Solution within other Nazi atrocities is a tactic typical of Holocaust deniers. As Supreme Court Justice Robert H. Jackson, the chief American prosecutor, said at the close of the Nuremberg trials: "The Nazi movement will be of evil memory because of its persecution of the Jews, the most far-flung and terrible racial persecution of all time." That verdict still stands, and Trump's statement shows his seeming blindness to lessons of the Holocaust as a 'Jewish story' and their relevance for the formulation of immigration and refugee policy today.[7]

Trump's ban violated the letter and spirit of the Immigration Act of 1965, which rejected nationality quotas and celebrated America's diversity by opening immigration equally to peoples across the globe. President Lyndon Johnson said at the signing ceremony that by ending quotas, the act "corrects a cruel and enduring wrong in the conduct of the American nation." It "will really make us truer to ourselves both as a country and as a people."

Nearly twenty years later, President Ronald Reagan celebrated this inclusive vision of the American dream: "The poet called Miss Liberty's torch 'the lamp beside the golden door.' Well, that was the entrance to America, and it still is. . . . Every promise, every opportunity, is still golden in this land." Every American president since Johnson—Nixon not excluded—has avowed similar ideals, just perhaps not as eloquently as Reagan.[8]

Although the president has broad powers to exclude dangerous aliens from the United States, the 1965 law states that no person can be "discriminated against in the issuance of an immigrant visa because of the person's race, sex, *nationality*, place of birth or place of residence." In 1995, the U.S. Court of Appeals for the District of Columbia ruled that in writing this clause, "Congress could hardly have chosen more explicit language." Any justification for an exception, "if possible at all, must be most compelling—perhaps *a national emergency*."[9]

Immigration from the seven covered nations is not a national emergency nor even a serious threat of any kind to the United States. Trump's justification for the ban cited that "numerous foreign-born individuals have been convicted or implicated in terrorism-related crimes since September 11, 2001." Yet nationals from the covered nations were not involved in the 9/11 hijackings and have not killed a single American in a terrorist attack since 1975.[10]

A Homeland Security study, first disclosed by Rachel Maddow of MSNBC and verified as authentic by DHS, concluded

that no amount of vetting will help keep America safe because "most foreign-born, U.S.-based violent extremists likely
radicalized several years after their entry to the United States,
limiting the ability of screening and vetting officials to prevent
their entry because of national security concerns." A study by
New American found that of persons charged with terrorist
and related activities in the U.S. or killed in the course of terrorism, 81 percent were U.S. citizens; 9 percent were refugees,
illegal immigrants or persons on nonimmigrant visas; and the
remainder were of unknown status. These findings show that
the way to prevent domestic terrorism is to work with the U.S.
Muslim community to prevent radicalization, not to alienate
and antagonize American Muslims.[11]

The seeming goal of Trump's order was to rally his anti-
immigrant base and to ratify his power as president, not to
protect Americans from terrorism.

Trump's other executive orders on immigration reinforced
the message of his travel ban. He has reinterpreted American immigration law to broaden the criteria for deportation
of any undocumented immigrant with a criminal violation,
no matter how trivial, as well as of those merely believed to
have committed "acts that constitute a chargeable criminal
offense." This order made some 11 million American residents vulnerable to deportation, their fates dependent on the
discretion of enforcement officers whose ranks Trump wants
to expand by some fifteen thousand.

Taken together, the travel ban, the new deportation push, the insistence on building a border wall, and the blindness to lessons of the Holocaust reinforced what Trump's chief strategist Stephen Bannon described as Trump's vision of a nationalist America united behind "a culture and a reason for being"—singular, not plural. Trump and Bannon have, effectively, turned back the clock to discredited policies of the xenophobic 1920s, when nativists battled against pluralistic, cosmopolitan forces that they believed threatened America's national identity.

The enemies may have changed in ninety years, but the anti-pluralist visions that animate the policies of this administration remain the same. In the 1920s, the alleged threats to American civilization came not from the Muslims or the Hispanics, from but from the Jews, the Catholics, and the Asians. Republican Warren Harding pledged in his successful presidential campaign of 1920 to govern as an "America First" president. In support of measures to close America's golden door to most immigrants, he said that, being mindful of "racial differences" among people, he would admit to the United States "only the immigrant who can be assimilated and thoroughly imbued with the American spirit." In 2016, Trump said, "I only want to admit people who share our values and love our people." [12]

In 1924, Congress prohibited the immigration of Asians, a people that it deemed inherently unfit for American citizenship, and set quotas for each nation of Europe. The law skewed those quotas to exclude Jews and Catholics from southern and eastern Europe; Poland, Lithuania, and Russia combined had an annual quota of less than ten thousand immigrants. During the Nazi era, even the more generous quota for Germany kept some 200,000 Jews stranded in Hitler's Third Reich. The waiting list for an American visa reached ten years. Many more Jews were trapped in lands that would become killing grounds in the Holocaust. On the home front anti-Semites who refused to raise the immigration quotas, warned of dangerous Jewish immigrant criminals, spies, and saboteurs. Most of the Jews stranded in Germany and elsewhere in Europe eventually perished in the Nazi death camps.[13]

Just as nativists once stereotyped Jews as subversive and Asians as unassimilable, Trump stereotyped Muslims from the banned countries as potential terrorists. During the campaign, he said that most Syrian refugees in the United States are "strong, young men. . . . You look at them. I'm saying. Where are the women? Where are the children?" In 2015, a State Department spokesperson said that only some two percent of Syrian refugees settling in America are single men; 78 percent are women and children. After issuing the ban, he spoke of "bad dudes," flooding into the United States from the embargoed nations, with the intent to harm Americans. Yet not a single refugee, Syrian or otherwise, has carried out a serious terrorist attack in the United States during the past forty years. An analysis by the Cato Institute found that the chances of an American being killed by a terrorist refugee from any land are 1 in 3.6 billion.[14]

Rumana Ahmed, an American-born Muslim woman and a professional National Security Council staffer who chose to stay on and work with the Trump team, found painfully personal its commitment to a singular American culture that rejected diversity. On the first day that she entered the offices of the new NSC, she recalls, "the new staff looked at me with a cold surprise. The diverse White House I had worked in became a monochromatic and male bastion."

She observed that the NSC's structure of nonpartisan analysis had collapsed, with orders coming from "a few in the West Wing." On the day she resigned, she told Trump's senior NSC communications adviser, Michael Anton, of her consternation with what she saw as the administration's anti-Muslim policies. In return, she said, "He looked at me and said nothing." Ahmed later learned that "he authored an essay under a pseudonym, extolling the virtues of authoritarianism and attacking diversity as a 'weakness,' and Islam as 'incompatible with the modern West.'" The Muslim in Trump's NSC had lasted on the job for all of eight days.[15]

A CONSTITUTIONAL VIOLATION

The Trump administration hastily drafted and implemented its travel ban with little regard for its human costs. Overnight, the ban produced chaos at America's airports and left stranded abroad even aliens with visas and the right of permanent legal residence in the United States. The ban separated families and kept men and women from their jobs and schooling in the United States. It rendered aliens afraid to leave the United States out of fear that the government would stop them from returning. It forced refugees to return to war-torn countries at the peril of their lives. Eventually, officials said that the ban did not cover legal residents after originally insisting that it did.

Civil rights groups and state governments immediately filed lawsuits to enjoin implementation of the ban. The state of Washington succeeded first. Senior Federal District Court Judge James L. Robart quickly issued a temporary injunction halting implementation of the ban nationwide. A three-judge panel of the Ninth Circuit Court of Appeals then unanimously rejected the government's pleading to lift Robart's injunction. Later, Federal District Court Judge Leonie M. Brinkema in Virginia independently issued another nationwide temporary injunction. At least for a time, the ban was dead.[16]

Judge Brinkema and the Ninth Circuit found that the plaintiffs were likely to succeed on the merits in a full trial because the ban suffered from fatal constitutional defects. The Circuit Court ruled that the order collides with the Fifth Amendment, which prohibits the government from depriving individuals of their "life, liberty, or property, without due process of law." It found that the government failed to show that the order complies with "what due process requires, such as notice and a hearing prior to restricting an individual's ability to travel." The Constitution's due process protections, the court said, apply not just to citizens, but to all persons within the United States, including aliens who might seek to leave and then reenter the country.

Additionally, Judge Brinkema found that the ban likely violates the First Amendment's prohibition against "an *establishment* of religion," which prohibits any government action that favors one religion over another. The order provided exemptions for members of minority religions in these mostly Muslim countries, thus in effect favoring non-Muslims over Muslims. The judge noted that Trump had confessed his discriminatory intent when asked by David Brody of the Christian Broadcasting Network about his refugee order: "As it relates to persecuted Christians, do you see them as kind of a priority here?" Trump replied, "Yes." He then falsely claimed that if "you were a Christian in Syria it was impossible, at least very tough to get into the United States. If you were a Muslim you could come in, but if you were a Christian, it was almost impossible." In a Fox News interview, Trump advisor Rudy Giuliani said that Trump had approached him for advice on how to draft a "Muslim ban" legally. After the election, Trump removed and then restored a link that calls for a "total and complete shutdown of Muslims entering the United States until our country's representatives can figure out what is going on."[17]

REJECTING TRUMP'S CLAIM OF ABSOLUTE PRESIDENTIAL POWER

Trump's lawyers also made the Nixonian claim of absolute presidential power. They argued that the courts lacked the authority to review a presidential decision "regarding what is in the national security and foreign policy interests of the United States." As in the Nixon litigation over his "executive privilege" to withhold the White House recordings from the special prosecutor, the courts rejected this disregard for the separation of government powers. In the Washington case, Judge Robart ruled that the judiciary must ensure "that the actions taken by the other two branches comport with our country's laws, and more importantly, our Constitution."[18]

The Ninth Circuit noted that the government is arguing not only that considerable deference should be granted to the executive, but more sweepingly that the president has "unreviewable authority to suspend the admission of any class of aliens." Like Judge Robart, the Ninth Circuit rejected such absolute presidential power, ruling that "There is no precedent to support this claimed unreviewability, which runs contrary to the fundamental structure of our constitutional democracy." It noted that, "neither the Supreme Court nor our court has ever held that courts lack the authority to review executive action in those arenas for compliance with the Constitution."

In support of its claim of overarching federal authority, the administration argued that the threat to national security posed by immigrants and refugees is whatever Trump thinks it to be. No evidence or proof is required. Judge Brinkema rejected this fact-free, or "alternative fact," version of the government's case. During the hearing on Virginia's lawsuit, the judge challenged Trump's lawyers to produce real evidence of the national security threat from the banned nations. "The courts have been begging you to provide some evidence, and none has been forthcoming," she said.[19]

In her order, Judge Brinkema ruled that the government has "not offered any evidence to identify the national security concerns that allegedly prompted this EO [Executive Order], or even described the process by which the president concluded that this action was necessary." The president, she also ruled, cannot hide the administration's lack of evidence by referring to classified information. Citing an earlier court ruling, she noted that "'Courts regularly receive classified information under seal and maintain its confidentiality. Regulations and rules have long been in place for that.'"[20]

TRUMP STIFLES DISSENT

To protect the one-man authority that Trump proclaimed in court, he stifled internal dissent within his administration and has branded as "enemies" any internal dissenters of conscience within the executive branch. In the polarized worlds of presidents Nixon and Trump, there are only enemies and loyalists—no friends, and no room in between for principled dissent. Nixon not only organized his Plumbers unit to plug leaks, but even illegally wiretapped members of his administration that he suspected of disloyalty.

In similar fashion, Trump has disregarded federal law and American traditions carved out to preserve a safe space for principled dissent. The Whistleblower Protection Act of 1989 protects the right of federal employees to act as whistleblowers and report misconduct, without retaliation or reprisals. The federal government's "Code of Ethics," which is posted in every agency, says that government employees must "put loyalty to the highest moral principles and to country above loyalty to persons, party, or Government." Within the State Department, internal regulations establish procedures for submitting a "dissent memo, without retaliation."[21]

In response to Trump's travel ban, some one thousand professional American diplomats exercised their right to submit such a dissent memo. It declared that Trump's ban "runs counter to core American values of nondiscrimination, fair play, and extending a warm welcome to foreign visitors and immigrants. Alternative solutions are available to address the risks of terror attacks which are both more effective and in line with Department of State and American values." White House Press Secretary Sean Spicer said that the signatories "should either get with the program or they can go." That is, shut up and march, or go hungry.[22]

Trump also fired Acting Attorney General Sally Yates, a Justice Department career lawyer for twenty-seven years, when she refused to defend his travel ban in court. Yates had not just a right but an obligation to reject the defense of an executive order that in good conscience she believed violated American law. In a colloquy during her confirmation hearings as the deputy attorney general, U.S. senator and now attorney general Jeff Sessions agreed on the need to reject on principle an unlawful order: "*You,* have to watch out because people [will] be asking you [to] do things you just need to say no about," Senator Sessions told Yates. "But if the views the president wants to issue are unlawful, should the *Attorney General* or *Deputy Attorney General* say no?" Yates responded, "Senator, I believe that the *Attorney General* and the *Deputy Attorney General* have an obligation to follow the law and the Constitution and to give their independent legal advice to the president."[23]

Just as Yates had an obligation to "say no" on principle to defending the order, Trump had an obligation to remove Yates and defend his order. Nonetheless, the manner of the firing—which presidential historian Julian Zelizer of Princeton University called Trump's "Monday Night Massacre"—inevitably raised comparison to Nixon's "Saturday Night Massacre."

In his letter sacking Yates, Trump showed that there can be no conscientious dissent on his watch. Trump said that she had "betrayed the Department of Justice," equating the principled right to say no with betrayal not just of her office but "his" Justice Department as well. He said, "It is time to get serious about defending our country," a charge that is akin to treason but has no bearing on the legal issue at stake. He accused Yates of "being weak on borders and very weak on illegal immigration," a gratuitous smear, which implied without evidence that politics rather than conscience motivated her dissent. He complained that Senator Sessions, his nominee for attorney general, was "being wrongly held up by Democratic senators for strictly political purposes." Nixon's former White House counsel John Dean said that Trump had exceeded even Nixon with this invective. "I've never read a White House statement as nasty as Trump's attack on acting AG Sally Yates—a new low."[24]

A VIOLATION OF THE SEPARATION OF POWERS

In drafting his order, Trump did not consult with the congressional leadership or chairs or members of the pertinent committees. Speaker of the House Paul Ryan said that he learned of the executive order "at the time it was being issued," and that he was briefed "as it rolled out." However, Trump recruited staff members of the House Judiciary Committee—which has oversight over the executive order—to assist in drafting the executive order, without prior consultation with their bosses. Press reports indicate that, without precedent in American history, Trump imposed on these congressional employees the same confidentiality agreements he had required of his ex-wives, his business employees, and his campaign workers. The unauthorized use of congressional staffers, and particularly the coercing of gag orders, violates the separation of powers between the executive and Congress, a key factor in the House's decision to impeach Andrew Johnson.[25]

In a more serious violation of checks and balances, Trump and his advisors responded by waging war against the judiciary. Following the model of their war against the press, they tried to undermine the credibility and legitimacy of the American judiciary. Just as he had earlier claimed that Judge Gonzalo Curiel could not impartially preside over the Trump University litigation because of Curiel's Mexican heritage, Trump now disparaged Judge Robart. He tweeted that "The opinion of this so-called judge [Robart], which essentially takes law-enforcement away from our country, is ridiculous and will be overturned!" George W. Bush appointed Judge Robart to the bench and the Senate unanimously confirmed him.[26]

Trump then ominously added, "Just cannot believe a judge would put our country in such peril. If something happens blame him and court system. People pouring in. Bad!" After the Ninth Circuit's ruling, Trump warned, "Right now, we are at risk because of what happened" in the courts; "THE SECURITY OF OUR NATION IS AT STAKE!" he tweeted in capitals. In effect, President Trump, the master of deflection, had preemptively piled blame on the courts for any future terrorist attack against the United States.[27]

Trump's disparagement of the judiciary raises concern that, in the event of another terrorist incident, which is almost inevitable, Trump will blame the courts and his political enemies as a pretext for taking charge under martial law. There is precedent for a president disregarding rulings of even America's highest court. Trump's hero Andrew Jackson, whose portrait now hangs in the Oval Office, famously ignored a Supreme Court decision against Indian removal, which drove Native Americans from their homes in the East and forced them to migrate westward. Jackson reportedly said, "[Chief Justice] John Marshall has made his decision;

now let him enforce it." Although the comment is likely apocryphal, Jackson did ignore the court's decision.[28]

ATTACKS ON THE PRESS

Donald Trump had once been the "Tabloid King" of the New York media. He shrewdly planted stories in the press, often demanding anonymity, and sometimes even posing as his own public-relations agent, using the fictitious names of John Miller and John Barron. As president, however, Trump has followed the opposite strategy of discrediting the press. To eliminate another check on his powers, Trump has taken to discrediting any reporting that does not follow his propaganda line, condemning it as "fake news" by the "very dishonest press." He has set himself as the arbiter and censor of news, saying, "I know what's good. I know what's bad. . . . The news is fake because so much of the news is fake." *In a direct blow against the Constitution.*[29]

The real news, in Trumpian doublethink, comes from the administration's "alternative facts." To stoke fear of alien Muslims and distrust of reporting, Kellyanne Conway said that the two Iraqis arrested in 2011 "came here to this country, were radicalized, and they were the masterminds behind the Bowling Green massacre. I mean most people don't know that because it didn't get covered." It wasn't covered because *it never happened.* The two men committed no crimes in the United States, and authorities arrested them in Bowling Green without incident. Conway later said that she had made a "slip of the tongue," but the context of her remarks refutes that claim, as this was, after all, the third time—and not the first—that she had referred to the "Bowling Green massacre" or "Bowling Green attack."[30]

By charging that the media has failed to cover terrorist attacks, apparently out of sinister, if unspecified, motives, Trump gave credibility to Conway's alternative facts. "They have their reasons, and you understand that," he said. The administration then released a list of alleged, uncovered terrorist atrocities. It included attacks in Paris; Nice, France; Orlando, Florida; and San Bernardino, California, that the media blanketly covered for days.[31]

Trump projects onto the press his own inveterate lying when he scoffs that what they report is "fake news." Through this tactic of classic Orwellian doublethink, falsehood becomes truth and truth becomes falsehood, all in the service of "Big Brother." Yet Trump is willing to accept news from the media that suits his purposes. At a campaign rally on February 18, 2017, to highlight the terrorist threat from refugees, Trump said, "You look at what's happening in Germany, you look at what's happening last night in Sweden. Sweden, who would believe this?" The Swedish government responded with consternation, saying there had been no terrorist incident the previous night and that officials had not elevated the terror threat level. Trump said he had garnered his information from a FOX News report.[32]

Trump has also exceeded Nixon by adopting Putin-style censorship of the media. On February 24, 2017, the White House barred from a press briefing selected outlets that it had castigated for reporting news critical of the administration, including CNN, *Politico*, the *New York Times*, and the *Los Angeles Times*. "Nothing like this has ever happened at the White House in our long history of covering multiple administrations of different parties," said Dean Baquet, the executive editor of the *New York Times*. That same day Trump threatened further suppression of the press, saying, "They shouldn't be allowed to use sources unless they use somebody's name." He added that the media "doesn't represent the people," and "we're going to do something about it."[33]

By discrediting the press, or at least the press he doesn't like, and stifling internal dissent, Trump ensures that he becomes the only source of information, however false, for the public. Leading newspapers and television news outlets, he said, are not just his enemy but, crucially, "the enemy of the American people in many ways." He said that the nation's leading journalists "make up stories and make up sources." His chief adviser Steve Bannon called the press "the opposition party."[34]

Trump is not acting from a place of ignorance. He is following *his own history* of largely unchecked behavior over nearly five decades in business and politics, with gag orders, shaming of critics, lawsuits, and threats of lawsuits.

GROUNDS FOR IMPEACHMENT

Faced with restrictions imposed on his power by the separation of powers and the free press, Mr. Trump appears to be quite unhappy. He seems to be moving toward creating conditions under which he could rewrite parts of the Constitution in the image of his personal and business life. To even get to the point at which that becomes possible, Trump would need for the country to be consumed by total chaos, and deep divisions to have formed among the country's social, political, and economic groups.

Chaos at this extreme level fits with the objectives of Trump's chief strategist, Steve Bannon, who has called for the "deconstruction of the administrative state." Per the recollection of conservative historian Ronald Radosh, in a 2013 conversation Bannon compared himself to Lenin, who, he said, "wanted to destroy the state, and that's my goal too. I want to bring everything crashing down, and destroy all of today's establishment." Lenin replaced the Russian state with rule he called "the dictatorship of the proletariat," the common people. In practice, this boils down to dictatorship by a few elite apparatchiks in the Kremlin. If "the system is totally broken," as Trump has said, he "alone can fix it."[35]

In multiethnic countries run by autocratic leaders, conditions conducive to concentrating power in one group's hand are often created by making one ethnic minority the target of dehumanization and fearmongering. The U.S. social structure does not lend itself to such ethnic division, thankfully, but in an alarming work-around, Trump has made immigrants into the surrogate for an ethnic minority. And, to ensure that the judiciary, the media, and persons of conscience within the executive branch do not get in his way, Trump has fallen back on intimidation to keep them in line.

Like authoritarians across the world, he has also fallen back on projecting abuses on others. In an early-morning tweet storm on March 4, 2017, Trump accused President Obama of tapping his phones at Trump Tower during the election. "How low has President Obama gone to tapp [sic] my phones during the very sacred election process," Trump tweeted. "This is Nixon/Watergate. Bad (or sick) guy!" Trump offered no evidence for this explosive allegation. Ironically, federal officials can wiretap domestic telephones, but only if they shows probable cause to a court that the phones were being used by foreign agents or by someone acting on behalf of foreign agents.[36]

Never before—we seem to use those words a lot for Trump—has a sitting president abused the bully pulpit of his office to claim that a predecessor committed a serious and at the time impeachable crime. "If the alleged illegal wiretapping by Obama would be impeachable if true, so must be the allegation if false," said Noah Feldman, a professor of constitutional law at Harvard University. "Anything else would give the president the power to distort democracy by calling his opponents criminals without ever having to prove it." [37] Even if President Trump does not brazenly violate the First Amendment through censorship, he can still be impeached for his war on the press as an abuse of presidential power. Although not a formal branch of government, the press is a necessary pillar of American democracy. Thomas Jefferson said, "The basis of our governments being the opinion of the people, the very first object should be to keep that right; and were it left to me to decide whether we should have a government without newspapers, or newspapers without a government, I should not hesitate a moment to prefer the latter." "Attacks on the press by Donald Trump as enemies of the people [are] more treacherous than Nixon's," concluded Carl Bernstein. [38]

Leading Republicans have warned Trump that an assault on the free press threatens a free people. Republican senator John McCain of Arizona said that the suppression of the free press is "how dictators get started," and "if you want to preserve democracy as we know it, you have to have a free—and many times adversarial—press." He added, "I'm not saying that President Trump is trying to be a dictator. I'm just saying we need to learn the lessons of history." Former president George W. Bush said, "I consider the media to be indispensable to democracy," adding, "power can be very addictive and it can be corrosive and it's important for the media to call to account people who abuse their power, whether it be here or elsewhere." He concluded, "It's kind of hard to, you know, tell others to have an independent free press when we're not willing to have one ourselves." [39]

Even if his arsenal of tactics for getting what he wants is bottomless, Trump may well be on his way to presenting a case for impeachment modeled on Nixon's—Article 2, Abuse of Power.

CHAPTER 10

The Unrestrained Trump

The Trump campaign is not about any cause, it is all about Trump. His campaign is all about him. How he treats other people is all about him—whether one is praised and patted on the head or cruelly mocked depends on what you have said about him.

> —*Peter Wehner, Conservative*
> *Political Analyst, June 2, 2016*

You think I'm going to change? I'm not changing.
> —*Donald J. Trump, May 31, 2016*

TRUMP DOESN'T CHANGE

On April 19, 2016, Donald Trump won a landslide victory in the New York State Republican primary. The media hailed his sober, respectful speech as evidence that he was changing, that a "new" Trump had emerged, one who would heed

---

the advice of his managers, stay on script, and appear "presidential." As a sign of his transformation, Trump referred to his opponent Ted Cruz as "Senator Cruz," rather than "'Lyin' Ted Cruz," and was applauded. The "new" Trump didn't last twenty-four hours. Within a day, he had called Cruz "'Lyin' Ted" a dozen times and was back to his undisciplined ways.[1]

THE WRONG TEMPERAMENT FOR A PRESIDENT

A president's behavior and decisions are held to a high standard, and Trump has shown no willingness to accept advice, to grow in his new role, or to internalize criticism and gain restraint. Trump may have claimed a landslide victory, but in truth, he lacks the protection of a wide popular mandate; postelection exit polls found that only 34 percent of voters believed that Trump had the right personality and temperament for the office of president.[2]

For five decades, mental health professionals have followed the so-called Goldwater rule against diagnosing a public figure from afar. The rule, sanctioned by the American Psychiatric Association, arose after *Fact* magazine, during the 1964 campaign, polled psychiatrists on the question of whether Republican candidate Barry Goldwater was mentally fit for the presidency. But some psychiatrists have since challenged this restraint. In a 2016 article published in the *Journal of the American Academy of Psychiatry and the Law*, psychiatrists said that the "Goldwater rule can be questioned, since third-party payers, expert witnesses in law cases, and historical psychobiographers make diagnoses without conducting formal interviews."[3]

Some professionals have expressed misgivings about Donald Trump's mental state, and the candidate himself made Hillary Clinton's mental capacities an issue in the campaign, charging that she "lacks the mental and physical stamina to take on ISIS." Politics attracts narcissistic personalities, but Trump breaks the mold, topping even his notoriously self-absorbed trio of campaign surrogates: Newt Gingrich, Rudy Giuliani, and Chris Christie. Trump appears to display what authorities in the field often refer to as narcissists who view others as extensions of themselves or tools for their own ends, and who are obsessed with personal enrichment and glorification. Trump revels in the cheers of a crowd and lashes back at even the mildest rebuke. Some extreme narcissists may verge on delusional in their lack of introspection or consideration related to the damage they wreak on others. They are often resistant to advice and hostile to criticism.[4]

Several historical figures have entered the public imagination as symbols of extreme narcissism. Consider the widely spoken of "Napoleon complex." The complex suggests that Napoleon's discomfort about his short stature led to his development of a ruthless personality, which in turn compelled him to conquer other peoples to reassure himself of his own worth. King Richard III of England, another larger-than-life personality, fascinated Shakespeare, who saw him as having developed a ruthless and brutal personality to compensate for insecurity about his crippled spine, which he believed made him appear weak.

These examples demonstrate what professionals know about extreme narcissism: that it typically results from deep-seated insecurity and in some cases shaming or neglect by a parent figure. Extreme narcissists seek to fill this gaping hole of self with power and prestige, but their insecurity can never be gratified, leaving them prone to rage over small or perceived slights. A "narcissistic injury" is a term describing these small or perceived slights that inspire rage in the narcissist and a desire for outsized punishment or revenge. These perceived injuries pierce the narcissist's thin skin, exposing his inner sense of smallness, which must be denied and protected at all costs. In his 2007 book *Think Big and Kick Ass in Business and Life,* Trump said, "When someone crosses you, my advice is get even. When people wrong you, go after those people because it is a good feeling and because other people will see you doing it. I love getting even."[5]

Trump showed his obsession with "smallness" when he retaliated after Marco Rubio's jest about his small hands. "He's like 6' 2", which is why I don't understand why his hands are the size of someone who is 5' 2"," Rubio joked. "Have you seen his hands? And you know what they say about men with small hands . . ." At a Detroit rally, holding up his hands, Trump said, "These hands can hit a golf ball 285 yards." Then, for all of America to see and hear at a presidential debate, Trump said, "Nobody has ever hit my hands. I have never heard of this." He again held up his hands and said, "Are they small hands? And he referred to my hands—if they are small, something else must be small. I guarantee you, there is no problem."[6]

This was not the first time someone had belittled Trump's hands. In 1988, *Vanity Fair* editor Graydon Carter had mocked Trump in *Spy* magazine as a "short-fingered vulgarian." With an understanding of the psychology of narcissism, Carter wrote that his purpose was "just to drive him a little bit crazy." It worked. "To this day," Carter said in 2015, "I receive the occasional envelope from Trump. There is always a photo of him—generally a tear sheet from a magazine. On all of them he has circled his hand in gold Sharpie in a valiant effort to highlight the length of his fingers."[7]

Even the validation of winning the presidency did not stop the insecure Trump from lashing out against any slight, no matter how trivial, no matter the source. He attacked the cast of *Saturday Night Live* for satirizing him, and the cast of the musical "Hamilton" for appealing to his vice presidential pick Mike Pence to "uphold American values." He belittled Arnold Schwarzenegger, as host of *Celebrity Apprentice*, for being "swamped" and "destroyed" in comparison to "the ratings machine, DJT." He lashed out at his old antagonist Graydon Carter, when *Vanity Fair* reviewed Trump Grill as "the worst restaurant in America."[8] He called actress Meryl Streep "one of the most overrated actresses in Hollywood" and a "Hillary flunky" after she criticized him in a speech at the Golden Globe Awards.[9]

After John Lewis, the African American civil rights icon and Democratic representative of Atlanta, questioned the legitimacy of Trump's presidency, Trump lashed out at Lewis personally. He said that Lewis was "All talk, talk, talk—no action or results. Sad!" In a reflection of his warped view that all African Americans live in hellholes of drugs and crime, he added that Lewis "should spend more time on fixing and helping his district, which is in horrible shape and falling apart (not to mention crime infested)."[10] Did I mention that Trump's vicious attack on Lewis occurred over MLK weekend?

Trump's unrestrained blasts, particularly against persons who are not his political rivals, have drawn sharp rebukes, including from Republicans and independent authorities on the presidency. Republican strategist Nicolle Wallace, who served as communications director for President George W. Bush, said of Trump's behavior: "It is cyberbullying. This is a strategy to bully somebody who dissents. That's what is dark and disturbing." Presidential historian Robert Dallek said that, "It's beneath the dignity of the office. He doesn't seem to understand that." Frank Sesno, director of the School of

Media and Public Affairs at George Washington University commented, "Anybody who goes on air or goes public and calls out the president has to then live in fear that he is going to seek retribution in the public sphere. That could discourage people from speaking out."[11] It may be too late for Trump to heed the admonition of President Abraham Lincoln during the Civil War, but he'd be wise to:

> If I were to read, much less answer, all the attacks made on me, this shop might as well be closed for any other business. If the end brings me out all right, what's said against me won't amount to anything. If the end brings me out wrong, ten angels swearing I was right wouldn't make any difference.[12]

The timing of Trump's tweets, which often post overnight or early in the morning, further discloses the extent of his extreme narcissism. During the day, when he is distracted and surrounded by a self-selected admiring audience, he feels temporarily fulfilled. As night falls, and he is left to his own thoughts and subconscious insecurities, his mind ruminates on his "enemies" and those who have harmed him. He is unable to stifle the strong urge to retaliate or crush his "opponent." This intense emotional response is a characteristic phenomenon of the narcissistic injury and its toxic repercussions for the narcissistic personality.

The final, frightening characteristic of extreme narcissism that Trump exhibits is delusional grandiosity, which for Trump manifests itself most visibly in bragging beyond reason or fact, even on matters that seem trivial. Eleven days before his inauguration, Trump boasted that anticipation for the event was so "unbelievable" and "record-setting" that "all of the dress shops are sold out in Washington." A quick survey by *New York Daily News* reporter Gersh Kuntzman found that D.C. shops were, in fact, well stocked, awash in "dresses to suit all tastes and price ranges."[13] Trump is even delusional about his delusions, saying, "I don't mind being criticized. I'll never, ever complain."[14]

When questioned at a news conference in February 2017 by Jewish publication *Ami Magazine*'s Jake Turx, about the administration's response to rising anti-Semitism, Trump couldn't just denounce anti-Semitism, but had to say "Number one, I am the least anti-Semitic person you've ever seen in your entire life," and, "Number two, racism, the least racist person." Even on International Women's Day, March 8, 2017, Trump couldn't resist turning the attention on himself. His tweet said, "I have tremendous respect for women and the many roles they serve that are vital to the fabric of our society and our economy."[15]

Fellow Republican senator Rand Paul of Kentucky said of Trump, "I think a little humility, a dose of humility, might be good for him. But I'm actually worried about the opposite. I'm worried that his narcissism exceeds nothing and that his delusions of grandeur have him saying that he can shoot people and people will still vote for him."[16]

In so many ways, Trump reveals his relentless need to protect his insecure sense of self. It is entirely possible that his internal conflicts make him incapable of admitting any lack of agency or power or inability to win—and that could prove dangerous. In response to North Korea's declaration that they will test missiles capable of reaching the United States, he said, simply, "it won't happen," as if the force of his belief in his personal power would keep the missiles from ever leaving the ground. Gross propaganda at best; delusional grandiosity at worst.[17]

Trump's delusional grandiosity, his black-and-white vision of the world, and his hair-trigger outbursts are frightening in a man who controls a nuclear arsenal with the power to end civilization. Trump's mania to be the biggest and the best, has led him to lie that his predecessor let us fall behind the Russians on nuclear weapons capacity. He's called for reigniting the nuclear arms race that brought the U.S. and the former Soviet Union close to annihilation in the 1980s.

If you were sitting in Beijing, Pyongyang, Moscow or Teheran, you might be frightened to hear the world's most powerful leader welcoming an arms race and also pledging to win wars, inflate his military, and cut diplomacy and foreign aid. And frightened people make bad decisions. Several times during the Cold War miscalculation and accident brought the U.S. and the Soviets close to mutual annihilation. With decision-time clocked in minutes, Americans have a right to ask whether the impulsive Trump would have the calm deliberation needed to respond to seemingly hostile blips on a radar screen.[18]

An ill-considered Trump response to a crisis or a manufactured crisis that heedlessly brings us close to nuclear war could lead to impeachment. Even absent such an incident, fears about Trump's custody of our nuclear arsenal could figure into the willingness of Congress to impeach the president on other grounds.

The roots of Trump's grandiosity extend far into his past. In his teens, Trump envisioned himself as a star, perhaps even the brightest star in the heavens. In a recorded interview with Michael D'Antonio, the Pulitzer Prize–winning author of *The Truth About Trump,* Trump bragged that, while in high school during the 1960s, he was the best baseball player in New York, if not the best athlete:

"I always knew I was good. I was always good at it. I was always the best athlete . . . Always the best player. Not only baseball, but every other sport too . . . I was the best baseball player in New York when I was young . . . Everybody wanted me to be a baseball player. But I was good at other things too. I was good at wrestling. I was really good at football. I was always good at sports. I was always the best at sports."[19]

Another sign of Trump's grandiose narcissism is his infamous tendency to deflect onto others all problems, difficulties, and failures. Hillary Clinton is responsible for the birther controversy. Loose security by the Democrats is to blame for Russia's meddling in the election on his behalf. Illegal voters cost him the popular vote. The media brought down General Flynn. The sex tape in which he bragged about sexually assaulting women is no big deal because "Bill Clinton has said far worse to me on the golf course—not even close." [20]

Trump's impulsivity, lack of insight, and poor judgment are dangerous for the country in multiple ways but may ultimately lead to his own undoing before leading to the country's. As pressure from the public mounts, he is likely to respond by doubling down on his outrageous assertions and dangerous behavior. The ease with which he distorts facts and misperceives his own power could cause him to reject threats to his presidency from those seeking his impeachment. He may not be able to help himself from responding in ways that will inflame arguments and criticism against him. He may not be able to tone down statements or arguments that offend others. He is unlikely to have the humility to recognize threats and to preemptively eliminate them before they become imminent.

As the legend of King Midas reminds us, the relentless search for wealth and power often alienates people who would be our closest allies. The office of President of the

United States is fundamentally a position of public service, and Trump is particularly unsuited to the role.

OF UNSOUND MIND

Issues surrounding Trump's temperament raise the question of whether he might be charged with "incapacity," one of the grounds for impeachment that James Madison cited in the Constitutional Convention. As in the precedent set by the case of Judge Pickering's impeachment, the charge would cite not a specific crime but Trump's erratic and bizarre behavior, which is already evident in the early days of his presidency. The House's fourth article of impeachment against Pickering charged him with being a man of "loose morals and intemperate habits," who in court "frequently, in a most profane and indecent manner, invokes the name of the Supreme Being to the evil example of all good citizens of the United States; and was then and there guilty of other high misdemeanors, disgraceful to his own character as a judge and degrading to the honor of the United States." Tweak a few of the words and it's easy to see how similar charges could be leveled against President Trump today.[21]

These psychological issues could also trigger the only other constitutional mechanism for removing a president from office. The Twenty-Fifth Amendment to the Constitution, adopted in 1967, provides a means for removing a president for disabilities—not limited to the physical—that render him unable to fulfill the duties of office. It's a Byzantine procedure that has never been used to remove a president and requires the cooperation of the vice president and the cabinet, both chosen by the president. Yet, in the newly dawned Trump era, precedent has counted for so little.

Under that amendment, the vice president and a "majority of either the principal officers of the executive departments or of such other body as Congress may by law provide" may, through a written submission to Congress, declare the president too incapacitated to carry out his duties. The vice president then assumes the role of president. The president can resume his office by declaring to Congress that he is fit to serve. The vice president and the cabinet can then challenge this declaration and the Congress can then, by a two-thirds vote, declare the president incapacitated. Otherwise the president resumes his office.[22]

Trump's hand-picked cabinet would, of course, have to turn against him to invoke the amendment, and he could fight back against it in the Republican Congress. It's a remote but possible scenario, given the unique psychology of President Trump and his willingness to offend either party, and it became slightly less remote when mental health professionals shattered the Goldwater rule to challenge Trump's mental fitness to govern the nation. An open letter, signed by thirty-five psychiatrists, psychologists, and social workers, most of them Ph.D.s or M.D.s, said that "We believe that the grave emotional instability indicated by Mr. Trump's speech and actions makes him incapable of serving safely as president." In accord with the analysis I present in this book, the authorities warned that "Mr. Trump's speech and actions demonstrate an inability to tolerate views different from his own, leading to rage reactions. His words and behavior suggest a profound inability to empathize. Individuals with these traits distort reality to suit their psychological state, attacking facts and those who convey them."[23]

CHAPTER 11

Memo: The Way Out

———

I'm capable of changing to anything I want to change to.
—*Donald J. Trump, February 10, 2016*

Mr. President, I'm aware that I've been hard on you, but as a reward for making it this far (it's common knowledge, of course, that you don't much like reading), I would like to offer you a way out of impeachment. My purpose is not to kill your spontaneity, and it's not to spoil your fun. My purpose, simply, is this: to give you a blueprint for surviving as president. People say that you are set in your ways, that a person can't change at the age of seventy, especially if that person is a president surrounded by yes-men. Yet you are very much your own man. "My primary consultant is myself," you once remarked. You've said that you can change, and that your life confirms your capacity for change when you believe it serves

———

your interest. What can be more important, I implore you, than changing to retain the presidency?

What follows is a short recap of the big life changes you've made over the years. (I figured, if you're willing to hear me out, I could spare you the effort of taking such a long walk down memory lane. You're the president of the most powerful country in the world, after all; you're a very busy man.) You've bailed on two marriages and the casino business. You've shifted your focus from building to licensing your name. You brilliantly turned to your own advantage the notion that President Obama was born outside of the United States. You switched from Democrat to Republican and became the first successful presidential candidate in history to make the shift from private businessman to political leader. You changed from pro-choice to pro-life and from banning *all* Muslim immigrants to more modest proposals.

Below is the plan of action that I propose you undertake, and immediately. It will not be an easy plan for you to follow, but nothing could be more in your interest, I assure you, than retaining the presidency and avoiding the stigma of impeachment.

1. DIVEST.

Divesting yourself from all your business interests and putting the proceeds into a genuine blind trust, managed by an independent administrator, is the *only* way for you to avoid the inevitable conflicts of interest that will expose you to impeachment. The trustee would also manage the divesture itself. Every modern president with substantial assets, from Ronald Reagan to George W. Bush, has adopted this safeguard.

Yes, with your far-flung illiquid assets and your valuable "Trump brand," you are in a class of your own. As your attorney Sheri Dillon said, "Selling his assets without the rights to the brand would greatly diminish the value of the assets and create a fire sale." However, a decline in the value of your brand does not turn on divestment. According to Walter M. Shaub, head of the nonpartisan Office of Government Ethics, "longstanding White House policy across Administrations prohibits the use of the President's name or image in advertising or for the endorsement of any commercial product or service."[1]

Dillon is correct that you would take a financial hit from divestment, but you have a multibillion-dollar cushion, and surely you will remain a billionaire once the lengthy and complex process concludes. David Reiss, director of Brooklyn Law's Center for Urban Business Entrepreneurship, put it bluntly when he said: "He has to make a choice. How much pain is he willing to take."[2]

Your attorney is also correct in that you are not bound by the laws that require divestment of other federal officials, but you are bound by the STOCK Act and the Emoluments

Clause, which Ms. Dillon much too quickly dismissed. And impeachment does not require the violation of a specific law. In response to your queries regarding conflicts of interest, ethics director Shaub wrote that, it has been a "consistent policy of the executive branch that a President should conduct himself 'as if' he were bound by this financial conflict of interest law." He added, "Given the unique circumstances of the Presidency, OGE's view is that a President should comply with this law by divesting conflicting assets, establishing a qualified blind trust, or both."[3]

Your son-in-law, Jared Kushner, set a fine example for you to study and follow. His lawyers worked with the ethics office to draft a practical approach to avoiding potential conflicts of interest. The office verified that he had, in fact, followed the strategy that you have avoided, of divesting himself from his private business holdings, not just stepping back from management. Even your critics Shaub and Eisen have blessed your son-in-law's "sensible" approach.[4]

But it will be so much work, I can hear you protesting. Mr. President, you don't have to go it alone. You can call on Congress to help you by enacting legislation that would provide you the same leeway provided other government officials for a tax-free trade of assets. It is true that at the end of this process, you will no longer have the Trump business empire. But your reward, which money cannot buy, is retaining the world's most important position.

---

2. SUPPORT A CARBON FEE AND
THE PARIS ACCORDS.

Even if events do not heat up in time for an impeachment case, you do not want to go down in history as the president who fiddled away while the planet burned. That you have always trusted science I am confident; otherwise, how ever could you have safely built Trump Tower and all those other iconic, striking structures? In 2009, you, Donald Jr., Eric, and Ivanka signed an open letter calling for "meaningful and effective measures to control climate change," in order "to protect humanity and our planet." Since then science on the matter has become even more convincing and the threat more urgent.

Now, before you object—there *are* ways to reaffirm your 2009 commitment to control climate change that will be consistent with your business-first principles. The adoption of a carbon fee would reduce carbon dioxide emissions through market principles, by making it more expensive to burn fossil fuels and encouraging the development of alternative sources of energy. A revenue-neutral fee would return proceeds to the American people, offsetting any rise in the price of carbon-based energy. Although it may seem counterintuitive, support for the Paris accords on climate change are consistent with your theme of "Make America Great Again." You've said that you want our allies to pay for their own defense and not just leech off the United States. Then, surely, too, you would want foreign nations to pull their own weight in combating climate change and not become free riders on the United States.

3. ADD A SHRINK TO THE
WHITE HOUSE PHYSICIANS.

As radical as it may seem, break precedent by including a doctor of psychiatry among your White House physicians. Tend to your mental health no less than your physical health. A psychiatrist at your disposal will provide you with valuable counseling and help you to restrain your more vulnerable tendencies and avoid the impeachment traps discussed in this book. Nobody blinks when a president seeks counseling from a minister; why should reaction to a psychiatrist be any different?

The assessment of the physical health of presidents and presidential candidates has become routine. You'll recall when you and Hillary Clinton released professional assessments of your physical fitness during the campaign, and the controversy that spawned. You said that Clinton lacked the "stamina" for leadership and that her supporters mocked your weight and your fast-food diet. Lost in this narrow focus on the flaws and strengths of the body is the no-less-significant mental side of health. History shows that presidents are more frequently plagued by mental rather than physical health problems. Abraham Lincoln suffered severe bouts of depression that confined him to bed and led to suicidal thinking. After the death of his beloved son in his second term, Calvin Coolidge suffered what psychiatrists termed a "major depressive episode" and "essentially abdicated his responsibilities as president," wrote his biographer Robert E. Gilbert. Richard Nixon had a doctor covertly prescribe for him Valium, which he then received indirectly from a psychiatrist.

Of course, the mere presence of a White House psychiatrist brings with it serious political risks. Opponents will challenge your decision-making abilities and claim that they were right all along about your temperamental unfitness for the presidency. Yet you have survived and thrived by defying the conventional political wisdom. Why not do it again? The result may be that your demonstration of humility and realism disarms rather than empowers your critics. Any consultations with a psychiatrist, as with any other physician, will be protected by doctor-patient confidentiality, and the doctor need not keep written records of his work with you.

Still not totally convinced? You even could go a step further and protect yourself politically by having Congress establish the Office of Presidential Psychiatrist. Although Americans today still view mental health challenges more negatively than physical ones, treatment no longer carries the grim stigma of lobotomies and shock therapy from bygone years. Lynn Rivers, who served four terms in the United

States Congress as a Democrat from Michigan, openly admitted to suffering from bipolar disorder, and freshman Democrat Ruben Gallego of Arizona has discussed seeking help for posttraumatic stress disorder. Congress, also, has recognized the reality, and ubiquity, of mental health issues. In 2008, Congress enacted a mental health parity law that required health insurance companies to cover mental and physical illness equally. In 2016, the Republican Congress enacted the Helping Families in Mental Health Crisis Act to expand and improve the federal government's role in mental health care.

4. USE A FACT-CHECKER.

You have done more for the employment of fact-checkers than any politician in the history of the country. You probably think that fact-checkers are another tool of the anti-Trump mainstream media. Not true. They're just wonks doing what they are being paid to do. Yes, you beat the debunkers by winning the White House, but you will face even more intense scrutiny as a president than as a candidate. The *Washington Post* has deployed a browser extension to add their fact-checks to your tweets in real time, and Google has introduced a new feature to tag and help users find "fact checking in large news stories." You've got to be more careful with the facts, Mr. President. That means no more "truthful hyperbole," either. Lies can lead directly to impeachment—as Clinton and Nixon learned first-hand—and they can cost you your credibility in the form of a House impeachment investigation or a Senate trial.

You can change your ways only by having your own wonk who independently checks your facts before speeches, interviews, rallies, news conferences—even tweets. That is, you need to beat the *Washington Post* and Google at their own game. I know this may slow you down and make the job less fun, but it's essential to your survival on the job.

5. TREAT WOMEN WITH DIGNITY AND RESPECT.

You have said that "nobody has more respect for women than I do," but your actions haven't matched your words. When you first contemplated running for president in 1999, you admitted to having a woman problem. Fast-forward to this most recent election, and that problem nearly torpedoed your candidacy after the release of the Howard Stern recordings, the *Access Hollywood* tape, and the many accusations made against you for sexual harassment and assault. You demeaned some of your accusers for their allegedly unflattering looks and you didn't treat Hillary Clinton with much respect as a woman during the campaign. In the tape, you also admitted to having an out-of-control libido, and that you just can't resist making nonconsensual advances on women.

It's time for a change. You need to treat women with the same dignity and respect that you would accord any man. Respect every woman's boundaries. That means not touching women in public or private in any way that might even seem unwanted or sexual in the slightest. Don't create an atmosphere in the White House that would lend credibility to any charges of assault or harassment, or that would encourage women to level such charges. This means you've got to stop making demeaning comments about women. Don't flirt or make sexual innuendos. Don't respond if a woman seems to be coming on to you. Don't judge women by their looks. Don't blame women for inviting sexual advances. Don't defend sexual harassers like former FOX News head Roger Ailes did. Don't suggest that female victims of sexual harassment at the workplace should just get another job; few have backup from a billionaire father. Don't make any comments about women's bodily parts, their breast-feeding, or their female cycle. Assume that all microphones are live and cell phones are everywhere.

Do increase the visibility of First Lady Melania Trump. Bring her back to the White House as soon as possible. Encourage her to adopt as her own a nonpartisan cause like Laura Bush did with literacy or Michelle Obama with child obesity. Don't give the impression that Ivanka is the surrogate first lady and that you are, de facto, a man on his own. This may all sound very boring to you, but you won't lack for other excitement as president of the United States.

If, like Bill Clinton, you are sued for sexual harassment while in office, don't do anything to turn it into grounds for impeachment. Don't fight. Don't threaten. Don't countersue. Settle, as you did with Justice's Fair Housing Lawsuit in the 1970s and the recent class-action lawsuit against Trump University. If you can't settle—think, for example, of that suit filed by feminist lawyer Gloria Allred—fine, but whatever you do, don't follow Bill Clinton's destructive path of lies and obstruction. The cover-up is usually worse than the deed.

6. CURB THE MUSSOLINI ACT.

I am not suggesting that you give up being a strong leader, but only that you moderate what appear to be your authoritarian tendencies. Edging too close to Mussolini territory will make you antagonistic enough for Congress and the public to want you gone, but not strong enough to overcome the check and balance of impeachment. America today is not Italy of the 1920s, and you are not Mussolini and don't want to be. No, really—you don't. We know how that ended for him: hanging upside down at a service station where people spit on his dead body.

Stop picking and choosing among companies based on the

allure of rewards and retributions. Let the free market work—ideally under better trade agreements, if you get them, that apply equitably across the American economy. Stop demeaning immigrants and minorities. You've come a long way to curb this tendency; don't revert. Remember it was once your German ancestors whom nativists denigrated as a threat to America. Get rid of your private security force—they smack too much of Mussolini's Black Shirts. Abandon your war on the press. Every dictator has killed off the free press. It's cliché at this point. Besides, you're going to need some press support if you get caught in an impeachment investigation; bullying won't cut it.

Stop attacking our democratic institutions. You won. You don't need to explain away a defeat, and having lost the popular vote will make no difference for your presidency. You'll be judged on how well you govern, not by the circumstances of your election. Don't believe me? Ask George W. Bush.

Stop demeaning judges. It is acceptable to criticize court decisions; many presidents, including such Democratic Party icons as Franklin Roosevelt and Barack Obama, have done so. But critiquing judges personally rather than on their decisions breeds completely unnecessary antagonism. In a democratic system, the courts are a check on tyranny no matter how vexing they may be. Unless you're planning to disregard court rulings and become a full-fledged dictator, ease up on the judges.

Stop saying you can't have a conflict of interest. Just stop. Maybe Mussolini got away with that, but a democratically elected president can always have a conflict if his private interests clash with those of the American people, and the remedy is impeachment.

Start using more inclusive rhetoric and downplay your cult of personality. I'm not suggesting that you swing across the spectrum to Clinton-style togetherness. But operating a bit against type will serve you well in the long run and will help to assure that you *have* a long run.

7. STEVE BANNON, YOU'RE FIRED.

There's no accounting for taste, so I'm not going to even try to understand your love for Steve Bannon. But we still need to talk about him. You think that he rescued your campaign and paved the way for your victory in November. Well, the campaign is over; it's time to start thinking about your presidency. Already, he's led you down the primrose path with a travel ban that only hurt your standing in the nation and across the world. Bannon will be a lightning rod for criticism and a bottomless source for discontent within your administration. He will be forever despised by the many Americans who loathed Breitbart News under his direction and who believe that he represents racism and anti-Semitism in America. Attention paid to Bannon's shortcomings won't deflect the focus away from your own, but it *will* reflect poorly upon you.

If it helps you to see where I (and most of America) am

coming from, picture Bannon as a bomb thrower who wants to upend American society and politics. Scary image, right? You don't need to go that far to make the changes that you promised the American people. Remember, you succeeded fabulously before the presidency—not by destroying the establishment, but by playing it brilliantly for your own ends. You want to continue to be president of the United States, not the commander of one faction in another American civil war. Bannon's agenda is not your own. Make that your mantra. You've already had one fiasco with Flynn; you can't risk another one with this guy. No one is better than you at firing people. It's time to exercise that skill with Steve Bannon.

8. PROTECT YOUR LEGACY.

I have one word for you in conclusion, Mr. President, and that word is *legacy*. It's easy to get swept up in the adulation and enthusiasm of the crowd. But you can't build a legacy on rallies and tweets. You need solid accomplishments that make America great and safe and that will secure your reelection in 2020.

Above all, you can't afford to ensnare yourself in an impeachment investigation, like the one that consumed the last two years of Clinton's presidency. The bar is, frankly, set so low for you that even the small changes I've suggested here would sufficiently disarm your critics and clear the path to a successful presidency. You can do this.

———

The Peaceful Remedy of Impeachment

"The President of the United States would be liable to be impeached, tried, and upon conviction of treason, bribery, or other high crimes and misdemeanors . . . The person of the King of Great Britain is sacred and inviolable: There is no constitutional tribunal to which he is amenable, no punishment to which he can be subjected without involving the crisis of a national revolution."

—*Alexander Hamilton,* The Federalist, *1788*

To impeach or not to impeach, that is the question: if the president's misdeeds are serious, not minor or technical, then the answer is yes. As students of history, the framers knew that power corrupts and they established impeachment as a legal and peaceful means for escaping tyranny without having to resort to revolution or assassination.

Benjamin Franklin made this point clear to his fellow

delegates at America's 1787 Constitutional Convention, and Hamilton reaffirmed it in *The Federalist Papers*. In the past, Franklin said, assassination removed tyrannical rulers. For the new nation, "It would be the best way therefore to provide in the Constitution for the regular punishment of the Executive when his misconduct should deserve it, and for his honorable acquittal when he should be unjustly accused."[1]

Recognizing that presidential misdeeds can take many forms, the delegates set the criteria for impeachment and removal broadly, trusting in the judgment of America's elected representatives.

Impeachment and trial did not unjustly harm Presidents Johnson or Clinton. Nor did they weaken the office of the president or sacrifice the common good. Andrew Johnson emerged from his acquittal a chastened and therefore better president than before. During the remaining months of his term, Johnson ceased his obstinate obstruction of congressional Reconstruction, which enabled Congress to continue the process of integrating free slaves into national life. Bill Clinton's public approval remained robust through the ordeal of investigation, impeachment, and acquittal. In the midterm elections of 1998, his Democratic Party gained seats in the House, the first time the party holding the White House had done so since 1934. The presidency emerged stronger than ever in the years following Clinton's impeachment—too strong, perhaps, for some critics of presidential authority.

The resignation of Richard Nixon, who was faced with the prospects of impeachment and conviction, removed from office a president who threatened America's constitutional order and likely had committed treason and crimes against humanity in Southeast Asia.

Trump need not match the level of misdeeds of Richard Nixon to warrant his impeachment. But Americans should be mindful of the distinction between that which merits punishment and that which is merely a matter of preference. For example, the president's unconventional style or his lack of "presidential" stature and demeanor might *offend,* but those are not offenses worthy of impeachment. Differences of policy and values do not make a case for impeachment, either. If he listens, Trump can yet change his ways.

Still, Trump's history and the path he's followed—as candidate, president-elect, and president—show that he is uniquely vulnerable to impeachment. It took three years for the House to impeach Andrew Johnson and more than five years for the impeachment of Bill Clinton and the near impeachment of Richard Nixon. Yet in the early stages of his presidency, Trump has already begun matching the abuses of President Nixon.

Is it shouting into the wind to make the case to a Republican Congress for impeaching a president of their own party? The answer is no. Once Trump becomes more of a liability than an asset to the GOP, the party may be willing to turn on him through impeachment. Republicans in Congress have no loyalty to Donald Trump, but they do have an agenda for the Trump presidency, and it's an agenda that could be side-tracked by the sound and fury of an impeachment. They've already gotten a conservative Supreme Court justice nominee to break the four-to-four, liberal-to-conservative deadlock. They are hoping to enact their legislative priorities now that the GOP has control of the presidency and Congress for the first time in a decade. Priorities include tax cuts, deregulation of business, the gutting of environmental laws, repeal and replacement of the Affordable Care Act, and a reordering of spending allocations from domestic to military.

If Congress achieves these goals and Trump becomes a liability, with dismal approval ratings, his fellow Republicans may be willing to impeach him, depending of course on the gravity of his offenses. Alternatively, if they fail to achieve their goals, they may seek the elevation of a more effective leader. Circumstances for Republicans today are far from those of 1868, when the controversial and polarizing Benjamin Wade would have become president in the event of Andrew Johnson's removal.

If the Senate removes Trump from office, then Vice President Mike Pence, a Republican dream president with experience in Congress rises to the White House. Pence is a predictable, standard-issue Christian conservative, with sterling Republican Party credentials. Under the Twenty-Fifth Amendment, Pence would also choose a replacement vice president. He could well pick Speaker Ryan, completing the ultimate dream team for Republicans.

As always in politics, complications lurk within every scenario. By supporting the impeachment of their president, Republicans will turn the very dangerous Trump into their enemy, which could have nightmarish consequences if he survives conviction in the Senate. They would risk the alienation of his loyal followers and the potential loss of dozens of House and Senate seats in the midterm elections of 2018. Still, if Democrats solidly back impeachment, only some two dozen House Republicans would have to join the Democrats for a voting majority.

When the House Judiciary Committee took a vote on articles of impeachment against Richard Nixon, it revealed that egregious transgressions can crack party loyalty; 6 of the committee's 17 Republicans joined all 21 Democrats in backing two of the three articles that the committee endorsed.[2]

Democrats would also be wise to think now about what they wish for when faced with the prospect of a Pence/Ryan administration in the event of Trump's impeachment and removal. Yet despite sharp policy differences, Democrats could likely trust Pence as president to respect the Constitution and the law, stand firm against Russian aggression, and not risk a nuclear war. The Democrats could also count on welcoming a split within the GOP's grassroots base that would open a path for a Democratic victory in the midterm elections of 2018 and the presidential election of 2020.

If Trump remains in office, a wave of popular revulsion against his presidency could conceivably power the Democrats into recapturing the House in 2018. But—and this is presuming that the Trump base remains predominantly Republican—the gerrymandering of House seats by Republicans who controlled most state legislatures and governorships after 2010 makes it very difficult for Democrats to gain the seats needed for a House majority.

Former lawyers in the Obama administration have formed a working group to monitor violations of the law and the Constitution by Donald Trump. But the fate of President Trump will ultimately rest with the democratic activism of the American people. Americans rightly celebrate their nation's founders: Thomas Jefferson for justifying independence; Washington for leading the Continental army to victory in the American Revolution. But it was the protests of ordinary colonials, men and women, whites and blacks, that turned public sentiment against King George III and ignited the revolution. "The Revolution was," as John Adams wrote, "in the minds and hearts of the *people*."[3]

The many robust demonstrations against President Trump

will be like smoke through a chimney unless, like the revolutionary protests, they are put to a purposeful end. If investigations uncover traitorous collusion with the Russians or Trump continues to clash with the law, the Constitution, the environment, and the nation's traditions and its security, the American people must demand his impeachment. In addition to mass protests, they should engage their representatives through petitions, e-mails, letters to newspaper editors, tweets, town hall gatherings, and face-to-face meetings, directed to the goal of impeachment. If Republicans in Congress remain recalcitrant, voters should be swift to dismiss them from office in 2018. Justice will be realized in today's America not through revolution, but by the Constitution's peaceful remedy of impeachment—but only if the people demand it.

Notes

AUTHOR'S NOTES

1. Max Farrand, *The Records of the Federal Convention of 1787*, vol. 2 (New Haven: Yale University Press, 1911). pp. 65–66.

2. Alexander Hamilton, "Federalist 65," in Clinton Rossiter, ed., *The Federalist Papers* (New York: Signet, 2003), pp. 394–95.

3. Arthur Schlesinger Jr., *The Imperial Presidency* (Boston: Houghton Mifflin, 1973), p. 415.

4. Prior to Trump, 43 men have held the presidency. The White House lists Barack Obama as the 44th president only because Grover Cleveland was elected to two nonconsecutive terms.

CHAPTER 1

1. *U.S. v. Nixon*, 506 US 224 (*1993*); For more details on impeachment, see Emily Field Van Tassel and Paul Finkelman, *Impeachable Offenses: A Documentary History From 1877 to the Present* (Washington, DC: Congressional Quarterly, 1999) and Raoul Berger, *Impeachment: The Constitution Problem* (Cambridge, MA: Harvard University Press, 1974).

2. Jared B. Cole and Todd Garvey, "Impeachment and Removal," *Congressional Research Service*, October 29, 2015, https://fas.org/sgp/crs/misc/R44260.pdf.

3. George Washington to Edmund Randolph, March 28, 1787, *Founders Online*, https://founders.archives.gov/?q=rheumatic%20complaint%20Author%3A%22Washington%2C%20George%22&s=1511311111&r=2.

4. Max Farrand, *The Records,* vol. 2, pp. 65–66.

5. Ibid., pp. 63–71, 545.

6. "Thomas Jefferson: Campaigns and Elections," *Miller Center of Public Affairs,* http://millercenter.org?/president/biography/jefferson -campaigns-and-elections.

7. Erwin C. Surrency, "The Judiciary Act of 1801," *American Journal of Legal History* 2 (1958), pp. 53–65; Jean Edward Smith, *John Marshall: Definer of a Nation* (New York: Henry Holt, 1996), pp. 1–20.

8. "From Thomas Jefferson to the House of Representatives, 3 February 1803," *Founders Online,* https://founders.archives.gov/documents /Jefferson/01-39-02-0381; on the impeachment see Lynn W. Turner, "The Impeachment of John Pickering," *American Historical Review,* 54 (1949).

9. Giles quoted in William H. Rehnquist, *Grand Inquests: The Historic Impeachments of Justice Samuel Chase and President Andrew Johnson* (New York: William Morrow, 1992), p. 27; Lynn W. Turner, "The Impeachment," p. 493.

10. Robert R. Blair and Robin D. Coblentz, "The Trials of Mr. Justice Samuel Chase," *Maryland Law Review* 27 (1967), pp. 365–86.

11. Joseph Story, *Commentaries on the Constitution,* 1833, "Impeachment Clauses," §762, http://press-pubs.uchicago.edu/founders /documents/a1_2_5s18.html.

12. On Lincoln, Johnson and Reconstruction, see Brooks D. Simpson, *The Reconstruction Presidents* (Lawrence: University Press of Kansas, 1998); "Second Inaugural Address of Abraham Lincoln," *Avalon Project,* http://avalon.law.yale.edu/19th_century/lincoln2.asp.

13. Andrew Johnson, "Address Upon Assuming the Office of President of the United States," April 17, 1865, *The Presidency Project,* University of California, Santa Barbara, http://www.presidency.ucsb.edu /ws/?pid=535.

14. *The Proceedings in the Trial of Andrew Johnson, President of the United States, Before the United States Senate, on Articles of Impeachment Exhibited by the House of Representatives with an*

Appendix. (London: The Christian Age, 1882), p. 311; Frederick Douglass, *Life and Times of Frederick Douglass* (Hartford, CT: Park Publishing, 1881), p. 355.

15. H. Lowell Brown, *High Crimes and Misdemeanors in Presidential Impeachment* (New York: Palgrave, 2010), p. 149; Elizabeth R. Varon, "Andrew Johnson and the Legacy of the Civil War," *Oxford Research Encyclopedia*, March 2016, http://americanhistory.oxfordre .com/view/10.1093/acrefore/9780199329175.001.0001/acrefore -9780199329175-e-11.

16. Michael Les Benedict, *The Impeachment and Trial of Andrew Johnson* (New York: Norton, 1973), p. 49.

17. "Tenure of Office Act," Thirty-Ninth Congress, Session 2, Chapter 153, 154. 1867. https://www.senate.gov/artandhistory/history/resources /pdf/Johnson_TenureofOfficeAct.pdf.

18. Andrew Johnson, "Special Message," February 22, 1868. Online by Gerhard Peters and John T. Woolley, *The American Presidency Project*, http://www.presidency.ucsb.edu/ws/?pid=72193.

19. *Congressional Globe*, Appendix, February 24, 1868, p. 160; Benedict, *The Impeachment*, Appendix A, pp. 184–88.

20. Ibid., Benedict.

21. *The Proceedings in the Trial of Andrew Johnson*, pp. 84, 645.

22. Ibid., p. 71.

23. Ibid., p. 756.

24. Ibid., pp. 42, 529, 780.

25. "Eliza McCardle Johnson," *White House*, https://www.whitehouse .gov/1600/first-ladies/elizajohnson.

26. Benedict, *The Impeachment*, p. 134.

27. In 1877, Congress repealed the Tenure of Office Act and in 1926, when overturning a similar law, the Supreme Court noted in dicta that the Act of 1867 was an invalid encroachment on presidential authority.

28. "Andrew Johnson Dead," *New York Times,* August 1, 1875, http:// www.nytimes.com/learning/general/onthisday/bday/1229.html.

CHAPTER 2

1. Allan J. Lichtman, *White Protestant Nation: The Rise of the American Conservative Movement* (New York: Grove/Atlantic, 2008), p. 283.

2. "Trump Says 'Amazing' Letter From Nixon Will Hang in Oval Office," *USA Today*, December 16, 2016, http://www.usatoday.com/story/news/2016/12/15/newser-trump-letter-nixon-hang-oval-office/95465212/.

3. Quoted in Carl Bernstein and Bob Woodward, "40 Years After Watergate, Nixon Was Far Worse Than We Thought," *Washington Post*, June 8, 2012, https://www.washingtonpost.com/opinions/woodward-and-bernstein-40-years-after-watergate-nixon-was-far-worse-than-we-thought/2012/06/08/gJQAlsi0NV_story.html?utm_term=.2388316ebd18.

4. Lichtman, *White Protestant Nation*, p. 290.

5. Ibid., p. 283, 291,

6. "Mission Incredible," *Washington Post*, June 21, 1972, p. 22

7. "Conversation: Nixon and John Ehrlichman," July 19, 1972, *President Nixon Remembers*, http://law2.umkc.edu/faculty/projects/ftrials/hiss/hissnixontapes.html.

8. "Transcript of the News Conference by the President," *New York Times*, August 30, 1972, p. 20.

9. Bob Woodward and Carl Bernstein, *All the President's Men* (New York: Simon & Schuster, 1974), pp. 105, 184–85.

10. "It's Inoperative, They Misspoke Themselves," *Time*, April 30, 1973, http://content.time.com/time/magazine/article/0,9171,907098,00.html.

11. Conversation, Nixon and Henry Kissinger, December 14, 1972, in Douglas Brinkley and Luke Nichter, *The Nixon Tapes, 1971–1972* (New York: Harper, 2014, p. 703; Lichtman, *White Protestant Nation*, p. 283.

12. Lichtman, *White Protestant Nation*, pp. 299–300.

13. Kate Reilly, "How Donald Trump's Firing of Sally Yates Compares to Nixon's Saturday Night Massacre," *Time*: History, January 31, 2017, http://time.com/4654930/saturday-night-massacre-donald-trump/; Arun Rath, "'I am not a Crook': How a Phrase Got a Life of its Own," *NPR*, November 17, 2013, http://www.npr.org/templates/story/story.php?storyId=245830047.

14. David J. Lynch, "Sessions Unfazed by White House-FBI Talks Over Russia Probe," *Financial Times*, February 27, 2017, https://www.ft.com/content/add66a32-fd3f-11e6-96f8-3700c5664d30.

15. A special prosecutor can coexist with independent investigations.

16. *U.S. v. Nixon*, 418 U.S. 683 (1974).

17. Lichtman, *White Protestant Nation*, p. 299.

18. "President Nixon's Resignation Speech," *PBS*, August 8, 1974, http://www.pbs.org/newshour/spc/character/links/nixon_speech.html.

19. Nixon to Reagan, August 13, 1987, White House Central Files, PR00502, Ronald Reagan Presidential Library, Simi Valley, California.

20. John A. Farrell, "Nixon's Vietnam Treachery," *New York Times*, Sunday Review, December 31 2016, https://www.nytimes.com/2016/12/31/opinion/sunday/nixons-vietnam-treachery.html?_r=0.

21. Peter Baker, "Nixon Tried to Foil Johnson's Vietnam Peace Talks in '68 Notes Show," *New York Times*, January 2, 2017, https://www.nytimes.com/2017/01/02/us/politics/nixon-tried-to-spoil-johnsons-vietnam-peace-talks-in-68-notes-show.html?_r=0; Robert "KC" Johnson, "Did Nixon Commit Treason in 1968? What the New LBJ Tapes Reveal, *History News Network*, January 25, 2009, http://historynewsnetwork.org /article/60446.

22. 1 Stat. 613, January 30, 1799.

23. "Article 7: Crimes Against Humanity," *International Criminal Court*, https://www.icc-cpi.int/resource-library/Documents/ElementsOf CrimesEng.pdf.

24. On the bombing campaign and the genocide see, Ben Kiernan, *How Pol Pot Came to Power* 2nd ed. (New Haven: Yale Univer-

sity Press, 2004), and *The Pol Pot Regime*, 3rd ed., (New Haven: Yale University Press, 2008); Nixon to Kissinger, December 9, 1970, Tape, *National Security Archive*, https://nsarchive.gwu .edu/NSAEBB/NSAEBB123/Box%2029,%20File%202,%20Kiss inger%20%96%20President%20Dec%209,%201970%208,45%20 pm%20%200.pdf.

25. Kiernan, *How Pol Pot Came to Power*, p. xxiv.

26. Ray Locker, *Nixon's Gamble: How a President's Own Secret Government Destroyed His Administration* (Lanham, MD: Rowman & Little-field, 2016), pp. 75–76; Greg Grandin, *Kissinger's Shadow* (New York: Henry Holt, 2015), p. 176.

27. John Vidal and Owen Bowcott, "ICC Widens Remit to Include Environmental Destruction Cases," *The Guardian*, September 15, 2016, https:// www.theguardian.com/global/2016/sep/15/hague-court-widens -remit-to-include-environmental-destruction-cases

28. Rick Perlstein, *Nixonland: The Rise of a President and the Fracturing of America* (New York: Scribner, 2008), pp. 26–29.

29. Sally Denton, "'Tricky Dick' vs. the Pink Lady,'" *The Daily Beast*, November 6, 2009, http://www.thedailybeast.com/articles/2009/11/16 /tricky-dick-vs-the-pink-lady.html.

30. Drew Pearson, "Cut-Throat California Campaign," *Washington Post*, October 28, 1950, p. B15.

31. Alan Rappeport and Noah Weiland, "White Nationalists Celebrate 'an Awakening' After Donald Trump's Victory," *New York Times*, November 19, 2016, https://www.nytimes.com/2016/11/20/us /politics/white-nationalists-celebrate-an-awakening-after-donald -trumps-victory.html?_r=0.

32. All citations can be found archived on www.Breitbart.com and were published in order on May 15, 2016, January 2, 2016, April 5, 2016, July 1, 2015, February 19, 2016, and July 6, 2016.

33. Allan J. Lichtman, *The Thirteen Keys to the Presidency* (Lanham, MD: Madison Books, 1990), p. 298.

34. Lichtman, *White Protestant Nation*, p. 231.

35. Richard Nixon, Press Conference, November 7, 1962, http://language log.ldc.upenn.edu/myl/RichardNixonConcession.html.

36. Lichtman, *White Protestant Nation*, p. 279; Joe McGinniss, *The Selling of the President 1968* (New York: Trident, 1969).

37. Mary Harris, "A Media Post-mortem on the 2016 Presidential Election," *mediaQuant*, November 14, 2016, http://www.mediaquant .net/2016/11/a-media-post-mortem-on-the-2016-presidential -election/.

38. See Locker, *Nixon's Gamble*, passim.

39. "Woodward and Bernstein: "40 Years After Watergate"; Perlstein, *Nixonland*, p. 526; Lichtman, *White Protestant Nation*, p. 289.

40. James Cannon, *Gerald R. Ford: An Honorable Life* (Ann Arbor, MI: University of Michigan Press, 2013), p. 27.

41. Madeline Conway, "Former Nixon Lawyer Predicts Trump Presidency 'Will End in Calamity,'" *Politico*, January 31, 2017, http:// www.politico.com/story/2017/01/john-dean-trump-presidency -234422.

CHAPTER 3

1. Megan Messerly, "Henderson Woman Shares Story as Housing Discrimination Tester at Trump Property," *Las Vegas Sun*, October 25, 2016, https://lasvegassun.com/news/2016/oct/25/henderson -woman-shares-housing-discrimination-stor/; "Decades-Old Housing Discrimination Case Plagues Donald Trump," *NPR*, September 29, 2016, http://www.npr.org/2016/09/29/495955920 /donald-trump-plagued-by-decades-old-housing-discrimination -case.

2. Ibid.

3. Michael Kranish and Robert O'Harrow Jr., "Inside the Government's Racial Bias Case Against Donald and How He Fought It," *Washington Post*, January 23, 2016, https://www.washingtonpost .com/politics/inside-the-governments-racial-bias-case-against -donald-trumps-company-and-how-he-fought-it/2016/01/23

/fb90163e-bfbe-11e5-bcda-62a36b394160_story.html?utm_term =.aaa46a33deec. Court documents on the case can be found at "United States v. Fred C. Trump, Donald Trump, and Trump Management, Inc.," *Civil Rights Litigation Clearinghouse*, https://www .clearinghouse.net/detail.php?id=15342.

4. Ibid.; settlements do not usually include admissions of guilt; otherwise, there would be no incentive to settle.

5. Drew S. Days III, Assistant Attorney General, to Roy M. Cohn, January 20, 1978, https://www.clearinghouse.net/chDocs/public /FH-NY-0024-0038.pdf.

6. David A. Fahrenthold, "Trump Boasts About His Philanthropy. But His Giving Falls Short of his Words." *The Washington Post*. Politics. 19 October 2016,. https://www.washingtonpost.com/politics /trump-boasts-of-his-philanthropy-but-his-giving-falls-short-of-his -words/2016/10/29/b3c03106-9ac7-11e6-a0ed-ab0774c1eaa5_story .html?utm_term=.6dcf1b03ff48.

7. State of New York–Department of Law, "Solicitation and Collection of Funds for Charitable Purposes," https://www.charitiesnys .com/pdfs/statute_booklet.pdf; Attorney General Eric T. Schneiderman, "Notice of Violation Directing Trump Foundation to Cease and Desist New York Solicitations," https://ag.ny.gov/press-release /new-york-attorney-generals-office-issues-notice-violation-directing -trump-foundation.

8. Kate Vinton, "Meet Linda McMahon, Wife Of WWE Billionaire And Trump's Pick For Small Business Administrator," *Forbes*, December 7, 2016, "http://www.forbes.com/sites/katevinton/2016/12/07 /linda-mcmahon-wife-of-wwe-billionaire-vincent-mcmahon-is -trumps-pick-to-head-his-small-business-administration/; David A. Farenthold, "Trump Used $258,000 From His Charity to Settle Legal Problems," *Washington Post*, September 20, 2016, https:// www.washingtonpost.com/politics/trump-used-258000-from-his -charity-to-settle-legal-problems/2016/09/20/adc88f9c-7d11-11e6 -ac8e-cf8e0dd91dc7_story.html.

9. David A. Fahrenthold, "Trump Directed $2.3 Million owed to Him to His Tax-Exempt Foundation Instead," *Washington Post,* September 26, 2016, https://www.washingtonpost.com/politics/trump -directed-23-million-owed-to-him-to-his-charity-instead/2016/09/2 6/7a9e9fac-8352-11e6-ac72-a29979381495_story.html.

10. Harper Neidig, "Trump Aide Defends Portrait Foundation Paid For: Trump Is 'Storing' It at Hotel," *The Hill*, September 27, 2016, http://thehill.com/blogs/ballot-box/presidential-races/298169 -adviser-claims-trump-is-storing-portrait-on-display-at; Kevin Sack and Sreve Eder, "New Records Shed Light on Donald Trump's $25,000 Gift to Florida Official," *New York Times,* September 14, 2016, https://www.nytimes.com/2016/09/15/us/politics/pam -bondi-donald-trump-foundation.html; David A. Fahrenthold, "Donald Trump Used Money Donated For Charity to Buy Himself a Tim Tebow–Signed Football Helmet," *Washington Post*, July 1, 2016, https://www.washingtonpost.com/news/post-politics /wp/2016/07/01/donald-trump-used-money-donated-for-charity -to-buy-himself-a-tim-tebow-signed-football-helmet/?utm_term =.548545368f80.

11. Harper Neidig, "NY AG: Trump Can't Dissolve Foundation Until Investigation Over," *The Hill*, December 24, 2016, http://thehill.com /blogs/blog-briefing-room/news/311773-ny-ag-trump-cannot -legally-dissolve-foundation-until.

12. David Farenthold, "Trump Foundation Admits to Violating Ban on 'Self-Dealing,' New Filing to IRS Shows," *Washington Post*, November 22, 2016, https://www.washingtonpost.com/politics/trump-foundation -apparently-admits-to-violating-ban-on-self-dealing-new-filing-to -irs-shows/2016/11/22/893f6508-b0a9-11e6-8616-52b15787add0 _story.html?utm_term=.1d199bd3e28b.

13. Kurt Eichenwald, "How Donald Trump's Company Violated the United States Embargo Against Cuba," *Newsweek,* September 29, 2016, http://www.newsweek.com/2016/10/14/donald-trump-cuban -embargo-castro-violated-florida-504059.html.

14. United States Government Accountability Office, "Economic Sanctions, Agencies Face Competing Priorities in Enforcing the U.S. Embargo on Cuba," November 2007, http://www.gao.gov/new.items /d0880.pdf; "Enforcement Of Penalties Against Violations Of The U.S. Embargo On Cuba," *Archive.org*, https://archive.org/stream /enforcementofpen00unit/enforcementofpen00unit_djvu.txt.

15. Karen Yi, "Trump Casino Empire Dogged by Bad Bets in Atlantic City," *USA Today*, July 5, 2016, http://www.usatoday.com/story /news/2016/07/05/trump-atlantic-city-usa-today-network-records -regulators/86717110/.

16. Daniella Diaz, "Trump: I'm Smart' for Not Paying Taxes," *CNN*, September 27, 2017, http://www.cnn.com/2016/09/26/politics/donald -trump-federal-income-taxes-smart-debate/; David Barstow, Susanne Craig, Russ Buettner, and Megan Twohey, "Donald Trump Tax Records Show He Could Have Avoided Taxes for Nearly Two Decades, The *Times* Found," *New York Times*, October 1, 2016, https://www.nytimes.com/2016/10/02/us/politics/donald-trump -taxes.html.

17. For a thorough analysis of the Trump University controversy, see Christopher L. Peterson, "Trump University and Presidential Impeachment," September 20, 2016, https://papers.ssrn.com/sol3/papers2 .cfm?abstract_id=2841306.

18. *Cohen v. Trump*, United States District Court, Southern District of California, No. 3:13-cv-02519-GPC-WVG, Deposition of Donald J. Trump, December 10, 2015, p. 274–75, https://papers.ssrn.com /sol3/papers2.cfm?abstract_id=2841306.

19. "Trump University Lawsuits: Frequently Asked Questions," http:// www.trumpuniversitylitigation.com/Home/faq#faq4.

20. Kelly Roesler, "Trump, Me? Trump U: Behind 'The Donald's' Online Real Estate Investing School," *Ottawa Citizen*, June 28, 2016, http://ottawacitizen.com/news/local-news/trump-me-trump-u.

21. "Trump Deposition, December 10, 2015," passim; *Makaeff v. Trump*, United States District Court, Southern District of Califor-

nia, 3:10-CV-00940-CAB(WVG), Declaration of Roald Schnack-enberg, September 16, 2012, pp. 1, 3, https://assets.documentcloud.org/documents/2850043/Schnackenberg.pdf.

22. Kate Reilly, "Donald Trump Calls Trump University Settlement 'Only Bad Thing' About Election Victory," *Fortune,* November 19, 2016, http://fortune.com/2016/11/19/donald-trump-university-settlement-timing/.

23. Massimo Calabresi, "What Donald Trump Knew About Undocumented Workers at His Signature Tower," *Time,* August 25, 2016, http://time.com/4465744/donald-trump-undocumented-workers/.

24. James West, "Former Models for Donald Trump's Agency Say They Violated Immigration Rules and Worked Illegally," *Mother Jones,* August 30, 2016, http://www.motherjones.com/politics/2016/08/donald-trump-model-management-illegal-immigration. All subsequent quotes are from this article.

25. Laura D. Francis,"Trump Modeling Agency's Visa Practices Questioned," *Bloomberg BNA*, September 6, 2016, https://www.bna.com/trump-modeling-agencys-n73014447354/.

26. Allissa Wickham, "Senator Calls for USCIS Probe into Modeling Agency," *Law 360,* September 7, 2016, https://www.law360.com/articles/837175/senator-calls-for-uscis-probe-into-trump-modeling-agency.

27. 156 *Congressional Record* S 10405, December 16, 2010, Session: 111- 2, Vol. 156 No. 167 p. S10405. The constitution applies the same standards for impeachment and conviction to all federal officials, including judges and presidents.

28. 105th Congress, 2nd Session, "Impeachment of William Jefferson Clinton: Report of the House Judiciary Committee," December 16, 1998, p. 158.

29. Associated Press, "Trump: Mattis' View on Torture Will Override His Own" January 27, 2017, http://www.foxnews.com/politics/2017/01/27/trump-mattis-view-on-torture-will-override-his-own-beliefs.html.

30. Theodore Schleifer and Barbara Starr, "Military Report: Trump Pick Michael Flynn Shared Classified Intel," *CNN*, December 15, 2016, http://www.cnn.com/2016/12/14/politics/michael-flynn-classified -intel-report/.

31. Cody Derespina, "Spicer Checks WH Phones for Leaks, Vows More Searches Coming," *FOX News*, February 26, 2017, http://www .foxnews.com/politics/2017/02/26/spicer-checks-wh-staffers-phones -for-leaks-vows-more-searches-coming.html.

32. Ryan Teague Beckwith, "President Trump Described Deporta-tions as Military Operation," *Time*, February 23, 2017, http://time .com/4680815/donald-trump-deportations-military-operation/; "18 U.S. Code §1385—Use of Army and Air Force as posse comitatus," *Law Information Institute*, https://www.law.cornell.edu/uscode/text /18/1385.

CHAPTER 4

1. Alexander Hamilton, *Pacificus*, No. VI, July 17, 1793, *Found-ers Online*, https://founders.archives.gov/documents/Hamilton /01-15-02-0081.

2. Ryan Lizza, "Will Trump Avoid A Constitutional Crisis?," *The New Yorker*, January 10, 2017, http://www.newyorker.com/news/ryan -lizza/will-trump-avoid-a-constitutional-crisis.

3. Emily Raulhala, "Duterte: During phone call, Trump praised my drug war as the 'right way,'" *Washington Post*, Decem-ber 3, 2016, https://www.washingtonpost.com/news/worldviews /wp/2016/12/03/duterte-during-phone-call-trump-praised-my -drug-war-as-right-way/?utm_term=.30ac2730a4bf; : VJ Bacungan, "Duterte Echoes Trump's 'dishonest' media claim," *CNN*, February 9, 2017 http://cnnphilippines.com/news/2017/02/09/duterte-trump -dishonest-media.html.

4. Yuji Vincent Gonzales, "French Paper Banners Duterte as 'Serial Killer President,'" *Inquirer.Net*, October 9, 2016, https://globalnation .inquirer.net/146418/french-paper-banners-duterte-as-serial

-killer-president; "UN rights experts urge Philippines to end wave of extrajudicial killings amid major drug crackdown," *UN News Centre,* August 18, 2016, http://www.un.org/apps/news/story .asp?NewsID=54707#.WJiZzbYrKAw; https://www.occrp.org /personoftheyear/2016; Agence France-Presse, "Philippine president -elect says 'corrupt' journalists will be killed," *The Guardian,* May 31, 2016, https://www.theguardian.com/world/2016/may/31 /philippine-president-elect-says-corrupt-journalists-will-be-killed; Felipe Villamor, "Duterte, Citing Hitler, Says He Wants to kill 3 million Addicts in Philippines," *New York Times,* September 30, 2016, https://www.nytimes.com/2016/10/01/world/asia/philippines -rodrigo-duterte-hitler-drugs.html?_r=0; "Philippines: Police De- ceit in Drug War Killings," *Human Rights Watch,* March 2, 2017, https://www.hrw.org/news/2017/03/02/philippines-police-deceit -drug-war-killings.

5. Stephanie Baker, Ben Brody, and Caleb Melby, "Trump's Busi- ness Partner Will Be Manila's Man in Washington," *Bloomberg,* November 22, 2016, https://www.bloomberg.com/politics/articles /2016-11-22/trump-s-business-partner-will-be-manila-s-man-in -washington.

6. Ibid.

7. Jeremy Venook, "The Story Behind Trump's Chinese Trademark," *The Atlantic,* February 22, 2017, https://www.theatlantic.com/business /archive/2017/02/trump-chinese-trademark/517458/.

8. Associated Press, "China Grants Preliminary Approval to 38 New Trump Trademarks," *AP,* March 8, 2017, https://apnews.com/8f54b1 4808a2459f9efcb0089f41f056.

9. "If Discovered, He May Be Impeached: President Trump and the Foreign Emoluments Clause," *American Constitution Society for Law and Policy,* February 2, 2017, http://www.acslaw.org /acsblog/%E2%80%9Cif-discovered-he-may-be-impeached %E2%80%9D-president-trump-and-the-foreign-emoluments -clause.

10. Zahraa Alkhalsi and John Defterios, "Dubai golf course developer: Trump 'doesn't discriminate,'" *CNN*, November 21, 2016, http://money.cnn.com/2016/11/21/news/dubai-trump-golf-course-developer/; Darren Samuelsohn, "White House Win Provides a Stimulus for the Trump Brand," *Politico*, January 10, 2017, http://www.politico.com/story/2017/01/donald-trump-brand-business-233385.

11. Jean Eaglesham and Lisa Schwartz, "Trump's Debts are Widely Held on Wall Street,Creating New Potential Conflicts," *Wall Street Journal*, January 5, 2017, https://www.wsj.com/articles/trump-debts-are-widely-held-on-wall-street-creating-new-potential-conflicts-1483637414.

12. Susanne Craig, "Trump's Empire: A Maze of Debts and Opaque Ties," *New York Times*, August 20, 2016, https://www.nytimes.com/2016/08/21/us/politics/donald-trump-debt.html; Jesse Eisinger, "Why Deutsche Bank Remains Trump's Biggest Conflict of Interest," *The National Memo*, February 10, 2016, http://www.nationalmemo.com/deutsche-bank-trumps-conflict-interest/. Matt Egan, "Scandal-Ridden Wells Fargo Wants Less Regulation," *CNN Money*, December 6, 2016, http://money.cnn.com/2016/12/06/investing/wells-fargo-trump-regulation-tim-sloan/.

13. Rosalind S. Helderman and Tom Hamburger, "Trump's presidency, overseas business deals and relations with foreign governments could all become intertwined," *Washington Post*, November 25, 2016, https://www.washingtonpost.com/politics/trumps-presidency-overseas-business-deals-and-relations-with-foreign-governments-could-all-become-intertwined/2016/11/25/d2bc83f8-b0e2-11e6-8616-52b15787add0_story.html?.

14. Jonathan A. Adler, "Does the Emoluments Clause Lawsuit Against Donald Trump Stand a Chance.?" *Washington Post*, January 23, 2016, https://www.washingtonpost.com/news/volokh-conspiracy/wp/2017/01/23/does-the-emoluments-clause-lawsuit-against-president-trump-stand-a-chance/?utm_term=.fc40731011be.

15. "S.2038-STOCK Act," *Congress.Gov*, https://www.congress.gov /bill/112th-congress/senate-bill/2038; Christina Wilkie and Paul Blumenthal, "This GOP-Backed Law Forbids Donald Trump From Using Presidency For Personal Profit," *Huffington Post*, December 13, 2016, http://www.huffingtonpost.com/entry/trump-private -profit-stock-act_us_585068c2e4b0e411bfd42094; "18 U.S. Code §227—Wrongfully Influencing a Private Entities Employment Decision," *Law Information Institute*, https://www.law.cornell.edu /uscode/text/18/227.

16. Jim Zarroli, "Trump's Businesses Could be Tripped Up by a 2012 Insider Trading Law," *NPR*, December 22, 2016, http://www.npr .org/2016/12/22/506497041/trumps-businesses-could-be-tripped -up-by-a-2012-insider-trading-law.

17. Isaac Arnsdorf, Josh Dawsey, and Ben White, "White House Leans into Trump Inc." *Politico*, February 9, 2017, http://www.politico .com/story/2017/02/trump-business-family-234874.

18. "Complaint," *Melania Trump v. Mail Media, Inc.*, Supreme Court, State of New York, County of New York—Commercial Division, February 6, 2017.

19. Tribune News Service, "Melania Trump's Lawyer's Cite 'Once-in-a-Lifetime Opportunity' For First Lady to Boost Her Personal Brand," *Chicago Tribune*, February 7, 2017, http://www.chicago tribune.com/news/nationworld/politics/ct-melania-trump-lawsuit -20170207-story.html.

20. "First Amended Complaint," *Melania Trump. v Mail Media, Inc.*, February 17, 2017, Index No. 650661/201.

21. Aidan Quigley, "Trump Blasts Nordstrom For Dumping Ivanka's Fashion Line," *Politico*, February 8, 2017, http://www.politico.com /story/2017/02/trump-nordstrom-tweet-ivanka-234791; Feliz Solomon, "Nordstrom's Isn't the Only Retailer Where Ivanka Trump's Sales are Tanking," *Fortune*, February 9, 2017, fortune.com/2017/02/09 /Ivanka-trump-nordstrom-amazon-sales-slump/.

22. Maxwell Tani, "Kellyanne Conway Encourages Americans to 'Go

Buy Ivanka's Stuff,' Potentially Violating Ethics Rules," *Business Insider*, February 9, 2017, http://www.businessinsider.com kellyanne-conway-go-buy-ivankas-stuff-2017-2; Sopan Deb, "Alec Baldwin Mocks Ivanka Trump (and Her Dad) on 'Tonight Show,'" *New York Times*, February 10, 2017, https://www.nytimes .com/2017/02/10/arts/television/alec-baldwin-trump-kellyanne -conway.html?_r=0.

23. Drew Harrell, Tom Hamburger and Rosalind S. Helderman, "White House says Conway has been 'counseled' after touting Ivanka Trump's products," *Washington Post*, February 9, 2017, https://www.washingtonpost.com/politics/conway-may-have-broken -key-ethics-rule-by-touting-ivanka-trumps-products-experts -say/2017/02/09/fd1cc64a-eeda-11e6-b4ff-ac2cf509efe5_story .html?utm_term=.632fd516dca9.

24. Francine McKenna, "Trump Counselor Conway Violates Ethics Laws, Congressional Leaders Say," *MarketWatch*, February 19, 2017, http://www.marketwatch.com/story/trump-counselor-conway -violates-ethics-laws-watchdog-says-2017-02-09.

25. "Ivanka's 'Seat at the Table' in the Oval Office Raised Eyebrows," *Twitter*, February 13, 2017, https://twitter.com/i/moments /831308717731766272.

26. *Trump Old Post Office v. CZ-National*, Superior Court for the District of Columbia, Case No. 2015 CA 005890 B, Deposition of Donald J. Trump, October 21, 2016, p. 15.

27. Bernard Condon and Chad Day, "White House Trump Organization Names Ethics Advisers," *Washington Times*, January 25, 2017, http://www.washingtontimes.com/news/2017/jan/25/white-house -trump-organization-name-ethics-adviser/.

28. Hui-Yong Yu and Caleb Melby, "Trump Hotels, Amid Calls to Divest, Instead Plans U.S. Expansion," *Bloomberg*, January 25, 2017, https://www.bloomberg.com/news/articles/2017-01-25/trump-hotels -to-triple-locations-in-u-s-expansion-ceo-says.

29. Jennifer Wang, "Donald Trump's Fortune Falls $800 Million

To $3.7 Billion," *Forbes*, September 28, 2016, https://www.forbes
.com/sites/jenniferwang/2016/09/28/the-definitive-look-at-donald
-trumps-wealth-new/#308078b947a5.

30. Antonin Scalia, "Memorandum to Kenneth A. Lazarus, Associate
    Counsel to the President," December 18, 1974, https://fas.org/irp
    /agency/doj/olc/121674.pdf.

31. Benjy Sarlin, "Donald Trump's Feud With Nordstrom's Sparks
    Warnings From Ethics Experts," *NBC News*, February 10, 2017,
    http://www.cnbc.com/2017/02/10/donald-trumps-feud-with-nord
    strom-sparks-warnings-from-ethics-experts.html.

CHAPTER 5

1. Philip Bump, "In 2008, Donald Trump said George W. Bush
   should've been impeached," *The Washington Post*, February 13,
   2016, https://www.washingtonpost.com/news/the-fix/wp/2016/02/13
   /in-2008-donald-trump-said-george-w-bush-shouldve-been
   -impeached/?utm_term=.14724f3057fd.

2. Donald Trump with Tony Schwartz, *Trump: The Art of the Deal*
   (New York: Ballantine, 1987), p. 58; Elliot Hannon, "The Easiest Way to Get to Know Donald Trump Is to Depose Him," *Slate*,
   July 29, 2016, http://www.slate.com/blogs/the_slatest/2015/07/29
   /donald_trump_depositions_give_insight_into_beliefs.html.

3. David A. Fahrenthold and Robert O'Harrow Jr., "Trump: A True
   Story," *Washington Post*, August 10, 2013, https://www.washington
   post.com/graphics/politics/2016-election/trump-lies/.

4. Jerry Useem, "What Does Donald Trump Really Want?" *Fortune*,
   April 3, 2000, http://fortune.com/2000/04/03/what-does-donald
   -trump-really-want/.

5. Daniel Roth, "Inside Donald Trump's Trophy Life," *Fortune*, April 19,
   2004, http://fortune.com/2004/04/19/donald-trump-business
   -enterprise/.

6. Susan Taylor Martin, "Buyers Still Feel Burned by Donald Trump
   After Tampa Condo Tower Failure," *Tampa Bay Times*, July 31,

2015, http://www.tampabay.com/news/business/realestate/buyers
-still-feel-burned-by-donald-trump-after-tampa-condo-tower
-failure/2239499.

7. Ibid.: Joshua Gillin, "Did Trump Bail on Building Condos in Florida?," *PolitiFact*, July 28, 2016, http://www.politifact.com/florida/statements/2016/jul/28/tim-kaine/did-trump-bail-building-condos-florida/; Jeff Harrington, "Trump Firms Up Plan to Tower Over Tampa," *Tampa Bay Times*, January 11, 2005, http://www.sptimes.com/2005/01/11/Tampabay/Trump_firms_up_plan_t.shtml.

8. Martin, "Buyers Still Feel Burned," *Trump v. O'Brien*, Superior Court, New Jersey, Trump Deposition, December 19, 2007, p. 91.

9. "Failed Project Lands Trump in Florida Court," *CBS Miami*, January 25, 2016, http://miami.cbslocal.com/2016/01/25/failed-project-lands-trump-in-florida-court/; Michael Finnegan, "Trump's Failed Baja Condo Resort Left Buyers Feeling Betrayed and Angry," *LA Times*, June 27, 2016, http://www.latimes.com/politics/la-na-pol-trump-baja-snap-story.html; Drew Griffin, "Buying a Trump? Better Read the Fine Print," *CNN*, February 22, 2016, http://www.cnn.com/2016/02/22/politics/trump-properties-investigation/.

10. Ibid.; Michael Sallah and Michael Vasquez, "Failed Donald Trump Tower Thrust in GOP Campaign for Presidency," *Miami Herald*, March 12,2016, http://www.miamiherald.com/news/politics-government/election/article65709332.html.

11. Emon Reiser, "Donald Trump Faces Federal Sanctions for not Disclosing $5 Million Policy on Failed Tower," *South Florida Business Journal*, June 20, 2014, http://www.bizjournals.com/southflorida/news/2014/06/20/donald-trump-faces-federal-sanctions-for-not.html; Dara Kim, "Court Sides With Trump in Failed Fort Lauderdale Project," *Sun Sentinel*, April 27, 2016, http://www.sun-sentinel.com/real-estate/news/fl-trump-suit-hotel-fort-lauderdale-20160427-story.html.

12. Jonathan Martin, "Trump Institute Offered Get-Rich Schemes with Plagiarized Lessons," *New York Times*, June 29, 2016, https://www

.nytimes.com/2016/06/30/us/politics/donald-trump-institute
-plagiarism.html.

13. Ibid. Infomerical at https://www.youtube.com/watch?v=6J1iC7Q
Fum0.

14. Lucas Jackson, "Donald Trump's Companies Destroyed Emails
in Defiance of Court Orders," *Newsweek,* October 31, 2016,
http://www.newsweek.com/2016/11/11/donald-trump-companies
-destroyed-emails-documents-515120.html.

15. Jeffrey M. Jones, "Huckabee, Trump, Romney, Set Pace for 2012
GOP Field," *Gallup,* April 15, 2011, http://www.gallup.com
/poll/147233/huckabee-trump-romney-pace-gop-field-2012.aspx.

16. Glenn Kessler and Michelle Ye Hee Lee, "Fact Checking Donald
Trump's Presidential Announcement Speech," *Washington Post,*
June 16, 2015, https://www.washingtonpost.com/news/fact-checker
/wp/2015/06/17/fact-checking-donald-trumps-presidential
-announcement-speech/?utm_term=.91f98e078ef5.

17. Ibid.; Heather Long, "Donald Trump's Wild Claim: Unemployment Is 42%," *CNN,* September 28, 2016, http://money.cnn
.com/2015/09/28/news/economy/donald-trump-unemployment
-42-percent/; Glenn Kessler, "Trump's Absurd Claim That 92 Million Americans Represent a 'Nation of Jobless Americans,'" *Washington Post,* September 16, 2016, https://www.washingtonpost.com
/news/fact-checker/wp/2016/09/16/trumps-absurb-claim-that
-92-million-americans-represent-a-nation-of-jobless-amer
icans/?utm_term=.0a8b61eb84dc.

18. Kessler and Lee, "Fact Checking."

19. "2015 Lie of the Year: The Campaign Misstatements of Donald
Trump," *PolitiFact,* December 21, 2015, http://www.politifact.com
/truth-o-meter/article/2015/dec/21/2015-lie-year-donald-trump
-campaign-misstatements/.

20. Glenn Kessler, "Trump's Outrageous Claim That 'Thousands' of
New Jersey Muslims Celebrated the 9/11 Attacks," *Washington
Post,* November 22, 2015, https://www.washingtonpost.com/news

/fact-checker/wp/2015/11/22/donald-trumps-outrageous-claim-that
-thousands-of-new-jersey-muslims-celebrated-the-911-attacks;
Mark Berman, "Donald Trump Says a 'Top Police Officer' in Chicago Said He Could Stop Surging Violence in a Week," *Washington Post,* August 23, 2016, https://www.washingtonpost.com/news/post
-nation/wp/2016/08/23/donald-trump-says-chicago-police-could
-stop-surging-violence-by-being-much-tougher.

21. Brian Tashman, "7 Other Times Donald Trump Suggested Obama Is a Secret Muslim and Terrorist Sympathizer," *Right Wing Watch,* June 15, 2016, http://www.rightwingwatch.org/post/7-other-times
-donald-trump-suggested-obama-is-a-secret-muslim-and-terrorist
-sympathizer/; C. Eugene Emory Jr. and Louis Jacobson, "Donald Trump's First TV Ad Shows Migrants 'At The Southern Border,' But They're Actually in Morocco," *PolitiFact,* January 24, 2016, http://
www.politifact.com/truth-o-meter/statements/2016/jan/04/donald
-trump/donald-trumps-first-tv-ad-shows-migrants-southern-/.

22. Jonathan Martin, "Officials Fight Donald Trump's Claims of a Rigged Vote," *New York Times,* October 16, 2016, https://www
.nytimes.com/2016/10/17/us/politics/donald-trump-election-rigging
.html.

23. "Studies Contradict Trump Claim That Voter Fraud Is 'Very, Very Common,'" *Fortune,* October 18, 2016, http://fortune
.com/2016/10/18/studies-contradict-trump-claim-that-voter-fraud
-is-very-very-common/; *Applewhite, et al., v. Commonwealth of Pennsylvania,* 333 M.D. 2012, Opinion.

24. Stephen Collinson, "Why Trump's Talk of a Rigged Vote Is So Dangerous," *CNN,* October 19, 2016, http://www.cnn.com/2016/10/18
/politics/donald-trump-rigged-election/; Jake Sherman and Steven Shephard, "Poll: 41 Percent of Voters Say Election Could Be 'Stolen' from Trump," *Politico*/Morning Consult, October 17, 2016. http://
www.politico.com/story/2016/10/poll-41-percent-of-voters-say-the
-election-could-be-stolen-from-trump-229871.

25. Mallory Shelbourne, "Trump Claims Voter Fraud Without Evi-

dence, Says 'I Won the Popular Vote,'" *The Hill*, November 27, 2016, http://thehill.com/homenews/campaign/307622-trump-i-would -have-won-popular-vote-if-people-had-not-voted-illegally; Michael Wines, "All This Talk of Voter Fraud: Across U.S., Officials Found Next to None," *New York Times*, December 18, 2016, https://www .nytimes.com/2016/12/18/us/voter-fraud.html?_r=0.

26. Louis Jacobson, "Donald Trump's Electoral College Victory Was Not A 'Massive Landslide," *PolitiFact*, 12 December 2016, http:// www.politifact.com/truth-o-meter/statements/2016/dec/12/donald -trump/donald-trumps-electoral-college-victory-was-not-ma/.

27. Arthur Sulzberger Jr., "To Our Readers, From the Publisher and Executive Editor," *The New York Times*, 13 November 2016, https:// www.nytimes.com/2016/11/13/us/elections/to-our-readers-from -the-publisher-and-executive-editor.html; Jonathan Lemire, "Contents of Folders Sparks Speculation," *Associated Press*, January 12, 2017, https://apnews.com/50b799be59cf4cf9b9b4e13414.

28. Jack Holmes, "A Trump Surrogate Drops the Mic: 'There's No Such Thing as Facts,'" *Esquire,* December 1, 2016, http://www.esquire .com/news-politics/videos/a51152/trump-surrogate-no-such-thing -as-facts/.

29. "Comparing Hillary Clinton, Donald Trump on the Truth-O-Meter," *PolitiFact*, http://www.politifact.com/truth-o-meter/lists/people /comparing-hillary-clinton-donald-trump-truth-o-met/. Trump's combined total of "false" and "pants on fire" was 186, while Clinton's was 36.

30. Jon Sharman, "Donald Trump: All the False Claims President Has Made Since His Inauguration," *Independent*, January 23, 2017, http://www.independent.co.uk/news/world/americas/donald-trump -us-president-false-claims-inauguration-white-house-sean-spicer -kellyanen-conway-press-a7541171.html; Mark Landler, "Trump Under Fire for Invoking Nazis in Criticism of U.S. Intelligence," *The New York Times*, January 11, 2017, https://www.nytimes .com/2017/01/11/us/donald-trump-nazi-comparison.html; Louis Jacobson, "Donald Trump Wrong That Murder Rate is Highest in

47 Years," *PolitiFact,* February 8, 2017, http://www.politifact.com /truth-o-meter/statements/2017/feb/08/donald-trump/donald -trump-wrong-murder-rate-highest-47-years/.

31. Theodore Schleifer, "Trump Falsely Claims (Again) Biggest Electoral College Victory Since Reagan," *CNN,* February 16, 2017, http://www.cnn.com/2017/02/16/politics/donald-trump-electoral -victory-claim/.

32. Charlie Savage, "Fact Check: Trump is Wrong About Guantanamo Detainees," *New York Times,* March 7, 2017, https://www.nytimes .com/2017/03/07/us/politics/guantanamo-bay-trump.html.

33. Eric Bradner, "Conway: Trump White House Offered 'Alternative Facts' on Crowd Size," *CNN,* January 23, 2016, http://www.cnn .com/2017/01/22/politics/kellyanne-conway-alternative-facts/.

34. Kyle Balluck, "Conway: 'We're Going to Have to Rethink Our Relationship with Press," *The Hill,* January 22, 2016, http://thehill.com /homenews/sunday-talk-shows/315523-conway-were-going-to-have -to-rethink-our-relationship-with-press; Kimiko de Freytas-Tamura, "George Orwell's *1984* is Suddenly a Best Seller," *New York Times,* January 25, 2017, https://www.nytimes.com/2017/01/25/books/1984 -george-orwell-donald-trump.html?_r=0.

35. *Clinton v. Jones,* 520 U.S. 681 (1997).

36. "Text of Clinton's Grand Jury Testimony," http://www.enquirer.com /clinton/complete_transcript.html.

37. Richard Lacayo, "When Is Sex Not 'Sexual Relations'?" *CNN Politics,* August 24, 1998, http://www.cnn.com/ALLPOLITICS/1998/08/17 /time/clinton.html.

38. Nick Penzenstadler and Susan Page, "Exclusive: Trump's 3,500 lawsuits unprecedented for a presidential nominee," *USA Today,* June 01, 2016, http://www.usatoday.com/story/news/politics/elections /2016/06/01/donald-trump-lawsuits-legal-battles/84995854/.

39. Edward-Isaac Dovere and Josh Dawsey, "Could Trump's 'Alternative Facts' Put Lives at Risk?," *Politico,* January 22, 2017, http://www .politico.com/story/2017/01/trump-alternative-facts-234011.

40. Aaron Blake, "Sean Spicer's Defense of Himself and Explanation of Donald Trump's Sensitivity, Annotated," *Washington Post,* January 23, 2016, https://www.washingtonpost.com/news/the-fix /wp/2017/01/23/sean-spicers-defense-of-himself-and-explanation -of-donald-trumps-sensitivity-annotated/?utm_term=.5ee99 a1abf5a; Erik Sherman, "'Alternative Facts' May Be the End of Trustworthy Government Data," *Forbes,* January 24, 2017, http://www .forbes.com/sites/eriksherman/2017/01/22/alternative-facts-may-be -the-end-of-trustworthy-government-decision-data/#13ea2b4c41f1.

41. Jim Rutenberg, "'Alternative Facts' and the Costs of Trump-Branded Reality," *New York Times,* January 22, https://www .nytimes.com/2017/01/22/business/media/alternative-facts-trump -brand.html?_r=0.

CHAPTER 6

1. "Trump Admits to Pre-Wedding 'Jitters,'" *Fox News,* January 21, 2005, http://www.foxnews.com/story/2005/01/21/trump-admits-to -pre-wedding-jitters.html.

2. Judie Hups, "Ivana Trump Biography; Republican Party Nominee Donald Trump's First Wife," *Donald Trump Buzz,* September 21, 2016, https://www.donaldtrumpbuzz.com/biography/ivana-trump -biographyrepublican-party-nominee-donald-trumps-first-wife/.

3. Rolando Pujol and Marvin Scott, "The War of the Trumps— THE Divorce of the 1990's," *PIX 11,* May 21, 2013, http://pix11 .com/2013/02/19/the-war-of-the-trumps-the-divorce-of-the-1990s -marvin-remembers/; Dana Schuster, "Ivana Trump on How She Advises Donald—and Those Hands," *New York Post,* April 3, 2016, http://nypost.com/2016/04/03/ivana-trump-opens-up-about-how -she-advises-donald-his-hands/; Howard Kurtz, "Trump Talks, Ivana Appears, Agreement 'Sealed in Gold,' Billionaire Says," *Washington Post,* February 15, 1990, p. B1.

4. Barbara Ross and Stephen Rex Brown, "Court Docs Reveal Donald Trump's 'Cruel' Treatment of Ivana," *New York Daily News,* Sep-

tember 17, 2016, http://www.nydailynews.com/news/politics/court
-docs-reveal-donald-trump-cruel-treatment-ivana-article-1.2796179;
Richard D. Hylton, "Trumps Settle; She Gets $14 Million Plus," *New
York Times,* March 21, 1991, http://www.nytimes.com/1991/03/21
/nyregion/trumps-settle-she-gets-14-million-plus.html.

5. Howard Kurtz, "Marla 'I Love Him,'" *Washington Post,* April 20,
1990, https://www.washingtonpost.com/archive/lifestyle/1990/04/20
/marla-i-love-him/24308105-1219-416f-b478-744b71cdf3d4/?utm
_term=.450ddfae0734; Michael Blowen, "Your 15 Minutes Are Up,
Marla," *Boston Globe,* June 27, 1991, https://www.highbeam.com
/ doc/1P2-7666455.html; Martha Sherrill, "Marla Gets Her Man,"
Washington Post, July 4, 1991, https://www.washingtonpost.com
/archive/lifestyle/1991/07/04/marla-gets-her-man/d6336b8c-7406
-496f-adf0-c45cfc7c2ce9/?utm_term=.582fae5deac7.

6. Maureen Dowd, "Liberties; Trump L'oeil Tease," *New York Times,*
September 19, 1999, http://www.nytimes.com/1999/09/19/opinion
/liberties-trump-l-oeil-tease.html; Erica Tempesta, "What to Buy the
Billionaire Who Has Everything! How Donald Trump and Ex Marla
Maples' Lavish 1993 Tiffany & Co Wedding Registry Listed Everything from a $530 Crystal 'Sail' Sculpture to a $1,250 BOWL," *The
Daily Mail,* November 14, 2016, http://www.dailymail.co.uk/femail
/article-3934520/What-buy-billionaire-Donald-Trump-ex-Marla
-Maples-lavish-1993-Tiffany-wedding-registry-listed-530-crystal
-sail-sculpture-1-250-BOWL.html; Amanda Prestigacomo, "WOW:
Here's how Trump's Ex Found Out He Was Divorcing Her," May 9,
2016, http://www.dailywire.com/news/5576/wow-heres-how-trumps
-ex-found-out-he-was-divorcing-amanda-prestigiacomo.

7. Bill Hoffman, "Marla to Ivana: Sorry—Regrets Swiping Her 'Ego-
Driven' Hubby," *New York Post,* October 19, 1999, http://nypost
.com/1999/10/19/marla-to-ivana-sorry-regrets-swiping-her-ego
-driven-hubby/.

8. Cameron Joseph, "Trump Says Cheating on Ivana with Marla Was
'Beautiful' in 1994," *Daily News,* October 8, 2016, http://www.ny

dailynews.com/news/politics/trump-cheating-ivana-marla-beautiful
-1994-article-1.2822695.

9. Carlos Lozada, "Donald Trump on Women, Sex, Marriage and
Feminism," *Washington Post,* August 5, 2015, https://www
.washingtonpost.com/news/book-party/wp/2015/08/05/donald
-trump-on-women-sex-marriage-and-feminism/?utm_term
=.e38ca7f13188.

10. Tina Brown, "Donald Trump, Settling Down," *Washington Post,*
January 27, 2005, http://www.washingtonpost.com/wp-dyn/articles
/A40186-2005Jan26.html.

11. Catherine Thompson, "Donald Trump Spreads the Message That
Hillary Clinton 'Can't Satisfy Her Husband," *Business Insider,*
April 17, 2016, http://www.businessinsider.com/donald-trump-via
-twitter-hillary-clinton-cant-satisfy-her-husband-2015-4; Ashley
Parker, "Donald Trump Says Hillary Clinton Doesn't Have 'a Presidential look,'" *New York Times,* September 6, 2017, https://www
.nytimes.com/2016/09/07/us/politics/donald-trump-says-hillary
-clinton-doesnt-have-a-presidential-look.html.

12. Angie Drobnic Holan, "In Context: Donald Trump's Lewd Remarks
from 2005," *PolitiFact,* October 8, 2016, http://www.politifact.com
/truth-o-meter/article/2016/oct/08/context-donald-trumps-lewd
-remarks-2005/.

13. Donald Trump and Kate Bohner, *The Art of the Comeback* (New
York: Random House, 1997), p. 116.

14. Natasha Stoynoff, "Physically Attacked by Donald Trump—A *People* Writer's Own Harrowing Story," *People,* October 12, 2016, http://
people.com/politics/donald-trump-attacked-people-writer/.

15. Stephanie Petit, "Revealed: 6 People Who Corroborate Natasha
Stoynoff's Story of Being Attacked by Donald Trump," *People,* October 19, 2016, http://people.com/politics/people-writer-attack-by
-donald-trump-corroborated-six-named-sources/.

16. Jon Greenberg, "Donald Trump Says Reports of Sexual Assault by
Him Have Been Disproven," *PolitiFact,* October 20, 2016, http://

www.politifact.com/truth-o-meter/statements/2016/oct/20/donald
-trump/donald-trump-says-reports-sexual-assault-him-have-/.

17. Jia Tolentino, "Trump and the Truth: The Sexual Assault Allegations," *The New Yorker,* October 20, 2016, http://www.newyorker
.com/news/news-desk/trump-and-the-truth-the-sexual-assault
-allegations; Dowd, "Liberties; Trump L'oeil Tease."

18. Madeline Farber, "Donald Trump Allegedly Walked In on Naked
Beauty Pageant Contestants," *Fortune,* October 9, 2016, http://fortune
.com/2016/10/09/trump-naked-beauty-pageant/.

19. Matt Broomfield, "Women's March Against Donald Trump is the
Largest Day of Protests in U.S. History, Say Political Scientists," *Independent*, January 23, 2017, http://www.independent.co.uk/news
/world/americas/womens-march-anti-donald-trump-womens-rights
-largest-protest-demonstration-us-history-political-a7541081.html;
Mahita Gajanan, "Read Aziz Ansar's *SNL* Monologue Taking on
Donald Trump," *Time*, January 23, 2017, http://time.com/4642747
/aziz-ansari-snl-monologue-transcript/; Nick Romano, "Watch Celebrities Attend Women's Marches Around the World," *Entertain-
ment*, January 22, 2017, http://ew.com/news/2017/01/21/celebrities
-womens-march/.

20. Christina Carterucci, "Russia Decriminalized Domestic Violence
With Support From the Russian Orthodox Chruch, *Slate*, February 8, 2016, http://www.slate.com/blogs/xx_factor/2017/02/08
/russia_decriminalized_domestic_violence_with_support_from
_the_russian_orthodox.html; Leila A. McNeill, "What Trump's Immigration Policies Mean for Domestic Violence Victims," *The Establishment*, February 22, 2017, https://theestablishment.co/what
-trumps-immigration-policies-mean-for-domestic-violence-victims
-a3e56248efcd#.v3tknrdil.

21. Daniella Silva, "Trump Accuser Summer Zervos Files Defamation
Suit Against President-Elect," *NBC,* January 7, 2017, http://www
.nbcnews.com/politics/politics-news/trump-accuser-summer-zervos
-files-defamation-suit-against-president-elect-n708031; WITW Staff,

"Contestant from *The Apprentice* Sues Donald Trump Over Sexual Assault Allegations," *New York Times,* January 17, 2017, http://nytlive.nytimes.com/womenintheworld/2017/01/17/contestant-from-the-apprentice-sues-donald-trump-over-sexual-assault-allegations/.

22. Brandy Zadrozny, "*Apprentice* Contestant Summer Zervos Slaps Donald Trump with Defamation Lawsuit," *The Daily Beast,* January 17, 2017, http://www.thedailybeast.com/articles/2017/01/17/apprentice-contestant-summer-zervos-slaps-donald-trump-with-defamation-lawsuit.html.

23. Jeremy Stahl, "The New Trump Defamation Lawsuit Is Daring Trump to Incriminate Himself in Court," *Slate*, January 17, 2017, http://www.slate.com/blogs/the_slatest/2017/01/17/the_new_trump_defamation_lawsuit_is_ daring_trump_to_incriminate_himself.html.

CHAPTER 7

1. Vidal and Bowcott, "ICC Widens Remit."
2. "Ruth Greenspan Bell on Why Climate Change Demands More Than the UNFCCC," *NewSecurityBeat,* June 19, 2015, https://www.newsecuritybeat.org/2015/06/no-precedent-human-history-ruth-greenspan-bell-climate-change-demands-nfccc/.
3. Display Ad, "Dear President Obama & The United States Congress," *New York Times*, December 6, 2009, p. 8.
4. Ross Konningstein and David Fork, "What it would Really Take To Reverse Climate Change," *IEEE*, November 18, 2014, http://spectrum.ieee.org/energy/renewables/what-it-would-really-take-to-reverse-climate-change; "Mainau Declaration 2015 on Climate Change," *Mainau Declaration*, July 3, 2015, http://www.mainaudeclaration.org/.
5. Jeremy Schulman, "Every Insane Thing Donald Trump Has Said About Global Warming," *Mother Jones*, December 5, 2016, https://www.washingtonpost.com/news/the-intersect/wp/2016/09/27/trump-didnt-delete-his-tweet-calling-global-warming-a-chinese-hoax/.

6. Aliyah Frumin, "Trump: Climate change is 'not one of our big problems,'" *MSNBC*, September 17, 2015, http://www.msnbc.com/msnbc/trump-climate-change-not-one-our-big-problems; John Siciliano, "Trump's plan to bring back coal country places EPA in crosshairs," *Washington Examiner*, November 14, 2016, http://www.washington examiner.com/trumps-plan-to-bring-back-coal-country-places-epa -in-crosshairs/article/2607222.

7. John Cook, et al., "Consensus on Consensus: A Synthesis on Consensus Estimates of Human-Caused Global Warming," *IOPscience*, April 13, 2016, http://iopscience.iop.org/article /10.1088/1748-9326/11/4/048002; John Cook, et al., "Quantifying the Scientific Consensus on Anthropogenic Global Warming in the Scientific Literature," *Environmental Research Letters* 8 (2013): W. Douglas Smith, "Climate Change is not Subject to Your Opinion," *Planet Experts*, November 16, 2015, http://www.planetexperts.com /climate-change-is-not-subject-to-your-opinion/.

8. Cook, et al., "Quantifying the Scientific Consensus"; Riley E. Dunlap and Aaron M. McCright, "Organized Climate Change Denial," in John S. Dryzek, Richard R. Norgaard, and David Schlosberg, eds., *The Oxford Handbook of Climate Change and Society* (New York: Oxford University Press, 2011), pp. 144–60.

9. Andrea Thompson, "Climate Experts Weigh in on Trump's Election Win," *Climate Central*, November 9, 2016, http://www.climate central.org/news/what-climate-experts-think-of-trumps-win-20860; Mary Bowerman, "Doomsday Clock Moves Closer to Apocalypse and 1 Person is to Blame," *USA Today*, January 26, 2017, http://www.usa today.com/story/news/nation-now/2017/01/26/doomsday-clock-end -world-nuclear-weapons-climate-change-donald-trump/97077736/.

10. "An America First Energy Plan" *The White House*, https://www .whitehouse.gov/america-first-energy; Annie Sneed, "Trump's First 100 Days: Climate and Energy," *Scientific American*, November 29, 2016, https://www.scientificamerican.com/article/trumps-first -100-days-climate-and-energy/.

11. U.S. Environmental Protection Agency, "Endangerment and Cause," https://www.epa.gov/climatechange/endangerment-and -cause-or-contribute-findings-greenhouse-gases-under-section -202a; Evan Lehman and Camille von Kaenel, "EPA Pick Sought to Unravel Endangerment Finding," E&E News, December 8, 2016, http://www.eenews.net/climatewire/2016/12/08/stories/10600 46865.

12. Brady Dennis, "Here's One Part of the EPA That the Agency's New Leader Wants to Protect," Washington Post, March 2, 2017, https://www.washingtonpost.com/news/energy-environment /wp/2017/03/02/heres-one-part-of-epa-that-the-agencys-new -leader-wants-to-protect/.

13. "The Little Syrian Boy: Here's Who He Was," NPR, September 3, 2015, http://www.npr.org/sections/parallels/2015/09/03/437132793 /photo-of-dead-3-year-old-syrian-refugee-breaks-hearts-around -the-world.

14. Mark Fischetti, "Climate Change Hastened Syria's Civil War," Scientific American, March 2, 2015, https://www.scientificamerican.com /article/climate-change-hastened-the-syrian-war/; Aryn Baker, "How Climate Change is Driving Migration to Europe, Time, September 6, 2016, http://time.com/4024210/climate-change-migrants/.

15. U.S. Department of Defense, "National Security Implications of Climate-Related Risks and a Changing Climate," July 23, 2015, http:// archive.defense.gov/pubs/150724-congressional-report-on-national -implications-of-climate-change.pdf?source=govdelivery.

16. Oliver Milman, "Scott Pruitt's EPA: a Dream for Oil and Gas Firms is Nightmare for Environment," The Guardian, December 8, 2016, https://www.theguardian.com/us-news/2016/dec/08/scott-pruitt -trump-administration-epa-oil-gas-environment; Coral Davenport, "E.P.A. Chief Doubts Consensus View of Climate Change," New York Times, March 9, 2017, https://www.nytimes.com/2017/03/09/ us/politics/epa-scott-pruitt-global-warming.html?_r=0.

17. Barmini Chakraborty, "Emails Reveal EPA Chief Pruitt's Work With

Oil, Gas Industries," *FOX News*, February 22, 2017, http://www
.foxnews.com/politics/2017/02/22/emails-reveal-epa-chief-pruitts
-work-with-oil-gas-companies.html; Eric Lipton, https://twitter
.com/EricLiptonNYT/status/834170859715702784.

18. Steph Solis, "Rick Perry, Who Said He Wanted to Scrap Energy Dept.,
Now Wants to Lead It," *USA Today*, December 13, 2016, http://www
.usatoday.com/story/news/politics/onpolitics/2016/12/13/trump
-nominate-rick-perry-secretary-energy-reports-say/95363672/;
Amanda Sakuma, "Skeptics Rip Rick Perry as Trump's Pick to Lead
Department of Energy," *NBC News,* December 15, 2016, http://
www.nbcnews.com/politics/politics-news/skeptics-rip-rick-perry
-trump-s-pick-lead-department-energy-n696056.

19. Shannon Hall, "Exxon Knew About Climate Change Almost 40
Years Ago," *Scientific American*, October 26, 2016, https://www
.scientificamerican.com/article/exxon-knew-about-climate-change
-almost-40-years-ago/.

20. Devin Henry, "Senate Committee Approves Zinke to lead interior," *The Hill*, January 31, 2017, http://thehill.com/policy
/energy-environment/317046-senate-committee-approves-zinke-to
-lead-interior.

21. *NASA*, "NASA, NOAH Data Show 2016 Hottest year on Record,"
January 18, 2017, https://www.nasa.gov/press-release/nasa-noaa
-data-show-2016-warmest-year-on-record-globally; Andrew
Freedman, "The Last Time CO_2 Was This High, Humans didn't ex-
ist," *Climate Central,* May 2, 2013, http://www.climatecentral.org
/news/the-last-time-co2-was-this-high-humans-didnt-exist-15938;
Brian Kahn, "Earth's CO_2 Passes the 400 PPM Threshold Maybe
Permanently," *Scientific American*, September 27, 2016, https://
www.scientificamerican.com/article/earth-s-co2-passes-the-400
-ppm-threshold-maybe-permanently/; James Hansen, Makkito
Sato, Pushker Kharecha, David Beerling, Robert Berner, Valerie
Masson-Delmotte, Mark Pagani, Maureen Raymo, Dana L. Royer,
and James C. Zachos, "Target Atmospheric CO_2: Where should

Humanity Aim?," NASA et al., https://arxiv.org/pdf/0804.1126 .pdf.

22. Bobby Magill, "Decoding Trump's White house Energy Plan," *Climate Central*, January 20, 2017, http://www.climatecentral.org /news/decoding-trumps-white-house-energy-plan-21097.

23. *U.S. Environmental Protection Agency*, Climate Impacts on Water Resources," https://www.epa.gov/climate-impacts/climate-impacts -water-resources; *CDC*, "Zika Virus," https://www.cdc.gov/zika/; Xiaoxu Wu, et al., "Impact of Climate Change on Human Infectious Diseases: Empirical Evidence and Human Adaptation," *Environmental International* 86 (2016), pp. 14–23.

24. Vidal and Bowcott, "ICC Widens Remit"; "States Parties-Chronological list," *ICC*, https://asp.icc-cpi.int/en_menus/asp/states%20parties/Pages /states%20parties%20_%20chronological%20list.aspx.

25. Linda Mogeni, "Gambia May Not Join African Withdrawals From ICC," *Inter Press Service*, December 9, 2016, http://www.ipsnews .net/2016/12/gambia-may-not-join-african-withdrawals-from-icc/.

26. Bob Berwyn, "Climate Change Concerns Prompt Court to Block Vienna Airport Expansion," *Inside Climate News*, February 17, 2017, https://insideclimatenews.org/news/14022017/climate-change -vienna-airport-paris-climate-agreement-james-hansen; Zahra Hurji, "Children's Climate Lawsuit Against U.S. Adds Trump as Defendant," *Inside Climate News*, https://insideclimatenews.org /news/09022017/climate-change-lawsuit-donald-trump-children.

27. Kristen Ellingboe and Ryan Koronowski, "Most Americans disagree with their congressional representative on climate change," *Think Progress*, March 8, 2016, https://thinkprogress.org/most-americans -disagree-with-their-congressional-representative-on-climate -change-95dc0eee7b8f#.oxtskbxr3.

CHAPTER 8

1. Molly K. McKew, "Putin's Real Long Game," *Politico Magazine*, January 1, 2017, http://www.politico.com/magazine/story/2017/01

/putins-real-long-game-214589; "OPEC Revises Russian 2017 GDP Growth Forecast, Up By 0.1 to 1%," *Sputnik International*, February 11, 2017, https://sputniknews.com/world/201702131050629237 -russia-gdp-growth-opec/; Adam Withnall, "Vladimir Putin Corruption," *The Independent*, January 26, 2016, http://www .independent.co.uk/news/people/vladimir-putin-corruption -five-things-we-learned-about-the-russian-presidents-secret -wealth-a6834171.html.

2. Farrand, *The Records*, vol. 2, p. 109; Robert F. Jones, "George Washington and the Politics of the Presidency," *Presidential Studies Quarterly* 10 (1980), 28–35.

3. Ashley Parker and David E. Sanger, "Donald Trump Calls on Russia to Find Hillary Clinton's Missing Emails," *New York Times*, July 27, 2016, https://www.nytimes.com/2016/07/28/us/politics/donald -trump-russia-clinton-emails.html?_r=0&mtrref=www.google.com &gwh=A1FC8163A563596B24B4F1B10A004FDE&gwt=pay; "Chapter 121—Stored Wire And Electronic Communications And Transactional Records Access," U.S. Government Publishing Office, https://www.gpo.gov/fdsys/pkg/USCODE-2010-title18/html /USCODE-2010-title18-partI-chap121.htm.

4. Josh Rogin, "Trump Campaign's Guts GOP's anti-Russia Stance on Ukraine," *Washington Post*, July 18, 2016, https://www.washington post.com/opinions/global-opinions/trump-campaign-guts-gops-anti -russia-stance-on-ukraine/2016/07/18/98adb3b0-4cf3-11e6-a7d8 -13d06b37f256_story.html?utm_term=.bf22caff6756; David Satter, "Trump and Russia," *National Review*, August 11, 2016, http://www .nationalreview.com/article/438885/donald-trumps-russia-policy -dangerously-na-ve-about-vladimir-putin.

5. Evgenia Pismennaya, Stepan Kravchenko and Stephanie Baker, "The Day Trump Came to Moscow: Oligarchs, Miss Universe, and Nobu," *Bloomberg*, December 21, 2016, https://www.bloomberg.com/news /articles/2016-12-21/the-day-trump-came-to-moscow-oligarchs -miss-universe-and-nobu; Rosalind S. Helderman, "Here's What We

Know About Donald Trump and his Ties to Russia," *Washington Post*, July 29, 2016, https://www.washingtonpost.com/politics/heres -what-we-know-about-donald-trump-and-his-ties-to-russia /2016/07/29/1268b5ec-54e7-11e6-88eb-7dda4e2f2aec_story .html?utm_term=.2d7e2cc2e769.

6. Ibid., Pismennaya, Kravchenko, and Baker, "The Day Trump Came to Moscow"; https://twitter.com/realdonaldtrump/status/399939505 924628480?lang=en, November 11, 2013.

7. Tom Burgis, "Dirty Money: Trump and the Kazakh Connec-tion," *Financial Times*, October 22, 2016, https://www.ft.com /content/33285dfa-9231-11e6-8df8-d3778b55a923; *People of the State of New York v. Bayrock Group, et al.* August 11, 2015, Index 1010478/15, https://assets.documentcloud.org/documents/3117825 /Qui-Tam-Complaint-With-Exhibit-a-and-Attachments.pdf; "Bay-rock Group," https://assets.documentcloud.org/documents/3117892 /Bayrock-Presentation.pdf.

8. Charles V. Bagli, "Real Estate Executive With Hand in Trump Proj-ects Rose From Tangled Past," *New York Times*, December 17, 2007, http://www.nytimes.com/2007/12/17/nyregion/17trump.html?.

9. Michael Bird and Zeynep Sentek, "Kazakh Moguls," December 16, 2016, *The Black Sea*, http://theblacksea.eu/index.php?idT=88&idC =88&idRec=1274&recType=story.

10. Trump Deposition, *Trump v. O'Brien*, pp. 410–12; Wayne Barrett, "Inside Donald Trump's Empire: Why He Didn't Run for President in 2012," *The Daily Beast*, May 26, 2011, http://www.thedailybeast .com/articles/2011/05/26/inside-donald-trumps-empire-why-he -wont-run-for-president.html; Gary Silverman, "US election: Trump's Russian riddle," *Financial Times*, August 14, 2016, https://www .ft.com/content/549ddfaa-5fa5-11e6-b38c-7b39cbb1138a; Richard Behar, "Donald Trump and the Felon: Inside His Business Deal-ings With a Mob-Connected Hustler," *Forbes*, October 25, 2016, https://www.forbes.com/sites/richardbehar/2016/10/03/donald -trump-and-the-felon-inside-his-business-dealings-with-a-mob

-connected-hustler/#583034e12282; *FEC*, Contributions, Sater, Felix, http://docquery.fec.gov/cgi-bin/qind/.

11. Ibid., Trump Deposition, pp. 584–99; See, for example, David E. Hoffman, *The Oligarchs: Wealth and Power in the New Russia* (New York: Public Affairs, 2011).

12. Mike McIntire, "Donald Trump Settles a Real Estate Lawsuit, and a Criminal Case Was Closed," *New York Times*, April 5, 2016, https://www.nytimes.com/2016/04/06/us/politics/donald-trump-soho-settlement.html.

13. *People of the State of New York v. Bayrock Group, et al.*; Supreme Court of the State of New York, County of New York, Index 1010478/15, incorporated civil complaint, August 11, 2015. In December 2016, federal District Court Judge Lorna G. Schofield denied a defendant's motion to dismiss the racketeering and other claims against Bayrock, Sater, Arif, and Schwarz. They dismissed only the racketeering conspiracy claims against Bayrock because it could act only through it agents. *Kriss v. Bayrock*, 10 Civ. 3959 (LGS) (DCF), Order and Opinion, December 2, 2016, https://iapps.courts.state.ny.us/nyscef/ViewDocument?docIndex=bkVEI0QZkhWfLcZhsgq5sQ==.

14. Ibid., *New York v. Bayrock Group*, pp. 2–3.

15. Ruth Sherlock, Edward Malnick, and Claire Newell, "Exclusive—Donald Trump Signed Off Deal Designed to Deprive US of Tens of Millions in Tax, *The Telegraph*, May 25, 2016, http://www.telegraph.co.uk/news/2016/05/25/exclusive-donald-trump-signed-off-deal-designed-to-deprive-us-of/.

16. Jeff Nesbit, "Donald Trump's Many, Many, Many, Many Ties to Russia," *Time*, August 15, 2016, http://time.com/4433880/donald-trump-ties-to-russia/; James S. Henry, "The Curious World of Donald Trump's Private Russian Connections," *The American Interest*, December 19, 2016, http://www.the-american-interest.com/2016/12/19/the-curious-world-of-donald-trumps-private-russian-connections/. (*note 1*)

17. See, for example, *New York v. Bayrock*, pp. 3, 26, 107, 117, 136, 140, 145, 154–55; Henry, "The Curious World," describes the Bay-

rock brochure; Ari Moses, "The Modern Puppet State," *Washington University Political Review*, March 14, 2014, http://www.wupr .org/2014/03/16/the-modern-puppet-state/; Reena Flores, "Kazakhstan: Trump Praised 'Miracle' Achieved Under Our President," *CBS News*, December 2, 2016, http://www.cbsnews.com/news/donald -trump-kazakhstan-nursultan-nazarbayev-miracle/.

18. The press has thoroughly covered Ross's Russian connections. See Kevin G. Hall, "Trump's Pick for Commerce Leaves Russia Questions Unanswered," *McClatchy*, February 26, 2017, http://www .mcclatchydc.com/news/politics-government/article135001434 .html; Kevin G. Hall, "Ross Confirmed for Cabinet, But White House Refuses to Release His Answers on Russia," *Kansas City Star*, February 27, 2017, http://www.kansascity.com/news/politics -government/article135344269.html; and in depth, James S. Henry, "The Troubling Russian Connections of Trump Nominee Wilbur Ross," *The National Memo*, February 27, 2017, http://www.national memo.com/ross-russian-connections/; "Global Tax 50: 2016," *International Tax Review*, http://www.internationaltaxreview.com/Article /3644898/Global-Tax-50-2016.html.

19. Ibid.; Karen Freifield and Arno Scheutze, "Deutsche Bank Fined for $10 Billion Sham Russian Trades," *Business News*, January 31, 2017, http://www.reuters.com/article/us-deutsche-mirrortrade-probe -idUSKBN15F1GT.

20. Steven Mufson and Tom Hamburger, "Inside Trump Adviser Manafort's World of Politics and Global Financial Dealmaking," *Washington Post*, April 26, 2016, https://www.washingtonpost .com/politics/in-business-as-in-politics-trump-adviser-no-stranger -to-controversial-figures/2016/04/26/970db232-08c7-11e6-b283 -e79d81c63c1b_story.html?utm_term=.500abf6161e0; Jeff Horowitz and Desmond Butler, "Manafort Tied to Undisclosed Foreign Lobbying," *AP*, August 17, 2016.

21. Andrew E. Kramer, Mike McIntire, and Barry Meier, "Secret Ledger in Ukraine Lists Cash for Donald Trump's Campaign Chief," *New*

York Times, August 13, 2016, https://www.nytimes.com/2016/08/15 /us/politics/paul-manafort-ukraine-donald-trump.html.

22. Kenneth P. Vogel, David Stern, and Josh Meyer, "Manafort Faced Blackmail Attempt, Hack Suggests," *Politico*, February 23, 2017, http://www.politico.com/story/2017/02/paul-manafort-blackmail -russia-trump-235275.

23. Kenneth P. Vogel, David Stern, and Josh Meyer, "Manafort's Ukrainian 'Blood Money' Caused Qualms, Hack Suggests," *Politico*, February 28, 2017, http://www.politico.com/story/2017/02/manaforts-ukrainian -blood-money-caused-qualms-hack-suggests-235473.

24. Julia Ioffe, "The Mystery of Trump's Man in Moscow," *Politico Magazine*, September 26, 2016, http://www.politico.com/magazine /story/2016/09/the-mystery-of-trumps-man-in-moscow-214283; "Donald Trump Ally Admits 'Back-Channel' Link to Wikileaks," *Miami Herald*, October 12, 2016, http://www.miamiherald.com /news/politics-government/election/donald-trump/article1078 82287.html#storylink=cpy.

25. "Joint Statement from the Department of Homeland Security and Office of the Director of National Intelligence on Election Security," October 7, 2006, https://www.dhs.gov/news/2016/10/07/joint-state ment-department-homeland-security-and-office-director-national.

26. *New York Times*: "Transcript of Second Debate," https://www .nytimes.com/2016/10/10/us/politics/transcript-second-debate.html; "Transcript of Third Debate," https://www.google.com/#q=transcript +third+presidential+debate+new+york+times&*.

27. "Assessing Russian Activities and Intentions in Recent US Elections," *ICA*, Intelligence Community Assessment, www.intelligence .senate.gov/sites/default/files/documents/ICA_2017_01.pdf.

28. Melissa Chan, "Julian Assange Says a '14-Year-Old Kid Could Have Hacked Podesta' Emails," *Time*, January 4, 2017, http://time .com/4621653/julian-assange-wikileaks-emails/.

29. Louis Jacobson, "Donald Trump's dubious claim that foreign governments had 'absolutely no effect' on election outcome," *PolitiFact*, Jan-

uary 8, 2017, http://www.PolitiFact.com/truth-o-meter/statements /2017/jan/08/donald-trump/donald-trumps-dubious-claim-foreign -governments-ha/.

30. Rebecca Savransky, "Trump in 2010 wanted 'death penalty' for WikiLeaks," *The Hill*, January 4, 2017, http://thehill.com/home news/campaign/312679-trump-in-2010-wanted-death-penalty-for -wikileaks; Jedd Legum, "Trump Mentioned Wikileaks 164 Times in Last Month Of Election, Now Claims it Didn't Impact One Voter," *Think Progress*, January 7, 2016, https://thinkprogress.org/trump -mentioned-wikileaks-164-times-in-last-month-of-election-now -claims-it-didnt-impact-one-40aa62ea5002#.m6o9xgndy.

31. Peter Bergen, "No, President-elect Trump: Russian hacking is not like the CIA's WMD fiasco," *CNN*, January 4, 2017, http://www.cnn .com/2017/01/04/opinions/russian-hacking-is-not-another-cia-fiasco -like-iraq-wmd-bergen/.

32. Ibid.

33. "Company Intelligence Report," 2016/080, https://www.document cloud.org/documents/3259984-Trump-Intelligence-Allegations .html, text of dossier. All citations to the dossier are from this docu- ment.

34. Abby Phillip, "O'Reilly Told Trump That Putin is a Killer: Trump's Reply: 'You Think Our Country Is So Innocent?'" *Washington Post*, February 4, 2017; Nick Allen, "Trump Defends Vladimir Putin Over Alexander Litvinenko Murder," *The Telegraph*, January 16, 2016, http://www.telegraph.co.uk/news/worldnews/us-election/12123600 /Donald-Trump-defends-Vladimir-Putin-over-Alexander-Litvinenko -murder.html.

35. "Trump Said Iranians Would Be Blown Out of Water and US Navy Just Opened Fire . . ." *Conservative Tribune*, http://conservativetribune .com/trump-iranians-us-navy/; Luis Martinez, "Russian Aircraft Buzzed U.S. Ship 3 Times in a Day," *ABC News*, February 14, 2017, http://abcnews.go.com/International/russian-aircraft-buzzed-us -navy-ship-times-day/story?id=45490605.

36. "Manafort Denies Trump Campaign Changed GOP Platform on Ukraine," *TPM*, August 1, 2016, http://talkingpointsmemo.com /livewire/manafort-ukraine-gop-platform.

37. Natasha Bertrand, "It Looks Like Another Trump Insider Has Significantly Changed His Story About the GOP's Dramatic Shift on Ukraine," *Business Insider*, March 3, 2017, http://www.business insider.com/jd-gordon-trump-adviser-ukraine-rnc-2017-3; Steve Reilly, "Exclusive: Two Other Trump Insiders Also Spoke With Russian Envoy During GOP Convention," *USA Today*, March 2, 2017, http://www.usatoday.com/story/news/2017/03/02/exclusive -two-other-trump-advisers-also-spoke-russian-envoy-during-gop -convention/98648190/; Tom Hamburger and Karen Tumulty, "WikiLeaks Releases Thousands of Documents About Clinton and Internal Deliberations," *Washington Post*, July 22, 2016, https:// www.washingtonpost.com/news/post-politics/wp/2016/07/22 /on-eve-of-democratic-convention-wikileaks-releases-thousands -of-documents-about-clinton-the-campaign-and-internal -deliberations/?utm_term=.8b475e8d7f1f.

38. Robert Mendick and Robert Verkaik, "Mystery death of ex-KGB chief linked to MI6 spy's dossier on Donald Trump," *The Telegraph*, January 27, 2016, http://www.telegraph.co.uk/news/2017/01/27/mystery -death-ex-kgb-chief-linked-mi6-spys-dossier-donald-trump/.

39. Jim Sciutto and Evan Perez, "Intelligence Officials Corroborate Part of Steele Dossier," *CNN*, February 10, 2017, Michael S. Schmidt, Mark Mazzetti, and Matt Apuzzo, "Trump Aides Had Repeated Contacts With Russian Intelligence," *New York Times*, February 14, 2017, https://www.nytimes.com/2017/02/14/us/politics /russia-intelligence-communications-trump.html?_r=0; Pamela Brown, Jim Sciutto, and Evan Perez, "Trump Aides Were in Constant Touch With Senior Russian Officials During Campaign, *CNN*, February 15, 2016, http://www.cnn.com/2017/02/14/politics/donald -trump-aides-russians-campaign/.

40. Brendan Naylor, " 'Nobody That I Know of': Trump Denies Cam-

paign Contacts With Russia," *NPR*, February 16, 2017, http://www
.npr.org/2017/02/16/515624391/nobody-that-i-know-of-trump
-denies-campaign-contacts-with-russia; John Kelly and Steve Reilly,
"Trump Team Issued at Least 20 Denials of Contacts With Russians," *USA Today*, March 2, 2017, http://www.usatoday.com/story
/news/politics/2017/03/02/trump-teams-many-many-denials
-contacts-russia/98625780/; Philip Bump, "The Web of Relationships
Between Team Trump and Russia," *Washington Post*, March 3, 2017,
https://www.washingtonpost.com/news/politics/wp/2017/03/03/the
-web-of-relationships-between-team-trump-and-russia/?utm
_term=.ebed01ed15c0.

41. Adam Entous, Ellen Nakashima, and Greg Miller, "Sessions Met
    With Russian Envoy Twice Last Year, Contacts he Did Not Dis-
    close," *Washington Post*, March 1, 2017, https://www.washingtonpost
    .com/world/national-security/sessions-spoke-twice-with-russian
    -ambassador-during-trumps-presidential-campaign-justice-officials
    -say/2017/03/01/77205eda-feac-11e6-99b4-9e613afeb09f_story
    .html?utm_term=.184675a9dd36.

42. Ibid.; Aaron Blake, "Transcript of Jeff Sessions's Recusal News Con-
    ference, Annotated," *Washington Post*, March 2, 2017, https://www
    .washingtonpost.com/news/the-fix/wp/2017/03/02/transcript-of-jeff
    -sessionss-recusal-press-conference-annotated/?utm_term=.6716fccb
    27ab; Letter available from *NBC News* at https://twitter.com/NBC
    NightlyNews/status/838875832693161984/photo/1; Paul Sonne, Re-
    becca Ballhaus, and Carol E. Lee, "Jeff Sessions Used Political Funds
    For Republican Convention Expenses," *Wall Street Journal*.

43. Ibid.

44. "Clinton's Acquittal: Excerpts—Senators Talk About Their Votes in the
    Impeachment Trial," *New York Times*, February 13, 2017, http://www
    .nytimes.com/1999/02/13/us/clinton-s-acquittal-excerpts-senators
    -talk-about-their-votes-impeachment-trial.html.

45. Max Greenwood, "Trump on Sessions: 'He Didn't Say Any-
    thing Wrong,'" *The Hill*, March 2, 2017, http://thehill.com

/homenews/administration/322136-trump-sessions-did-not-say
-anything-wrong; "Like 'Mccarthyism': Lavrov Slams US 'Witch
Hunt-Like' Scrutiny Of Russian Ambassador's Contacts," *RT*,
March 3, 2017, https://www.rt.com/news/379334-lavrov-mccarthyism
-ambassador-witch-hunt/.

46. For Kleindienst and Mitchell, see James Rosen, *The Strong Man:
John Mitchell and the Secrets of Watergate* (New York: Doubleday,
2008), pp. 329, 536–37.

47. Greg Miller, Adam Entous, and Ellen Nakashima, "National Security Advisor Flynn Discussed Sanctions With Russian Ambassador Despite Denials, Officials Say," *Washington Post*,
February 9, 2016, https://www.washingtonpost.com/world/national
-security/national-security-adviser-flynn-discussed-sanctions
-with-russian-ambassador-despite-denials-officials-say/2017/02/09
/f85b29d6-ee11-11e6-b4ff-ac2cf509efe5_story.html?utm
_term=.8945a349c2ed.

48. Ibid.

49. Andrew Roth, "Putin Says He Won't Deport U.S. Diplomats as he
Looks to Cultivate Relations With Trump," *Washington Post*, December 30, 2016, https://www.washingtonpost.com/world/russia
-plans-retaliation-and-serious-discomfortoverus-hacking-sanctio
ns/2016/12/30/4efd3650-ce12-11e6-85cd-e66532e35a44_story
.html?utm_term=.a3f5f837d95e.

50. Jordan Fabian and Lisa Hagen, "Trump: Flynn Treated Badly by
'Fake Media,'" *The Hill*, February 11, 2017, http://thehill.com
/homenews/administration/319666-trump-flynn-treated-badly-by
-fake-media.

51. Mark Landler and Richard Pérez-Peña, "Flynn Was Brought Down
by Illegal Leaks to Media, Trump Says," *New York Times*, February 9, 2017, https://www.nytimes.com/2017/02/15/us/politics/trump
-condemns-leaks-to-news-media-in-a-twitter-flurry.html; "Trump
Fumes About Anonymous Sources After Anonymous Briefing,"
Bloomberg, February 24, 2017, https://www.bloomberg.com/politics

/articles/2017-02-24/trump-assails-fake-news-blasts-media-use-of
-anonymous-sources.

52. Eric Wemple, "Trump's Attack On 'Nine Sources' Sounds A
Lot Like The News Story That Started Flynn Chaos," *Washington Post*, February 24, 2016, https://www.washingtonpost.com
/blogs/erik-wemple/wp/2017/02/24/president-trump-attacks-nine
-sources/?utm_term=.110b5d9a26c1.

53. Adam Entous, Ellen Nakashima, and Philip Rucker, "Justice
Department Warned White House That Flynn Could be Vulnerable to Russian Blackmail, Officials Say," *Washington Post*, February 13, 2017, https://www.washingtonpost.com/world/national
-security/justice-department-warned-white-house-that-flynn
-could-be-vulnerable-to-russian-blackmail-officials-say/2017/02/13
/fc5dab88-f228-11e6-8d72-263470bf0401_story.html?utm
_term=.81b91d03dafe.

54. Megan Twohey and Scott Shane, "A Back-Channel Plan for Ukraine
and Russia Courtesy of Trump Associates," *New York Times*, February 19, 2017.

55. Ken Dilanian, "Lawyer Confirms Meeting Ukrainian, Denies
Carrying Peace Plan," *NBC News*, February 20, 2017, http://www
.nbcnews.com/news/us-news/trump-lawyer-confirms-meeting
-ukrainian-denies-carrying-peace-plan-n723386.

CHAPTER 9

1. "Interview: Watergate Veterans—Just Like Nixon, Donald Trump
Appears to Think he is Above the Law," *NPR*, January 31, 2017, https://
www.democracynow.org/2017/1/31/watergate_veterans_just_like
_nixon_donald.

2. James Pfiffner and Joshua Lee, "Trump Pledged to Reverse Obama's
Executive Orders," *Washington Post*, January 23, 2017, https://www
.washingtonpost.com/news/monkey-cage/wp/2017/01/23/trump
-pledged-to-reverse-obamas-executive-orders-heres-how-well-past
-presidents-have-fulfilled-that-pledge/?utm_term=.caed4659077e;

John Ratcliffe, "Separation of Powers Act Key to Rebalancing Government," *The Hill*, June 6, 2016, http://thehill.com/blogs /congress-blog/judicial/284123-separation-of-powers-restoration -act-key-to-rebalancing.

3. Jacob Pramuk and John W. Schoen, "Trump Just Signed a New Travel Ban. Here's What Changed," *CNBC*, March 6, 2017, http:// www.cnbc.com/2017/03/06/trump-signs-new-travel-ban-targeting -six-countries.html.

4. *State of Washington v. Donald Trump*, "Complaint for Declaratory and Injunctive Relief," filed January 30, 2017. "Full Text of Trump's Executive Order on 7-Nation Ban, Refugee Suspension," *CNN*, January 27, 2017, http://www.cnn.com/2017/01/28/politics/text-of-trump -executive-order-nation-ban-refugees/.

5. "ISIS is Reportedly Calling Trump's Travel Ban 'the Blessed Ban,'" *The Nation*, February 9, 2017, http://nation.com.pk /international/09-Feb-2017/isis-is-reportedly-calling-trump-s -travel-ban-the-blessed-ban; Daniel Benjamin, "Donald Trump is Spreading Racism—Not Fighting Terrorism," *Time*, February 3, 2017, http://time.com/4658366/donald-trump-terrorism-racism/; Eliza Mackintosh, "Trump Ban is Boon for ISIS Recruitment Former Jihadists and Experts Say," *CNN*, January 31, 2017, http://www .cnn.com/2017/01/30/politics/trump-ban-boosts-isis-recruitment/.

6. Jeff Stein, "Top Republicans Denounced Trump's Muslim Ban on the Trail," *Vox*, January 28, 2017, http://www.vox .com/2017/1/28/14424758/ryan-pence-ban; Associated Press, "Iraqi Parliament Approves 'Reciprocity' to U.S. Ban," *Politico*, January 30, 2017, http://www.politico.com/story/2017/01/iraq-parliament -approves-reciprocity-to-us-ban-234354.

7. John Robert Badger, "World View: The Nuremberg Trials," *Chicago Defender*, September 7, 1946, p. 15.

8. "President Lyndon B. Johnson's Remarks at the Signing of the Immigration Bill," October 3, 1965, http://www.lbjlibrary.org/lyndon -baines-johnson/timeline/lbj-on-immigration; *The Public Papers of*

the Presidents of the United States: Ronald Reagan, June 30 to December 31, 1984, "Remarks, August 23, 1984," p. 1181, https://www.reaganlibrary.archives.gov/archives/speeches/1984/82384f.htm.

9. *Legal Assistance v. Department of State*, 45 F.3d 469 (D.C. Cir. 1995). Congress since modified the anti-discrimination provision by authorizing the government to set the "procedures" and "locations" for processing visas. But Trump's order far exceeds such authority.

10. "No Terrorist Attacks Post-9/11 by People From Countries in Trump's Travel Ban," *PolitiFact*, January 29, 2017, http://www.politifact.com/truth-o-meter/statements/2017/jan/29/jerrold-nadler/have-there-been-terrorist-attacks-post-911-countri/.

11. Greg Sargent, "In Leaked Document the Case for Trump's 'Muslim Ban' Takes Another Huge Hit," *Washington Post*, March 3, 2017, https://www.washingtonpost.com/blogs/plum-line/wp/2017/03/03/in-leaked-document-the-case-for-trumps-muslim-ban-takes-another-huge-hit/?utm_term=.5424442b8def. "Who are the Terrorists?" *New America*, https://www.newamerica.org/in-depth/terrorism-in-america/who-are-terrorists/.

12. Lichtman, *White Protestant Nation*, p. 8; Susan Jones, "Trump: 'I Only Want to Admit People Who Share Our Values and Love Our People'," *CNS News,* June 22, 2016, http://www.cnsnews.com/news/article/susan-jones/trump-i-only-want-admit-people-who-share-our-values-and-love-our-people.

13. Allan J. Lichtman and Richard Breitman, *FDR and the Jews* (Cambridge, MA: Harvard University Press, 2013), pp. 161–83; "German Jews During the Holocaust," *U.S. Holocaust Memorial Museum*, https://www.ushmm.org/wlc/en/article.php?ModuleId=10005469.

14. Jared Goyette, "It's now Clear That Most of the Syrian Refugees Coming to the United States are Women and Children," *PRI*, August 8, 2016, https://www.pri.org/stories/2016-08-08/it-s-now-clear-most-syrian-refugees-coming-united-states-are-women-and-children; Alex Nowrasteh, "Terrorism and Immigration: A Risk Analysis," *Cato*

Institute, September 13 2016, https://www.cato.org/publications /policy-analysis/terrorism-immigration-risk-analysis#full.

15. Rumana Ahmed, "I Was a Muslim in the Trump White House— and I lasted Eight Days," *The Atlantic*, February 23, 2017, https:// www.theatlantic.com/politics/archive/2017/02/rumana-ahmed -trump/517521/#article-comments; Hunter Walker, "Michael Anton is the Most Interesting Man in the White House," *Yahoo News*, February 16, 2017, https://www.yahoo.com/news/michael-anton-is-the -most-interesting-man-in-the-white-house-211930901.html.

16. *State of Washington v. Trump, et al.*, United States District Court Western Division of Washington, No. 2:17-cv-00141 (JLR), "Defendants' Opposition To Plaintiff State Of Washington's Motion For Temporary Restraining Order," and "Temporary Restraining Order," February 3, 2017; *Tareq Aqel Mohammed Aziz, et al. v. Donald Trump*, "Memorandum Opinion," U.S. District Court for the Eastern Division of Virginia, 1:17-cv-116 (LMB/TCB), February 13, 2017; *State of Washington v. Trump, et al.*, Court of Appeals of the Ninth Circuit, No. 17-35105, Order.

17. Rebecca Savransky, "Giuliani: Trump Asked Me How To do a Muslim Ban 'Legally,'" *The Hill*, January 29, 2017, http://thehill .com/homenews/administration/316726-giuliani-trump-asked-me -how-to-do-a-muslim-ban-legally; David Brody, "Brody File Exclusive: President Trump Says Persecuted Christians Will be Given Priority as Refugees, *Christian Broadcasting Network*, January 27, 2017, http://www1.cbn.com/thebrodyfile/archive/2017/01/27 /brody-file-exclusive-president-trump-says-persecuted-christians -will-be-given-priority-as-refugees; Noah Bierman, "Trump's Muslim Ban Was Removed From His Website, But It's Back," *Los Angeles Times*, November 10, 2016, http://www.latimes.com/nation/politics /trailguide/la-na-updates-trail-guide-so-what-s-the-deal-with -donald-trump-s-1478812963-htmlstory.html.

18. *State of Washington v. Trump, et al.*; Laura Jarrett, Eli Watkins, and Rene Marsh, "Justice Department to Challenge Judge's

Halt of Travel Ban," February 3, 2017, *CNN*, http://www.cnn
.com/2017/02/03/politics/federal-judge-temporarily-halts-trump
-travel-ban-nationwide-ag-says/.

19. Rachel Weiner, "Federal Judge: Courts 'Begging' for Evidence to
Support Trump's Travel Ban," *Washington Post*, February 10, 2017,
https://www.washingtonpost.com/local/public-safety/federal-judge
-in-virginia-presses-for-evidence-to-support-need-for-trump-travel
-ban/2017/02/10/e99202e2-ef17-11e6-9662-6eedf1627882_story
.html?utm_term=.562000bf38e9.

20. *Aziz v. Donald Trump,* Order.

21. Whistleblower Protection Act of 1989, Congress.gov, https://www
.congress.gov/bill/101st-congress/senate-bill/20/text; Joe Davidson,
"To Resist or Not, The Federal Employee's Dilemma," *Washington Post*, January 31, 2017, https://www.washingtonpost.com/news
/powerpost/wp/2017/01/31/to-resist-or-not-the-federal-employees
-dilemma/?utm_term=.f137e34ec4ca; "Code of Ethics for Government Service," https://www.law.cornell.edu/cfr/text/39/appendix
-A_to_part_3000.

22. Jeffrey Gettleman, "State Dept. Dissent Cable on Trump's Ban
Draws 1,000 Signatures," *New York Times*, January 31, 2017, https://
www.nytimes.com/2017/01/31/world/americas/state-dept-dissent
-cable-trump-immigration-order.html?_r=0; Elise Labott, "WH
Tells Career US Diplomats Who Oppose Trump to Get Out," *CNN*,
January 30, 2017, http://www.cnn.com/2017/01/30/politics/career
-diplomats-dissent-memo/.

23. Euan McKirdy, "Jeff Sessions Grilled Sally Yates on Constitutional
Duties During 2015 Hearing," *CNN*, January 31, 2017, http://www
.cnn.com/2017/01/31/politics/sally-yates-jeff-sessions-deputy
-attorney-general-hearing/.

24. Julian Zelizer, "Monday Night Massacre is a Wake-Up Call to
Senate Democrats," CNN, January 31, 2017, http://www.cnn
.com/2017/01/30/opinions/monday-night-massacre-wake-up-call
-to-senate-democrats-zelizer/; Paulina Firozi, "Nixon White House

Lawyer: Trump's Firing of Acting AG Yates a 'New Low,'" *The Hill*, January 31, 2017, http://thehill.com/homenews/news/317029-nixon-white-house-lawyer-trumps-firing-of-acting-ag-yates-a-new-low.

25. Rachael Blade, Jake Sherman, and Josh Dorsey, "Hill Staffers Secretly Worked on Trump Immigration Order," *Politico*, January 30, 2017, http://www.politico.com/story/2017/01/trump-immigration-congress-order-234392; Benjamin Siegel and John Parkinson, "House Staffers Worked on Trump Immigration Order: Allegedly Signed Non-Disclosure Agreements," *ABC News*. January 31, 2017, http://abcnews.go.com/Politics/house-staff-worked-trump-immigration-order-allegedly-signed/story?id=45168089.

26. Thomas Fuller, "'So-called Judge' Criticized by Trump is Known as a Mainstream Republican," *New York Times*, January 31, 2017, https://www.nytimes.com/2017/02/04/us/james-robart-judge-trump-ban-seattle.html?_r=0.

27. Alexis Simendinger, "Trump: Judge Biased if His Order Is Blocked," *Real Clear Politics*, February 8, 2017, http://www.realclearpolitics.com/articles/2017/02/08/trump_judges_biased_if_his_order_is_blocked_133024.html; Adam Boult, "'See You In Court'—Trump's Furious Tweet Mocked on Social Media," *The Telegraph*, February 10, 2017, http://www.telegraph.co.uk/news/2017/02/10/see-court-trumps-furious-tweet-mocked-social-media/.

28. Ronald N. Satz, *American Indian Policy in the Jacksonian Era* (Norman, OK: University of Oklahoma Press, 2002).

29. Jeff Stein, "9 Things It's Actually Hard to Believe The President of the United States Actually Just Said," *Vox*, February 17, 2017, http://www.vox.com/2017/2/16/14640772/president-trump-quotes-presser; Stephen Collinson, "An Amazing Moment in History: Donald Trump's Press Conference," *CNN*, February 16, 2017, http://www.cnn.com/2017/02/16/politics/donald-trump-press-conference-amazing-day-in-history/.

30. Aaron Blake, "Kellyanne Conway's 'Bowling Green Massacre' Wasn't A Slip of The Tongue. She Has Said It Before," *Wash-*

ington Post, February 9, 2017, https://www.washingtonpost.com
/news/the-fix/wp/2017/02/06/kellyanne-conways-bowling-green
-massacre-wasnt-a-slip-of-the-tongue-shes-said-it-before/?utm
_term=.6983b1d342f4.

31. Kim Hjelmgaard, "Media Covered Most of 78 Terror Attacks Trump said 'Not Even Being Reported,'" *USA Today*, February 7, 2017, http://www.usatoday.com/story/news/politics/onpolitics/2017/02/07/white-house-78-terror-attacks-list-trump/97582018/.

32. Eric Bradner, "Trump's Sweden Comment Raises Questions," *CNN*, February 20, 2017, http://www.cnn.com/2017/02/19/politics/trump-rally-sweden/. The FOX news report was actually an interview with a filmmaker, not a study of crime and immigration in Sweden.

33. Michael M. Grynbaum, "White House Bars *Times* and Other News Outlets From Briefing," *New York Times*, February 24, 2017, https://www.nytimes.com/2017/02/24/us/politics/white-house-sean-spicer-briefing.html?_r=0; Eric Levitz, "Trump Praises First Amendment, Calls for Media Suppression and Fewer Protests," *New York*, February 24, 2017, http://nymag.com/daily/intelligencer/2017/02/trump-praises-first-amendment-calls-for-media-suppression.html.

34. Julia Horowitz, "Carl Bernstein: Trump's Attacks on the Media are 'More Treacherous' Than Nixon's," *CNN*, February 19, 2017, http://money.cnn.com/2017/02/19/media/carl-bernstein-trump-nixon-reliable-sources/.

35. Philip Rucker and Robert Costa, "Bannon Vows a Daily Fight for Deconstruction of the Administrative State," *Washington Post*, February 25, 2017; Andrew O'Heir, "Steve Bannon, Bolshevik: Maybe Donald Trump's alt-right Svengali Really is a 'Leninist'" *Salon*, November 19, 2016, http://www.salon.com/2016/11/19/steve-bannon-bolshevik-maybe-donald-trumps-alt-right-svengali-really-is-a-leninist/. Bannon did not disavow the quote, but says that he did not remember talking to Radosh.

36. "Trump, Citing No Evidence, Accuses Obama of Nixon/Watergate Plot to Tap Trump Tower," *Washington Post*, March 4, 2017,

https://www.washingtonpost.com/news/post-politics/wp/2017/03/04
/trump-accuses-obama-of-nixonwatergate-plot-to-wire-tap-trump
-tower/?utm_term=.fa6ca3a37eeb.

37. Noah Feldman, "Trump's Wiretap Tweets Raise Risk of Impeachment," *Bloomberg*, March 6, 2017, https://www.bloomberg.com
/view/articles/2017-03-06/trump-s-wiretap-tweets-raise-risk-of
-impeachment.

38. Bernstein, "Trump Press Attacks"; Thomas Jefferson to Edward
Carrington, January 16, 1787, *Founders Online*, https://founders
.archives.gov/documents/Jefferson/01-11-02-0047.

39. Amy B. Wang, "'That's how dictators get started': McCain
criticizes Trump for calling media the enemy," *Washington Post*, February 18, 2017, https://www.washingtonpost.com
/news/the-fix/wp/2017/02/18/thats-how-dictators-get-started
-mccain-criticizes-trump-for-calling-media-the-enemy/?utm
_term=.451999b056cf; Peter Baker, "Former President George W.
Bush Levels Tacit Criticism at Trump," *New York Times*, February
27, 2017, https://www.nytimes.com/2017/02/27/us/politics/george-w
-bush-criticism-trump.html.

CHAPTER 10

1. Tierney McAfee, "No More 'Lyin' Ted'? Trump's Turn Toward 'Presidential' Talk Lasts Less Than 24 Hours," *People,* April 20, 2016,
http://people.com/celebrity/donald-trump-hailed-as-presidential
-after-ny-speech-but-soon-goes-after-lyin-ted/.

2. Dan Morrow, "President Trump's Fourteen Points," *Globalist,* November 12, 2016, https://www.theglobalist.com/trumps-fourteen-points/

3. J. Kroll and C. Pouncey, "The Ethics of APA's Goldwater Rule,"
Journal of the American Academy of Psychiatry and the Law, 44
(2016), pp. 126–35.

4. Caitlin MacNeil, "Trump Challenges Clinton to Release Health
Records," *TPM*, August 29, 2016, http://talkingpointsmemo.com
/livewire/trump-clinton-health-records-tweet; Joshua D. Miller,

W. Keith Campbell, and Thomas A. Widiger, "Narcissistic Personality Disorder and the DSM-V," *Journal of Abnormal Psychology* 119 (2010) pp. 640–49.

5. Donald Trump and Bill Zanker, *Think Big and Kick Ass in Business and Life* (New York: Collins, 2007).

6. Emily Shapiro, "The History Behind the Donald Trump 'Small Hands' Insult," *ABC News,* March 4, 2016, http://abcnews.go.com/Politics /history-donald-trump-small-hands-insult/story?id=37395515; Curt Mills, "Trump: 'These Hands Hit a Golfball 285 Yards!,'" *Washington Examiner,* March 5, 2016, http://www.washingtonexaminer.com /trump-these-hands-hit-a-golfball-285-yards/article/2585030; Federalist Staff, "Watch Donald Trump Repeatedly Insist That His Hands (and Manhood) Are Not Tiny," *The Federalist,* March 4, 2016, http:// thefederalist.com/2016/03/04/watch-donald-trump-repeatedly-insist -that-his-hands-and-manhood-are-not-tiny/.

7. Graydon Carter, "Steel Traps and Short Fingers," November 2015, http://www.vanityfair.com/culture/2015/10/graydon-carter-donald -trump.

8. Amber Jamieson, "Schwarzenegger Proposed Job Swap After Trump Takes Jab at Apprentice Ratings," *The Guardian,* February 2, 2017, https://www.theguardian.com/us-news/2017/feb/02/arnold-schwarzen egger-donald-trump-apprentice-ratings; Tina Nguyen, "Trump Grill Could Be the Worst Restaurant in America," *Vanity Fair,* December 14, 2016, http://www.vanityfair.com/news/2016/12/trump-grill -review.

9. Chris Isidore and Danielle Wiener-Bronner, "Trump Unleashes Tweet on Carrier Union Boss Who Blasted Him," *CNN,* December 7, 2016, http://money.cnn.com/2016/12/07/news/companies /trump-carrier-plant-mexico-union/; Lisa Respers France, "Donald Trump Attacks Streep for Speech at Golden Globes," *CNN,* January 15, 2017, http://www.cnn.com/2017/01/09/entertainment/donald -trump-meryl-streep-golden-globes/.

10. Aaron Blake, "John Lewis Says Donald Trump Isn't a Legiti-

mate President, and Trump Hits Back Hard," *Washington Post,* January 14, 2017, https://www.washingtonpost.com/news/the-fix /wp/2017/01/13/john-lewis-doesnt-think-donald-trump-is-a-legitimate -president/?utm_term=.2ef768ad6af0.

11. Michael D. Shear, "Trump as Cyberbully in Chief? Twitter Attack on Union Boss Draws Fire," *New York Times,* December 8, 2016, https://www.nytimes.com/2016/12/08/us/politics/donald-trump -twitter-carrier-chuck-jones.html.

12. Francis B. Carpenter, *The Inner Life of Abraham Lincoln: Six Months at the White House* (Lincoln, NB: University of Nebraska Press, 1995) pp. 258–59.

13. Gersh Kuntzman, "Trump Lies! There Are Plenty of Dresses in D.C.," *Daily News,* January 9, 2017, http://www.nydailynews.com /news/politics/trump-lies-plenty-dresses-article-1.2941495.

14. Brian Stetler, "Donald Trump: 'I Have Very Thick Skin,'" *CNN,* September 24, 2015, http://money.cnn.com/2015/09/24/media/donald -trump-new-day-rich-lowry/.

15. "'Least Racist Person' Trump Stirs Row with Black Reporter," *CNN,* February 18, 2017, http://www.bbc.com/news/world-us-canada -39004005.

16. Jesse Byrnes, "Rand Paul Knocks Trump's 'Delusions of Grandeur,'" January 25, 2017, http://thehill.com/blogs/ballot-box/presidential -races/266888-rand-paul-knocks-trumps-delusions-of-grandeur.

17. Melanie Zanona, "Trump on North Korea Missile Threat: 'It Won't Happen,'" *The Hill,* January 2, 2017, http://thehill.com/homenews /administration/312428-trump-on-north-korea-missile-threat -it-wont-happen.

18. Jonathan Landay, "Experts Dispute Trump's Assertion that U.S. Nuclear Arms Capability is Lagging," *Reuters*, February 24, 2017, http:// www.reuters.com/article/us-usa-trump-nuclear-idUSKBN1632L4; Michael D. Shear and David Sanger, "Trump Says U.S. Would 'Outmatch' Rivals in a New Nuclear Arms Race," *New York Times*, December 23, 2016, https://www.nytimes.com/2016/12/23/us/politics

/trump-nuclear-arms-race-russia-united-states.html;Helene Cooper and Peter Baker, "Critics Assail Cuts in Foreign Spending As Trump Moves to Boost Military, *New York Times*, February 27, 2017, https://www.nytimes.com/2017/02/27/us/politics/trump-foreign-military-spending-cuts-criticism.html; Geoffrey Forden, "False Alarms in the Nuclear Age," *Nova*, November 6, 2011, http://www.pbs.org/wgbh/nova/military/nuclear-false-alarms.html.

19. Rachel Maddow, "Donald Trump: Greatest Baseball Player in NY," *NBC News*, October 27, 2016, http://www.nbcnews.com/video/donald-trump-greatest-baseball-player-in-ny-795427907978.

20. Ian Johnston, "Trump Claims Bill Clinton Said 'Far Worse to Me' Amid Storm Over Lewd Remarks About Women," *Independent*, October 7, 2016, http://www.independent.co.uk/news/world/americas/donald-trump-women-grab-them-bill-clinton-far-worse-a7351376.html.

21. "CRS Report for Congress," *The United States Senate*, October 29, 1998, https://www.senate.gov/CRSpubs/dfe6ac8e-78ad-4e59-bcda-d612c382ec2f.pdf.

22. "U.S. Constitution: 25th Amendment," *Cornell University Law School*, https://www.law.cornell.edu/constitution/amendmentxxv.

23. Lance M. Dodes, M.D., et al., "Letter to the Editor," *New York Times*, February 13, 2017, http://www.lancedodes.com/new-york-times-letter.

CHAPTER 11

1. Walter M. Shaub to Thomas R. Carper, December 12, 2016, https://www.oge.gov/web/oge.nsf/Congressional%20Correspondence/092B59EFD6EC27608525808800724288/$FILE/Carper%20response.pdf?open.

2. Katy O'Donnell and Lorraine Woellert, "Selling His Empire Would Cost Trump Money. A Lot of It," *Politico*, January 9, 2017, http://www.politico.com/story/2017/01/trump-ethics-divest-business-233332.

3. Shaub to Carper.

4. Ari Melber, "Kushner Took a Stricter Approach on Ethics Than Trump, Emails Show," *NBC News*, February 19, 2017, http://www.nbcnews.com/politics/politics-news/kushner-took-stricter-approach-ethics-trump-emails-show-n723046.

CONCLUSION

1. Farrand, *The Record,* vol. 2, p. 65.
2. "Analysis of House Judiciary Impeachment Votes," *Watergate.info*, http://watergate.info/impeachment/analysis-judiciary-committee-impeachment-votes.
3. Edward-Isaac Dovere, "Obama Lawyers Form 'Worst-Case Scenario Group' to Tackle Trump," *Politico,* February 23, 2017, http://www.politico.com/story/2017/02/obama-trump-lawyers-worst-case-235280; John Adams to H. Niles, February 13, 1818, http://teachingamericanhistory.org/library/document/john-adams-to-h-niles/.